Ina Coolbrith

Ina Coolbrith

The Bittersweet Song of California's First Poet Laureate

Aleta George

Shifting Plates Press

Design by Meadowlark Publishing Services.

Front cover image: William Keith, *With a Wreath of Laurel*, 1900–11, oil on cardboard, 15¾ x 20 inches. Collection of the Saint Mary's College Museum of Art, Gift of Cochrane Browne, Jr., 0-154. It is likely that Ina Coolbrith inspired this painting given its title and the likeness of the subject. Coolbrith published a poem, "With a Wreath of Laurel," in the *Overland Monthly* in 1870 after she and Joaquin Miller gathered California bay laurel leaves in Sausalito to make a laurel crown for Lord Byron's gravesite in England.

Publication of this book is supported by a generous grant from the Ina Coolbrith Circle, a nonprofit organization of poets and historians founded by Ina Coolbrith in 1919.

Published by Shifting Plates Press.

Manufactured in the United States of America.
ISBN: 978-0-9861240-1-3 (Paperback)
978-0-9861240-2-0 (Hardcover)
978-0-9861240-0-6 (Centennial Edition)

Published 2015.

For Dave, who heard most of these stories on the trail

Contents

Contents

Foreword:
Ina Coolbrith—California's
Literary Champion

As America ponders the possibility of electing its first female president, here's Aleta George with *Ina Coolbrith: The Bittersweet Song of California's First Poet Laureate*—a fresh and compelling new biography about an astonishing woman who achieved many firsts, some of them before women enjoyed the right to vote.

In 1852 when she was eleven years old, Ina Donna Coolbrith was one of the first children to come to California over what is now called Beckwourth Pass. Her first poem was published in the *Los Angeles Star* when she was just fifteen, and by her early twenties she was well on her way to becoming California's first lady of poetry.

Coolbrith was the first woman invited to read a commencement ode for a University of California graduation ceremony, and became the city of Oakland's first public librarian. Youthful readers who looked to her for guidance included a boy named Jack London, who later described her as the noble goddess who gave him "the keys to the pathway to knowledge."

Coolbrith was also first among those who sought to nurture the poetry of California and the West. Whether located in San Francisco or Oakland, her home was open to California poets, writers, and artists, as well as to those visiting or passing through the Golden State. The famous or to-be-famous who admired Coolbrith's poetry, enjoyed her company, and called her friend included Mark Twain, Bret Harte, Ambrose Bierce, George Sterling, Charles Warren Stoddard, Mary Austin, John Muir, William Keith, Gertrude Atherton, Isadora Duncan, and many lesser known writers and artists.

Coolbrith's most impressive first, however, came late in life when in 1915 she was named California's first poet laureate during the Panama-Pacific International Exposition, an honor that was confirmed by the state legislature four years later.

Aleta George is keenly aware of the difficulties Coolbrith faced in trying to write and achieve success in a male-dominated literary world. A talented daughter was expected to provide for the family when men were unable or disinclined to do so. Ina was no exception, working fourteen hours a day, six days a week for many years. Her poet friend Joaquin Miller so assumed his male-given right to roam the world and write unencumbered that he thought it only natural that Ina, being a woman and therefore maternal, should add the task of raising his daughter to her many responsibilities!

And then there was a devastating stroke of bad luck when Coolbrith lost almost everything in the fire that followed the 1906 earthquake, including a completed manuscript of the history of California literature, a book that would certainly have sold well and eased her financial burden.

What's most exciting about George's biography is that she seamlessly combines her considerable narrative talent with a zest for meticulous research; for whatever one thinks of Coolbrith's poetry, her life is so captivating that it has been waiting not just for another biographer, but for a first-rate storyteller. There are secrets in this poet's life that, as George notes, Ina was "good at keeping." George is equally good at revisiting secrets that have already been partially revealed, as well as uncovering some that were previously overlooked. Her respect and affection for her subject are best realized by her care in assuring that we experience not just the facts about Coolbrith's life, but her thoughts and feelings at every crossroad in what is perhaps better called a saga than a story.

Speaking of firsts, I did not know that Coolbrith corresponded with her cousin "Joe" Smith (who would later become head of the Mormon Church and husband to five wives) and that he proposed marriage to her. Although she was still a teenager, Coolbrith's firm, mature rejections of his bullying attempts to get her to accept the doctrine of polygamy increased my admiration for her and helped me understand that it was not just her physical beauty and impressive poetry but her indomitable spirit that allowed her to appear as one of the brightest stars in the literary galaxy wherein she moved.

Although it can't be absolutely proven, George convinces me that Coolbrith was in love with poet Charles Warren Stoddard, exploring for the first time her bittersweet understanding and acceptance of the fact that Stoddard was gay. The poet's ability to overcome her own disappointment and go on to joke about having a double gay marriage (Charlie marrying his male lover; Ina an overly affectionate devotee) surprises me with its rare glimpse into the poet's playful sense of humor and generosity of spirit. True love.

One of the disappointments for those of us who admire Coolbrith's life is that her poetry, though celebrated in her own day, now appears—with notable exceptions—relatively minor. George increases our admiration for the poet's unflinching honesty by allowing us to feel Coolbrith's keen sense of falling short. Coolbrith is not merely being overly modest when she tells poet Lorenzo Sosso that "no one can have a more humble opinion of the quality of my verse than myself"; nor is she merely complimenting a friend when she tells George Sterling that he should have been California's poet laureate. My admiration for Coolbrith as a *reader* of poetry grows—and I understand why so many writers were eager to show her their work and seek her approval, knowing that her response would not be colored by self-interest or jealousy—that it really meant something.

In 2011, the City of Oakland installed a huge sculpture by Mario Chiodo in a downtown park with busts and faces of thirty-nine "Champions of Humanity," including Abraham Lincoln, Mahatma Gandhi, Mother Teresa, Nelson Mandela, Elie Wiesel—and, yes, the heroine of *Ina Coolbrith: The Bittersweet Song of California's First Poet Laureate*. Aleta George's fascinating new biography goes a long way toward explaining why California's literary champion deserves her inclusion there.

David Alpaugh
The Ina Coolbrith Circle

Preface

I first learned about Ina Donna Coolbrith in 1999 while doing research at the San Francisco Performing Arts Library. I immediately wanted to know more about the woman Charles Warren Stoddard called "the pearl of all our tribe," a tribe that included Stoddard, Bret Harte, Mark Twain, Joaquin Miller, and John Muir. That introduction led me to do more research, and the more I learned the more I was convinced that her story needed retelling. The only biography about her was published in 1973 and is now out of print. *Ina Coolbrith: Librarian and Laureate of California* by Josephine DeWitt Rhodehamel and Raymund Francis Wood was written with a librarian's keen eye for detail (Rhodehamel was a librarian at Oakland Public Library six decades after Coolbrith's tenure there) and serves as a rich resource of Ina's life, but since the publication of that book, new materials and new scholarship have become available to enrich the telling of her story.

Writing a biography is an intimate affair. I love spending time with Coolbrith, her friends, and her times. Her devotion to poetry in a place and time when few women led literary lives made her a trailblazer, and her struggle to balance art, family, and work still resonates today. She loved California and worked to capture its natural beauty in language, something that I also strive for in my work. I lived in San Francisco when I started this book, and my love of early San Francisco history continued throughout the writing of it. My immersion in Coolbrith's story also led me to explore Beckwourth Pass, where she entered California; Marysville, where she lived for two winters; and Los Angeles, where she married, divorced, and buried a child. My husband and I took the train to New York City on tracks that followed the same route she did on her six trips to the city more than a hundred years ago. While in New York, I toured the opulent rooms of the National Arts Club and haunted the hotels where she lived.

I traveled throughout California to read her letters, the majority of which are collected at The Bancroft Library at the University of California in Berkeley, and The Huntington Library, in San Marino. One of my favorite places for research was the Oakland Public Library, the same institution where Coolbrith worked for nearly twenty years (though the building in which she worked is long gone). Every time I arrived prior to opening, I waited with a crowd of about fifty people. A good sign for libraries! Inside, I worked at a worn wooden table in the Oakland History Room surrounded by old books, some of which Coolbrith herself certainly ordered. I shared space with high school students, city employees, fellow researchers, and the occasional street person. My table was tucked into a corner near the reference librarian's desk, where the librarian was on hand to help people as they walked in the door, and within shouting distance of kids running down the halls. "No running in the library!" was a common refrain I heard throughout the day while reading thousands of clipped articles and poems that Coolbrith pasted in her folio-sized leather scrapbook more than a century ago. The scrapbook is one of her few belongings that survived the fire following the great 1906 earthquake.

When I learned more about her, I understood that there were two kinds of letters missing: those that burned in the 1906 fire and those she had destroyed. There are holes in her story—intentional ones—but there are still good stories to tell and that's why I wrote this book. My goal is to share her epic story not to critique her work. I'll leave that to others who are more qualified than I. Personally, I grew to appreciate her poetry as I came to love her mind.

I have spent a decade with California's first poet laureate, and I look forward to sharing her with you on the centennial of her crowning. I hand this book to you with the respect, admiration, and love that are due to California's first lady of letters. One of my readers, Anne Cole, gave me the greatest compliment of all when after reading the book she said, "I now know and love a woman I had never met until I read your book."

Happy anniversary, Ina Coolbrith.

A.G.

Acknowledgments

The writing of this book has been a long and pleasurable journey, and I want to thank those who joined me for all or part of it. (Please forgive me if I've missed someone!)

The librarians come first. As a rule, all reference librarians are a pleasure to work with, but there are several who stand out: Dorothy Lazard and Kathleen DiGiovanni, Oakland Public Library; Crystal Miles, The Bancroft Library; Christopher Adde and Sue Hodson, The Huntington Library; Karma Pippin and Janice Braun, Mills College; Patricia Keats, Society of California Pioneers; and Mary Morganti, California Historical Society. Thanks also to the librarians at the Braun Research Library, Autry National Center of the American West; Berkeley Historical Society; California State Library; Honnold/Mudd Library, Claremont University Consortium; Holt-Atherton Special Collections, University of the Pacific; San Francisco History Center, San Francisco Public Library; and the Western Railway Museum. Julie Armistead at Saint Mary's College Museum of Art was also a pleasure to work with. A special word of appreciation goes to the Church History Library at The Church of Jesus Christ of Latter-day Saints, whose determination for transparency has greatly enriched this story.

Several writing communities have supported this work along the way. Blue Mountain Center in New York's Adirondacks gave me a room of my own and a place at the table to start the book. Brett Hall Jones, Lisa Alvarez, Sands Hall, and Barbara Hall of Squaw Valley Community of Writers lent their support and encouragement through the years. Workshop leaders Gerald Haslam and James D. Houston gave me a boost of confidence and many good ideas, and Ray March of Modoc Forum was generous and supportive throughout. Thanks to Kay Flavell for the month-long writing retreat at the New Pacific Studio in Vallejo. Other productive writing retreats were made possible by the generosity of family and friends who offered their homes while they were out of town. Thanks to Lanny, Liz, Nycholes, and Nolan Brown; Mary Houghteling; Lori and Bill Pottinger; and Jill Sturm.

The poetry communities that have enfolded me into their ranks include the Ina Coolbrith Circle (ICC) and the Valona Deli Second Sunday Poetry Series. ICC offered several opportunities to speak about my work in progress. They also contributed a generous grant to help with production. I owe special thanks to ICC member David Alpaugh, who championed this project from the beginning. ICC members Sherry Sheehan and Claire J. Baker gave me a glad word all along, and I won't soon forget the pilgrimage to Coolbrith's grave with poets Claire Baker and Mary Rudge, Alameda's first poet laureate, who died last year.

Early on I brought the manuscript to writing classes led by Linda Watanabe McFerrin and Janis Cooke Newman, both of whom brought intelligence and expertise to the book. Leslie Keenan and her Master Writer's Class at Book Passage helped me push the book to completion. Readers who provided invaluable insight included Mia Armstrong, Leslie Batson, Kathy Briccetti, Suzanne Bruce, Anne Cole, Mary Edwards, Dave George, Rick Gray, Mary Houghteling, Lori Pottinger, and Jill Sturm. Those who gave generous helpings of encouragement included Dana Damas (who opened her beach home for each Los Angeles research trip), Dawn Hartsock, Janet Manalo, and Dru Powell. Kerry Petersen shared his love of research and knowledge of Mormon history and suggested reading material that I may not have found without his lead. Greg Whitman was generous to share much of his own research into Ina's life.

My family has been supportive and patient through all these

years I have devoted to Ina. My sister, Chrystal Rodriguez, thinks of Ina like a sister; my niece, Avalon Rodriguez, advises me on Facebook and acts like my manager at events; Asta, Lindsey, and Austin George brought intelligence and interest to the mix; and my husband, Dave George, offered support, a love of history, and a willing ear for stories before they hit the page. He is my friend, my business partner, and the love of my life.

Sheridan McCarthy and Stan Nelson of Meadowlark Publishing Services helped me in shaping the manuscript into the finished project you hold in your hands. They did it with humor, expertise, and a seemingly never-ending amount of patience—a helpful trait to exhibit when working with an anxious first-time author. Thanks to Amy Murphy Indexing and Editorial for a thorough job and superhuman turnaround.

My biggest thank-you goes to Ina Coolbrith, whose passion for literature, creativity, and California continues to inspire. She was a mentor in life, and continues to be one after her death.

Prologue:
Leaving California

One with the starry chime
Earth keeps her rhythmic beat—
Our mother, old as time
With heart still young and sweet.

—Ina Coolbrith, "Renewal," 1909

The sway of the Pullman cars lulled most of the passengers to sleep on the eastbound *Overland Limited* train, but it is unlikely that Ina Donna Coolbrith slept. The seventy-eight-year-old poet had crossed the Nevada desert by foot and wagon nearly seven decades earlier when her family came west to California on the Overland Trail in 1852. How could she sleep when the train slipped under the same night sky she had watched as a girl? Somewhere in these sands she had buried her doll after it took a tumble and split its head. All the children of the wagon train attended the funeral as the doll was lowered into its grave.

Ina was crowned California's first poet laureate in 1915, and four years later she left her adopted state for New York and did not know when she would return. She was once known for her beauty and physical vitality, but now Ina's joints ached with rheumatoid arthritis and the years showed in her down-turned mouth and double chin. In public she wore a white lace mantilla to cover her thinning hair. She hated how she looked as an old woman, but others saw her differently. One reporter described her as having "clear, luminous eyes, very sensitive and expressive hands, and a young voice, quick, animated, and fluent."[1]

As the desert miles clicked off, Ina remembered crossing the rivers as a child. In the Nevada desert her party was lost and dangerously low on water when a Shoshone Indian offered to guide the party to the Humboldt River. While still several miles from the river, the guide noticed that the oxen's nostrils had flared, a sign that they sensed nearby water. The Shoshone advised the drivers to unyoke, and when the drivers did the unhitched oxen stampeded for the water. When the wagon party reached the river they found several oxen lying on the sand dying, their bellies distended from drinking too much, too quickly.

At the Truckee River on the eastern side of the Sierras, the party confronted a swift and swollen conveyor of ice and melted snow. Ina remembered her mother's lips moving in prayer as they crossed the river in the raft the men had built to get the wagons, women, and children across. Once safely on the other side, Ina sat on a rock to watch the men drive the oxen through the rough water. She felt helpless when several of the animals were carried downstream and drowned.

Although the going was rough, Ina fell in love with poetry on the Overland Trail. Under vast skies she read Lord Byron and Shakespeare from two slim volumes that her stepfather carried in his law library, and soon she was composing original verses in her head. "I began making songs before I could write them," she later told a reporter.[2] She published her first poem at age fifteen in Los Angeles, and by the age of twenty-one had published twenty-six more. She moved to San Francisco where she played a key role in that city's vibrant literary scene alongside Bret Harte, Mark Twain, and Charles Warren Stoddard. She was one of the few writers of the American West to publish in magazines back east, and her literary career seemed assured until her fortunes changed. Out of necessity after her sister died, Ina became the breadwinner for her family, and at age thirty-three took on the support of her ailing mother, her sister's two children, and writer Joaquin Miller's half-Indian daughter. Seventy-hour workweeks left Ina little time to write. "The bird forgot its notes and the wings their flight," she told her brother.[3]

Nevertheless, she published two collections of verse, most of which she had written in her twenties, and as the years passed her celebrity grew. During the 1915 Panama-Pacific International Exposition, she was crowned California's beloved poet, a gesture that made her the first state laureate in the nation.

Four years later she decided to leave California. Her most immediate reason for leaving was to get away from Josephine Zeller, her live-in employee. For nearly twenty years, Zeller had cooked, cleaned, and cared for Ina when Ina was bedridden with arthritis. Josie kept a meticulous house, planted the backyard garden, and was famous among Ina's friends for her pies. But Josie had a mean streak, and her tirades had become violent. Ina also wanted to be near Carl Seyfforth, a young pianist living in New York on Ina's dime. She called Seyfforth her "boy," but he was no boy. He was a passionate, egotistical, and handsome young man who relied on the gifts and attention of patrons. In his autobiography he wrote, "An artist is a parasite, the orchid of humanity, and should be subsidized."[4] Ina was his primary patron, even though she was not a woman of means.

The most pressing reason for her escape was to find the time and solitude she needed to write poetry. Her role as wage earner, and then years of a debilitating illness, had kept her from doing much literary work. In New York, she hoped that a change in climate would bring relief from rheumatism and free her to write. "If I am ever to do anything at the end of my life in my literary work, or its perpetuity, it must be done now," she told a friend before leaving San Francisco.[5]

On the second day of travel, the *Overland Limited* stopped in Ogden, Utah, a Mormon community where Ina and her family had lived before coming to California. If any local Mormons had known about her heritage, they may have greeted her at the station, but few knew that Ina Coolbrith, California's beloved poet, was a niece of Joseph Smith, the founder of the Church of Jesus Christ of Latter-day Saints. Although she was born Josephine Donna Smith, daughter of Don Carlos, the prophet's youngest brother, Ina chose to keep her

Smith heritage a secret after the age of twenty-one. She later told a Mormon relative that she did so because the affiliation had caused her problems in school, in marriage, and in work. She asked her relatives to keep her secret while she lived, and after she died. To one reporter who asked where she was born she replied, "I've been told I was born in Springfield. I have no personal memory, but I wish you'd say Illinois. That's near enough and gives me the whole state!"[6] In truth, Ina was born in the Mormon community of Nauvoo, Illinois.

She was good at keeping secrets. Some might argue that it would be best to honor her request and not highlight the parts of her life that she wanted to keep private. But in order to celebrate Ina's accomplishments, and to see what manner of person came to the young state of California an uneducated girl, and grew to become the state's matriarch of arts and letters, we need to delve into her story, secrets and all.

Part I:

Searching for Home

But who shall dare to tread where Shakespeare trod,
Or strike the harp he sounded?

—*Edward Pollock (1823–58), American poet*

1

"California is a Poem"

On a hot July afternoon in 1856, fifteen-year-old Ina Coolbrith walked home from school in Los Angeles. In one hand she carried a book satchel, and with the other she fanned her face with a hat. Her damp cotton dress clung to her tall frame, and her curly dark-brown hair fell from where she had pinned it that morning. "The day was tired out with the heat and I was glad to reach one of the small streets," she later said. "Tho' the pepper, lime and locust trees along the sides were drooping, the brea [tar] dripping from porch and roof eaves, and the sidewalks, of the same material, in a mood of such melting tenderness that the brown, bare-limbed little *muchachos* and *muchachas* no longer printed them with their small toes, but were resting their roly-poly bodies in the open doorways."[1] When it cooled down later in the day, entire families would bathe in *la zanja madre*, the local watering hole where *vaqueros* galloped up to the water in dusty storms.

Ina was attending a public school for the first time. She had learned to read and write at home, but never studied arithmetic, grammar, or the rules of composition. Her mother, Agnes Moulton Coolbrith Smith Pickett, could read and write, but used no punctuation in her letters. Ina's two years of schooling in Los Angeles would be the only formal education she would ever receive. She remembered the school, Los Angeles's first, as a "square brick building set

3

upon the open plain, with, as yet, no tree or vine to modify its ugliness, or oven-like comfort."[2] The isolated site at Second and Spring streets was chosen to keep students away from the distractions of the plaza, the heart of *El Pueblo de Nuestra Señora la Reina de Los Angeles*. Los Angeles had changed since California joined the Union six years earlier, but it was still more a pueblo than a city. Cattle roamed fenceless hills, and vineyards and orchards sprawled across the surrounding countryside. Within the city limits there were at least seventy-five vineyards, and in autumn the scent of the crush filled the air as Indians stomped on the grapes in large vats from dawn to dusk. The majority of the people who lived in Los Angeles were direct descendants of the eleven families of Indian, African, and Mexican descent who had come to Alta California from Mexico in 1781. The landowners of the rancheros that surrounded the pueblo owned second homes on the plaza, where they flashed their wealth with silver-studded saddles and hosted fiestas that could last a week. Cockfights were common, as was *correr el gallo*, a popular form of entertainment that required participants to grease the neck of a rooster, bury it up to its neck on the side of the road, and grab it while riding by at full speed.

With the Gold Rush came Anglo-Americans who changed the names of Calle Principal and Calle Primavera to Main and Spring streets, where saloons, gambling halls, and whorehouses were established to serve the incoming miners, outlaws, and gamblers. The newly arrived Americans had marginalized much of the Mexican population, and bandits resistant to the takeover roamed the mountains east of Los Angeles. Nearly everyone armed themselves with pistols and bowie knives in what had become the most lawless town in the West. "This is an awful—awful town, Joseph, to live in, an *awful* town," Ina wrote her cousin. "I dont [sic] believe there is another place in the world, so small as this town is, that has more crimes committed in it every day."[3]

If her sensibilities resisted the rougher elements of the pueblo, Ina was already being changed by the landscape and cultural charms of the place. Sixty years later she told a reporter, "As a girl I lived in Los Angeles when Los Angeles was still a Spanish town, but the old saying that in familiar places there are no wonderful things was exemplified in my case. I was brought up in the midst of wonderful things and did not realize it until they had all passed away."[4] Before coming to California, Ina played only Scottish songs on her guitar. In Los Angeles she learned to strum songs of romance and heartache in the Spanish style. She also learned to speak the dominant language of the pueblo, and for the rest of her life wove Spanish words and phrases into her poems, letters, and speech. The landscape of Southern California seared images into her brain so crisp that even seventy years later she wrote about cactus fences, gardens with fountains, and the shimmering Los Angeles River that flowed to the sea. The pueblo provided her with stories, such as the one repeated by Ella Sterling Cummins (later Mighels) in *The Story of the Files*:

> [Ina] was standing by the road one day when some
> Mexican-Californians came riding by, with jingling
> spur, and embroidered saddle, and arms full of flow-
> ers. "See the pretty little Americana," called out
> one of the gallant swarthy race, and as he spoke, he
> showered his flowers upon her.[5]

On another occasion, Ina attended a ball with her older sister, Agnes Charlotte. To kick off the festivities, Don Pío Pico, the twice-appointed Mexican governor of Alta California, bowed before Ina and said, "Will the *Muchachita Americana* do me the honor of opening the ball?"[6] Ina accepted and joined Pico in dancing the fandango, a lively form of flamenco that starts slow and increases to triple time as the dancers keep pace with clicking castanets and beating tambourines. Writer Gertrude Atherton wrote, "An uglier man than Pío Pico rarely entered this world."[7] Ina never mentioned Pico's looks when she described what for her had been an auspicious occasion.

On that hot July afternoon when Ina walked home from school, she turned the corner and a weak breath of wind delivered a scrap of newspaper to her feet. She discovered that the clipping contained a profile of Edward Pollock, a self-educated man who had come to California from Philadelphia in 1852 and become the most widely known California poet. Ina was so engrossed by what she read that she forgot about the need to find shade. Years later, in a lecture called

"Gossip: Personal Reminiscences of Early California Writers," Ina told her audience why the clipping was significant. She explained that as a girl she loved poetry, and called herself "its child lover."[8] She believed that poetry permeated the realm of lofty ideals and quixotic love, and was "so fine an essence as to belong to those akin to the Immortals."[9] She pictured poets as mythical beings who wrote about shores she had never seen. While it was standard to find poetry in California newspapers in the 1850s, the majority of those poems were either written by famous (and dead) English poets, or by local scribblers who imitated them. Pollock's poems were different. "Evening" was set in San Francisco and began, "The air is chill, and the hour grows late / And the clouds come in through the Golden Gate."[10] Before moving to Los Angeles at age thirteen, Ina had lived in San Francisco for a short time and had seen the fog rolling in through the Gate. Pollock's poem was set in a place she knew, and that cracked open a landscape of possibility inside of her. It served as a "revelation that poetry was, or could be, written in California."[11]

That night Ina pasted the clipping in her scrapbook, a used patent office report she filled with scraps of verse. Her stepfather, William Pickett, was quick to criticize her use of the office ledger. "Tut! Tut! Spoiling a mighty good book, Sis, spoiling a mighty good book!"[12] This from a man who only quoted Robert Burns's "Highland Mary."

Several weeks later, Ina's teacher, Miss Hayes, asked the class to write about their childhoods. Ina chose to complete the assignment in verse. Perhaps she felt emboldened by "Chandos Picture," Pollock's tribute to Shakespeare, in which he said, "But who shall dare to tread where Shakespeare trod / Or strike the harp he sounded?"[13] Ina did dare and wrote an eight-stanza poem called "My Childhood's Home." It began, "Sweet home of my childhood, the home of my heart / Fond mem'ry oft turneth to thee."[14] She didn't name her childhood home, but it is clear that her nostalgia was meant for the Mormon city of her birth, Nauvoo, Illinois, nestled into a bend of the Mississippi River.

Ina was born Josephine Donna Smith on March 10, 1841. Her parents, Agnes Coolbrith Smith and Don Carlos Smith, gave her the name Josephine to honor her uncle Joseph Smith Jr., the founder of the Church of Christ, a name that was changed to The Church of Jesus Christ of Latter-day Saints. Donna, her middle name, was given to recognize her father, Don Carlos, the prophet's youngest brother. Her family nicknamed her Inez, which she later clipped to Ina.[15] Ina had two older sisters, Agnes Charlotte, four, and Sophronia, two. The family lived a few blocks from the Mississippi river, and a stream ran through the cellar of their house. In the cellar, Don Carlos edited and printed *Times and Seasons*, a monthly Mormon newspaper. Adjacent to Nauvoo was an eight-hundred-acre swamp buzzing with mosquitoes, and until the Mormons drained and filled the swamp several years later, hundreds of people died of malaria. They did not know that the scourge came from mosquito bites. It would be another fifty years before scientists discovered that mosquitoes were the vectors of the disease.

Four months after Ina was born, malaria hit her family. Don Carlos nursed his wife and children back to health, but he died on August 7, 1841, one week after his sixth wedding anniversary. He was twenty-five years old. Two years later, Sophronia died of scarlet fever, and Agnes buried her second child next to her husband. The family's grief lasted for years. One month before Ina's fourth birthday, John Smith, Don Carlos's uncle, gave Ina a patriarchal blessing that recognized their losses, but it is unknown if his blessing brought her comfort. She found her own source of solace. Even at an early age, Ina turned to the natural world to salve her grief and find healing. In "My Childhood's Home" she described a spot in Nauvoo that had "a wildwood, by the murmuring rill / That flowed through the green, grassy glade." It was a peaceful place, hidden by flowers and ivy, where as a girl she played in the "calm, evening hours." The most striking feature of the wildwood was an "old, old oak" with great arms and a wide canopy where she played, and where her community came to pray. She rested on a little white cot among the flowers, vines, and moss to watch the light through the trees and listen to the water melodies: "Music—rich, soft and low, that has power to impart / A pure, holy calm to the sorrowing heart."[16]

When Ina's teacher read "My Childhood's Home," she thought Ina had plagiarized it. Ina recreated her teacher's reaction in her lecture, "Gossip."

"Where did you get this?" said Miss Hayes.

"I made it up," said Ina.

"Why did you write it in this way?"

"Because it was easier," said Ina, who started to cry because she thought she had done something wrong.[17]

Miss Hayes sent Ina to the principal, who summoned Ina's mother. Agnes assured the principal that Ina was capable of producing verse, and explained that Ina had been reciting original poetry to her dolls for years. The principal sent "My Childhood's Home" to Henry Hamilton, the new editor of the *Los Angeles Star*. Hamilton ran it, and it was Ina's first published poem. She was fifteen. The principal also sent the poem to John Rollin Ridge, poet, author, and editor. Ridge reprinted Ina's poem in the *Marysville Express* with words of praise: "[Los Angeles is a] beautiful and vine-clad country, rich in its native wines and in the possession of as sweet a young poetess as ever sung—we mean Ina, God bless her!"[18]

Ina had not met Ridge—not yet anyway—but she did know Marysville. She had lived in that town when she first came to California with her mother, Agnes; her stepfather, William Pickett, whom her mother had married when Ina was seven years old; her seventeen-year-old sister, Agnes Charlotte; and her twin half brothers, six years old. Pickett took the family to Marysville before he left for the mines and was snowed in for the winter. Agnes sewed dresses for local prostitutes to earn money to feed her children.

One day Ina walked to town for groceries on the only levee path not covered in water. The Yuba and Feather rivers met in Marysville and frequently flooded the town. The Pickett cabin was on a rise, and for three days and nights Agnes tied a boat to the cabin in case the rivers rose any higher. Agnes also gave temporary shelter to Old Thompson, a former slave from Virginia whose laundry-service tent had been taken away by the floods. As Ina walked on the soft edge of

Ina Coolbrith, c. 1852. Courtesy Oakland Public
Library, Oakland History Room.

the levee, it gave way and she fell into the icy water. She floundered
in the muddy water until Old Thompson heard her cries and saved
her. Several years later, Ina's family had an opportunity to return the
favor when Thompson showed up ill at their place in San Francisco.
Agnes rented a room for him in the house next door and nursed him
until he recovered. Ina visited him in the evenings to play her guitar. Agnes's lack of prejudice toward Thompson was unusual for the
time, and Ina shared her mother's humanity. Years later, Ina wrote
an inscription for writer Charles Fletcher Lummis, "Birth and death

unto all are given … Indian, Afric, Mongol, Saxon / Within are the heart and soul of Man."[19]

Later than spring, Pickett returned to Marysville and took the family to his Grass Valley gold claim, which he had named "Ina's Ledge." While in the mountain camp that summer, Ina took her twin brothers for a walk. She wandered off the path to look at wildflowers such as silver bush lupine, larkspur, and wild iris. As the sun fell behind the mountains she realized she could not find her way back to camp. The boys cried and Ina told them to stay calm and sit down. She was certain they would be rescued if only they stayed put. When Agnes realized the children were lost, a rescue party set out in the dark. They found the children at the base of a tree with the twins, asleep. The miners asked Ina if she was afraid of mountain lions. "No, I was not afraid. We were tired and hungry that's all. But I felt bad about mother."[20]

Ina's Ledge did not pan out, and the whole family returned to Marysville. After another flooded winter, Pickett and family boarded a San Francisco–bound steamer on the Sacramento River in the spring of 1854. In San Francisco, Pickett took a job as a printer for the *Daily Bulletin* and built a house near Mission Dolores, where goats roamed the open plains. The ticketed bull and bear fights in nearby fields were popular entertainment, even for the children who squeezed between the legs of the densely packed adults.

Agnes was pleased to find old friends in San Francisco. At the same time the majority of Mormons had left Illinois and prepared to head west on what became known as the Mormon Trail, a small group of Mormons left New York by ship in 1846 to sail to the Mexican territory of Alta California, where they could live outside of federal rule. Samuel Brannan was the appointed leader of the Mormons on the *Brooklyn* as it made its fourteen-thousand-mile journey down to Cape Horn and back up to California. While the ship was at sea, the United States declared war on Mexico and federal troops took possession of San Francisco. By the time the *Brooklyn* entered San Francisco Bay six months after leaving New York, Brannan saw the American flag waving at Fort Presidio and said. "There's that damned flag again."[21]

When the *Brooklyn* passengers learned that their brethren had settled in Utah, most of them headed overland. A small group stayed in San Francisco, where a bell ringer in Portsmouth Square (today's Chinatown) summoned them for Sunday worship. Agnes discovered that Caroline and Jonathan Crosby, friends she had known in Kirtland, Ohio, and Nauvoo, Illinois, were in San Francisco. From Caroline Barnes Crosby's daily diary we learn that Ina and her family socialized with the Mormons in San Francisco. Caroline wrote that the "Smith girls" visited the Crosby home frequently to sew quilts and join in evenings of lively music and prayer. Ina was multitalented. In addition to writing poetry she played the guitar and accordion, and sang. Caroline wrote in one entry, "I admired their appearances much. The youngest [Ina] plays the accordion and is a very good singer."[22]

That summer, Ina's cousin Joseph F. Smith stopped in San Francisco on his way to the Sandwich Islands (Hawaii) to serve on a mission. Cousin Joe's father, Hyrum Smith, had been murdered in 1844 alongside his brother Joseph Smith at the Carthage jail in Illinois. Ina and her cousin Joe saw each other frequently during his two-month stay in San Francisco. They socialized with other young people who gathered at the Crosby house for food, music, and hymns. Joe also visited Ina at her house, and found that Pickett, a lukewarm Mormon to start, had turned against the church. On one occasion, Pickett showed his disdain for the Mormon prohibition of alcohol and sent his twins out for a bottle of brandy, which he drank like water in front of Joe. "G—D— Brigham Young, G—D— Bill Walker, G—D— P. P. Pratt. I will blow daylight through them the first time I ever catch them out of Zion," railed Pickett.[23] Cousin Joe held his tongue but did speak up on another occasion when he helped Pickett fix a wagon. While holding up one side of the wagon, Joe said, "I am a better man than you are, and now, sir, if you once more open your mouth to me against Brigham Young or others, I will knock daylight out of your head."[24]

Shortly thereafter, Pickett's house burned to the ground and Pickett sent Agnes and the children to live in Los Angeles while he stayed in San Francisco to pay off his debts. Agnes and her four children boarded the steamship *America* and landed in the Southern California port of San Pedro. It was 1855, a year in which historian William A. Spalding calculated that death by violence in Los Angeles averaged one a day. If Pickett sent Agnes money, it wasn't enough, and she sewed to feed her children.

2

Blood Atonement

More than twenty earthquakes rocked the pueblo during the first two weeks of January 1857. Ina wrote her cousin Joe in Hawaii that the tremors were less shocking than the events that followed. She explained that the Los Angeles sheriff and his deputies had gone after a group of outlaws who were stealing horses, murdering men, and terrorizing San Juan Capistrano, a community fifty miles to the south. When the smoke cleared after a shootout, the popular sheriff and his deputies lay dead and Juan Flores and Pancho Daniel rode off with their men.

Ina wrote poems about cultural events only on rare occasions, but her third published poem was an exception. "Lines on the Recent Massacre," printed in the *Los Angeles Star* on January 26, 1857, reflected the city's mood for revenge:

> Is there no one true *man*,
> *Not one*, to act as the avenger
> Of the four noble beings who lost their own lives
> In defending *this* people from danger ...
>
> Then O! While the sod is yet damp on their graves
> Go forth, in God's name, and avenge them.[1]

Ina hardly needed to incite a community in which vigilante justice was the norm, particularly when it came to laying blame on working-class Mexican Americans. The majority of lynchings that took place in the 1850s were of Mexican Americans at the hands of the newly arrived Anglos, and the murder of the popular sheriff was an excuse to let prejudices explode. An armed foot patrol guarded the city while hundreds of men set out to find Flores, Daniel, and their gang. William H. Peterson, a lawyer, undersheriff, and Agnes Charlotte's fiancé, tracked Daniel to San Jose. Disguised as a Mexican and speaking perfect Spanish, Peterson captured Daniel during a card game and took him to jail. While awaiting trial, vigilantes took Daniel from his cell and lynched him. The story of Peterson's capture of Daniel was passed down to his children, Ina's niece and nephew.

In all, the vigilantes captured fifty-two Mexicans. They brought the captured men back to Los Angeles, where mock trials consisted of a judge who named the accused and turned to the crowd for a sentence. If someone yelled, "Hang him," the judge called for those in favor to say "Aye!" Eleven men were executed this way based on little or no evidence. When Flores was captured, he was tried and given a hanging date. On February 21, Flores was hung on Fort Hill (where the Federal Building now stands) as three thousand people watched, with Ina certainly among them.

Ina's call for revenge may have been inspired by "blood atonement," a tenet engrained among early Mormons. The belief espoused by founder Joseph Smith holds that the most heinous of crimes can only be avenged by spilling the blood of the perpetrator, and ideally on the soil where the crime was committed. Brigham Young continued the tenet after the men tried for the murders of Joseph and Hyrum Smith were acquitted. "It belongs to God and his people to avenge the blood [of His] servants," said Young.[2]

Ina turned sixteen on March 10, 1857, and one month later she and Agnes Charlotte took the sixty-mile eastbound stagecoach ride to San Bernardino, where Caroline and Jonathan Crosby had moved. San Bernardino was the largest Mormon settlement outside Utah. Brigham Young had established it as a fair-weather route from the sea to Salt Lake, but his support for the colony had eroded as the city's popularity increased. He came to refer to it as a gathering place for those too weak to withstand the rigors of Zion. Others praised it. The *Daily Alta California* named it the "most beautiful city of California."[3]

Upon arrival in San Bernardino, the Smith girls visited the Crosbys. "We enjoyed the evening very agreeably, had music both instrumental and vocal," Caroline wrote in her journal. "Josephine played the guitar, William the violin, and Ellen [Caroline's niece] the accordion."[4] It is easy to imagine that Ina showed her poems to Caroline, and that Caroline encouraged her to write more. Caroline loved poetry and music. She wrote in her journal that she liked to paste poems on her wall and read them aloud when she felt blue. Caroline was also close friends with Eliza Snow, the most popular Mormon poet and one of Brigham Young's plural wives. The girls stayed in San Bernardino for over a month, and in early June Agnes and the twins joined them for several weeks. The whole family returned to Los Angeles mid-June.

In late June, Ina received a letter from cousin Joe, who admonished that she never forget that the "highest blood in the world" flowed through her veins.[5] She replied that she hadn't forgotten, and was proud to be known throughout California as the "Los Angeles poetess, Ina Smith, niece of the Prophet."[6] Joe also told her she should live in Utah, not California. On this she disagreed. "Why are you so anxious for us to leave Cal. and go to Salt Lake?" she replied. "We can worship God, and love His blessed Son as well *here*, as we could anywhere else; and a simple, heart-felt prayer offered up in the private of my own room, is just as acceptable to Him, as it would be were it offered up in the Tabernacle of Salt Lake City."[7]

As Ina saw things, it wasn't she and her family who had abandoned their Utah relatives, but they who had banished her family. She told Joe that she had written more than twenty letters to relatives in Salt Lake, and not one had replied. "They have blotted their California relatives out of their hearts and memories. Although in California we have not forgotten the existence of God or his church."[8] Joe told Ina that it was God's will for Mormons to gather together, and even if her family and friends in Utah weren't responding to her letters, they were her only true friends. Given her attitude, he added, no one in Salt Lake would be sorry if she stayed in California. "Indeed, Mademoiselle, I do not know that we are particularly in need of you back there."[9]

He also accused her of being boastful about her published poems, to which Ina replied:

> If I have won myself a name, Joe, yet, I am not to be praised for it. All honor is due to *Him* who gave me the power and abilities to be able to write. Even those in this place who are averse to Mormonism have been heard to remark, 'Whether Joseph Smith was a man of God or not, they could not tell, but one thing was sure, that God had bestowed great genius upon the Smith family.' So if I have contributed to gaining even that much of an opinion in favor of our family, and Mormonism, I have at least done no *harm*, and *may have* done *some good*.[10]

Her argument had merit. The Gentiles' resentment toward Mormons had grown, primarily over the issue of polygamy. Founder Joseph Smith had begun the practice in secret, and Brigham Young continued to live and promote the doctrine in private until 1852 when he became the governor of the Utah Territory and told the outside world about the principles of plural marriage. It was a brazen move, given that polygamy was a felony in the United States and most Americans sided with Congressman John Alexander McLernand, who said polygamy was a "scarlet whore" that needed to be removed.

Ina was personally opposed to polygamy and told Joe that she didn't like what she had seen in polygamous households in Utah. "You have not lived at Salt Lake, in the very midst of it, and not have known [sic] how unhappy were those who were connected with it ... Thank God, I have a little common sense left, and as long as I have one particle, I will not go back there!"[11]

Her assertiveness was unique to the women in her family. Agnes and Agnes Charlotte conveyed a meeker tone in their letters to Joe, whom they called Joseph, his given name. It is hard to know where Ina gained the confidence of her convictions. She was not afraid to argue, and to build her case to Joe she quoted passages from the *Book of Mormon*: "Wherefore, O my brethren, hear me, and hearken unto the words of the Lord: *for there shall not any man among you have save it be one wife.*"[12]

Her own words were even more effective:

> Did not Uncle Joseph himself say that "it was not *commanded* him, but was *permitted* him"... Is it right for a girl of 15 or even 16 to marry a man of 50 or 60 ... I think I see *myself*, vowing to *love* and *honor*, some old driveling idiot of 60, to be taken into his *harem* and enjoy the pleasure of being his *favorite Sultana* for an hour, and then thrown aside, whil'st my *Godly* husband, is out Sparking *another* girl, in hopes of getting *another victim* to his despotic power. *Pleasant prospect, I must say.* This, Joe, *this is of God, is it? No, never, never, never!*[13]

"What would you make our Uncle Joseph to be? Wicked, sensual? And devilish? I thought you loved his 'blood,' was proud of it!" said Joe.[14]

"You may *preach*, you may talk to me from now to Eternity, but you *never* will make me believe that polygamy is true," she said.[15]

"What do you mean by 'believing in polygamy?'" he spat back. "What am I to understand by what you term 'belief'? That you will not accept it as from God? Or that you will never obey it whether it is from God or not? In either case you are condemnable and culpable. Do not believe you mean it Josephine! It is from God!"[16]

Joe had reason to take her anti-polygamy stance personally. He had asked Ina to marry him, and she had said no. Hints of his proposal, and her refusal, are in their letters.

"Remember me not as a lover," he wrote.

"As a sister remembers a brother / So I will remember thee," she replied, saying that she still had his ring and would keep it safe until she could return it.[17] Years later, he told a relative that had Ina accepted his proposal she would have been his first wife, a title that was considered an honor.

Joseph Smith, Brigham Young, and other Mormon men warned women (and girls) that they must believe in plural marriage or be damned for all time. Cousin Joe followed that line with Ina and cursed her, "I swer [sic] most solemnly in the name of Jesus and authority of the priesthood I hold, unless you awake, repent, and reform, God will blight your prospects, cross your path with sorrow and afflictions, and scurge [sic] you to humility and penitence."[18] Ina's reaction to Joe's curse is unknown.

It is unclear if Ina knew as a teenager that her mother had been a plural wife. Five months after Ina's father died (and before she married Pickett), Agnes became Joseph Smith's sixth plural wife. Brigham Young officiated and wrote cryptically about the event, "I was taken into the lodge J Smith was Agness."[19] Joseph was powerful, influential, mesmerizing, and handsome, and Agnes had small children to support. How could she say no when he told her that God had chosen her to be one of his wives, and that a union between them would be a Levirate marriage, a traditional practice from the Old Testament in which a man marries the widowed wife of his brother? Could she deny his assertion that the gates of heaven would be closed to her and her children if she resisted? If the relationship was consummated, it is unknown if Agnes felt betrayal or betrothal. Either way, it is unlikely that Joseph gave Agnes any true comfort or security, for in the year following Don Carlos's death Joseph took a total of thirteen plural wives—and he was just getting started. He had at least thirty plural wives by the time he wrote Doctrine and Covenant, Section 132, the revelation that codified the principle of plural marriage.

Polygamy would be Joseph Smith's ultimate undoing. When Emma, his first wife, learned about D&C 132 she threw the document in the fire, even though it stressed that God would reward the wife who obeyed the covenant and destroy the wife who did not. She told William Law, a respected member of the inner circle, about Joseph's covenant, and Law published a single edition of a newspaper that revealed polygamy to the wider community. A few days later, two hundred members of Smith's army, the Nauvoo Legion, destroyed Law's printing press and set the building that housed it on fire. The deed had dire consequences. Early Americans were adamant about protecting the freedom of the press, and the Gentiles around Nauvoo responded to the destruction of the press by threatening to remove the Mormons from Illinois. Joseph and Hyrum were arrested and taken to jail. While awaiting trial in Carthage, mobs stormed the jail and killed them.

Brigham Young took over as president, and Agnes sewed to support her daughters. One month before Ina's fifth birthday, Agnes became the eighth wife of George A. Smith, Don Carlos's cousin. Plural marriages get complicated for widows. A woman can only be sealed for eternity to one man. If she remarries, a ceremony is performed to renew the eternal seal to her husband, while her new husband stands in as proxy. The double standard is clear. A man can have multiple wives for eternity, and is in fact said to earn extra points for having them, while a woman is not rewarded for having multiple husbands on Earth or in Heaven.

The anti-Mormon mobs were not content with the murders of Joseph and Hyrum Smith; they wanted all the Mormons out of Nauvoo. In February 1846, Young led the majority of Mormons out of Illinois. Agnes was among a small group who did not follow. "I want to come and I do not want to come," she wrote George Smith. "I feel all alone if there was a Carlos a Joseph or Hyrum there how quickly would I be there I love the Church of Christ I love to be with my Brethren but alas there is an aching void that seem[s] never can be filld."[20]

Ina was five years old when an armed mob surrounded Nauvoo to force the remaining Mormons out. Fortunately for those under attack, a group of Gentiles came to their defense. Among the defenders was William Pickett, Ina's future stepfather. Pickett was an English-born lawyer who had come to Nauvoo as a newspaper correspondent. He was taller than Don Carlos, and ornery by nature. When an officer tried to arrest him on trumped-up charges, Pickett drew his gun and said, "I hope God will strike me dead if I don't shoot the man that serves a writ to me!"[21] Pickett led a ragtag group of volunteers called the "Kill Devil Company." During one skirmish, the Kill Devils began to retreat and Pickett held the front of the line alone until one of his men yelled, "Why, who wouldn't follow Pickett!"[22] It seems that guile and bravery ran in Pickett's family. He was a second cousin to General George E. Pickett, the man who would lead Lee's infamous charge at Gettysburg.

A deal was eventually struck that guaranteed safe passage to the remaining Mormons as long as they left town within days. A special clause held that Pickett was to leave within the hour. Agnes took her two daughters to St. Louis, Illinois, and married William Pickett, who had joined the Mormon Church. When Agnes became pregnant, Pickett took a second wife but the arrangement didn't last. Agnes bore twin boys on December 11, 1847, and Pickett announced the births to Brigham Young. "I last spring married an old acquaintance of yours, and was last week presented by her with two sons at one birth!... I have named the eldest Don Carlos and the other for myself."[23]

When news of gold in California reached St. Louis, Pickett left Agnes to fend for herself and her four children. Two years later he returned to take his family to California. On the way they stopped in Utah, and Agnes and the children lived in Ogden during the spring and summer of 1851 while Pickett went to California's goldfields. He returned in the fall to practice law and serve on a commission that codified church rules. An incident occurred that caused Pickett to leave Utah in a hurry. Cousin Joe claimed that Pickett was run out of town because he had been drinking, argued with a judge, and was declared in contempt of court. The March *Journal History* said only that the commission did not accomplish anything until "Pickett threw up his commission and left the territory."[24] Ina said that Pickett sent money to Agnes after he left, but it was confiscated by Brigham Young.[25] Joseph refuted the charge.

One month after Ina's eleventh birthday on March 10, 1852, she and her family joined a California-bound train of seventeen wagons and met Pickett on the Overland Trail, where makeshift graves and bleached oxen bones marked their way. While the party rested at the eastern base of the Sierra Nevada range, James Pierson Beckwourth rode into camp. Born to an African American slave and an officer in the Revolutionary War, Beckwourth came west and served as chief scout for General John C. Frémont and fought in the California Revolution. He also became an honorary chief of the Crow Nation. Ina remembered that he had candy in his pockets for the children, and that he called her his "princess." Beckwourth told the party that he had recently cleared a trail that was the shortest, easiest, and lowest in elevation of any pass across the mountains, and offered to take the party over the pass personally.

Legend has it that Ina's party was the first to take the new trail, and that Ina was the first white child to enter California over Beckwourth's Pass. But facts don't support the legend. In his autobiography, Beckwourth said that after finishing the trail in 1851 he contracted a painful skin infection, and was so sick that he accepted his coming death and wrote out his will. A wagon party discovered him on the eastern side of the Sierras, and the women of the party nursed him back to health. It was this party that he first took over the mountain.

Ina came to California one year later. She described the man who rode into camp as being one of the most beautiful men she had ever seen. She said Beckwourth was a tall, dark-skinned man wearing beaded leather clothing and braided shoulder-length hair, and riding a saddle-less horse. She never mentioned a painful, blistering skin rash or that the women in her party nursed a sick man until he was well.

Although she was mistaken in claiming that hers was the first party to enter California over the pass, she certainly was one of the first, and Beckwourth did take point position on their three-day journey over the Sierras. As they neared the summit, Beckwourth rode alongside the Pickett wagon and asked if Ina and Agnes Charlotte could ride with him. When they reached the summit, Beckwourth gestured to the Feather River below, and with the smell of sage in the mountain air, he said, "Here is California, little girls. Here is your kingdom.[26]

After arriving in California, Ina lived in Marysville, Grass Valley, San Francisco, and Los Angeles. She attended school, studied hard, and became a young poet of note. She sang, played two musical instruments, and was socially active. She believed in God, could quote the Book of Mormon, and socialized with Mormons in San Bernardino. Clearly she did not deny her Mormon heritage before coming to California as many sources claim. Although she never said so herself, it is likely that the event that led her to hide her heritage was the Mountain Meadows Massacre, a slaughter in Utah of 120 Gentile emigrants en route from Arkansas to California.

It took years to piece together what happened at Mountain Meadows, a popular spot for wagon trains to stop and rest before crossing the desert into California. When the Baker-Fancher wagon train passed through Utah tensions were high. President Buchanan had replaced Brigham Young with a new governor in an attempt to curtail polygamy and control Young's power, and the new governor was on his way to Utah with armed troops. Young feared a confrontation equal to that which had happened in Missouri. He incited the Mormons to arm themselves, defend their territory, and deny help to any Gentiles who passed through Utah on their way to California. The friction was heightened by a long drought and food shortages, and by the Mormon Reformation, a period of conservatism then at its peak when followers were asked to recommit to the Church's doctrines, including polygamy and blood atonement.

With the federal troops bearing down on Utah, George A. Smith traveled through the Southern Utah territories to tell citizens to prepare for battle. He also told the Paiute Indians that federal troops were on the way to kill them. Smith and his men camped near the Baker-Fancher party, who were endowed with twelve hundred head of cattle, a prize-winning racehorse, and gold coins. The Mormons told the party that Mountain Meadows was a good place to rest. The party took their advice but instead of finding rest they were attacked by Paiutes and Mormons dressed to look like them. The emigrants formed a defense. The Paiutes left after the first day of fighting, but the Mormons stayed and continued the offense. After several more days of entrenched volleying, Mormon leader John D. Lee entered the emigrant camp on September 11 with a white flag and promised to lead the party to safety. The Mormons formed the travelers into two groups, one of men and the other of women and children. Then they led the emigrants away from the wagons in single file and shot all fifty men point blank in the head, and murdered twenty women and fifty children by shooting them or stabbing them with knives. After the carnage, the Mormons stripped the Gentiles of their valuables, rode off with their horses and cattle, and left the dead to the buzzards on the mountain. The only souls allowed to survive were those under the age of five, children who were taken to Mormon households to be raised.

After this incident, Young expected a war and called all Mormons to Utah, and the entire community of San Bernardino made preparations to leave. Cousin Joe had stopped in San Bernardino on his way back to Utah from Hawaii, and one night rode a horse sixty miles from San Bernardino to Los Angeles to tell Agnes that he had acquired a wagon and four-mule team to take her and her children to Utah. Agnes turned him down.

When news of the massacre hit Los Angeles, its citizens gathered on the plaza, and with William Peterson serving as secretary, drew up a resolution that asked President Buchanan to execute punishment on the Mormons. It was not safe to be a Mormon or to be associated with Mormons outside Utah after the Mountain Meadows Massacre. A Mormon missionary who passed through Los Angeles was nearly hanged even though he had nothing to do with the attack. A year after the massacre, an investigation found enough incriminating evidence to indict the Mormons. Lead investigator James Henry Carleton wrote in his report that the Mormons were an "ulcer" that needed "excision, complete and thorough."[27] Ina later told John Smith that her heritage caused her to be "shunned" in school, and played a role in her sister's troubled marriage.[28] In public, the family distanced themselves from the Mormon Church; in private, they continued to communicate with family.

3

"An Unfinished Poem"

Ina and Agnes Charlotte demonstrated their separation from the church by choosing Gentile husbands. On March 3, 1858, Agnes Charlotte, twenty-one years old, married William Peterson. On April 21, 1858, about a month after her seventeenth birthday, Ina married twenty-five-year-old Robert Carsley, an ironworker and part-time minstrel player. Ina and her handsome husband moved into a small house near Salamander Iron Works, Carsley's foundry, close to the plaza and her sister's home. According to Ina's niece, neither Pickett nor Peterson liked Carsley; they even tried to stop her from marrying him.

At first, Ina published poems at the same rate as before. During her first eight months of marriage she placed five in the *Los Angeles Star*. Then her publishing slowed. In all of 1859 she published only one, six months into the year. In 1860 she published eight poems in *California Home Journal*, a San Francisco weekly (though these could have been written earlier), and in 1861 she published just two poems. Only one poem written during her marriage revealed anything about her relationship with Carsley. In "How I Came to Be a Poet," published in 1859, Ina credited love as her muse. Later poems tell a different story. She set "Fragment from an Unfinished Poem," published in 1864, in Los Angeles where "love's blossom budded, bloomed, and died." She described a walk with her lover under a night sky in a "spectral glen" where "jagged gashes of gray rock whirled shriekingly." She and her lover found a "weird magnificence even amid its horrors," because what "seemed most darksome and unlovely, were, by our great love, transfigured to divine." The ominous landscape contrasts with that usually associated with first love:

> The amber moon hung low i' the mid-heaven;
> Long, crimson blossoms of pomegranate boughs
> Swung, censor-like, above us; and we saw,
> Afar in the dim south, the long, sharp line
> Of castellated rocks, keen-piercing through
> The silver-veined tissues of the night.[1]

Other later poems described love's entrapment. In one she wrote how "Love's white arms, with soft caress / Round my neck were twining,"[2] and in another suggested that a lover is like a spider, "weaving his cruel web in the sun."[3]

It isn't clear exactly how soon after she wed Carsley that her marriage began to unravel. In a photograph of her taken around this time her skin looks soft, her curly shoulder-length hair is pulled back from her face, and a red rose is tucked into the bodice of her dress. The slow exposure of the emulsified glass plates bore into the truth of her troubles and revealed resignation in her lips, a glazed and unengaged look in one of her eyes, and an unmistakable air of sadness. Evidence of Carsley's temper is found in a letter to one of his clients, Abel Stearns, one of the wealthiest men in town. Carsley had opened Salamander Iron Works with a partner in March 1858, one month before he married Ina, and dissolved the partnership a year later. In May 1859, Carsley wrote Stearns that difficulties with his partner made it impossible to proceed with the job he was doing for Stearns. "I consider it advisable for your security that you remove at once all the tools, material, and finished and unfinished work in and about our shop belonging to you," Carsley warned.[4] One year later, Stearns sued Carsley for unsatisfactory work, and a judge decided in Stearn's favor. Carsley was forced to sell a piece of land to pay the debt.

It is logical to assume that the reason Ina stopped publishing

Ina Coolbrith, c. 1861. Courtesy Oakland Public Library, Oakland History Room.

poetry after eight months of marriage was due to being pregnant and the subsequent care of her newborn infant. The exact birthdate of Ina's child is unknown. City and county birth records did not yet exist, and there are no birth or death announcements of the Carsley's baby in the *Los Angeles Star*. Announcements for other children did occasionally appear, however, such as Agnes Charlotte's son, Henry Frank Peterson, whose birth was announced on January 28, 1859. The only information about Ina's child is anecdotal and comes from her family. Ina Lillian Peterson Cook, Ina's niece, said in a lecture that Ina's marriage did not last long, "though there was a little child born."[5] Ina Graham, Ina's grandniece, told Ina's biographer Josephine DeWitt Rhodehamel that her great-aunt had lost her only child. Ina's cousin H. S. Salisbury mentions the death of Ina's child in the January 1950 issue of *Improvement Era*. And in 1965, Ina's relative Jessie Winter Smith told an interviewer about the child and suggested that Carsley was responsible for its death.[6] There is no second source to corroborate his accusation.

Ina alluded to her child in the mysterious vault of her poetry. In "Rebuke," she wrote that the answer to the world being cruel was "The innocent gold of my baby's head / And the lisp of a childish prayer."[7] In the first stanza of her poem "The Mother's Grief," a mother "laughs in careless pleasure" as her baby boy, who is old enough to sit up and lisp his words, tries to catch sunbeams shining through an open cottage door, where behind him the "golden tassels of the corn / danced in the breath of morning." The second stanza finds the mother at the child's wake, where a sunbeam reaches for her child's hands, "crossed in rest forever."[8]

Los Angeles's first graveyard has long since been paved over. When the interred bodies were moved to make way for the growth of the city, workers found thirty toddler-sized caskets, each with a little window to give a last look at the child's face. Children died frequently in those days. On March 30, 1861, the *Los Angeles Star* wrote, "an unusual number of deaths [were] reported this week, with children the principal sufferers." If Ina's child had been born eleven months after she was married, and if the child was among that group of dead, he would have been two, old enough to lisp and sit in a doorway catching sunbeams. Outside of her family, Ina kept her dead child a secret all of her life, but the loss of it contributed to a deep melancholia.

Her sadness brought about by the loss of her child only added to the weight she carried from her own childhood and the empathy she felt for her mother. In July 1861, when Ina was twenty, she wrote an ode for her mother's fiftieth birthday. "In the Night: To My Mother" was the last poem in which Ina directly referenced her childhood. In the thirty-two-stanza poem she crowned herself a "child of suffering and song," and conjured up her "sainted" father, who was "loved—

yet never known," and her sister Sophronia, "golden-hair'd and
violet-eyed," both buried in "that far-off fairyland."[9]

The bulk of the poem, however, was dedicated to her mother and
communicated how much Ina loved her:

> Let thine arms enfold me, Mother,
> Lay my head upon thy breast;
> In the wide world I can never
> Find so sweet a place of rest ...
>
> Oh, my mother—how I love thee!
> Dearer than all else beside,
> Thou, my life's sweet guardian angel,
> Parent—teacher—friend and guide![10]

The poem referred to an incident that occurred two years before Ina was born that was an important part of her family's lore.
Ina's father, Don Carlos, was away on a mission when on October
18, 1838, a gang of men kicked down the door of Agnes's house in
Millport, Missouri. She grabbed her daughters, Agnes, two years old,
and six-month-old Sophronia, and escaped in nothing more than
a nightdress. With no moon to light her way, Agnes ran on ground
covered with three inches of snow as her house burned behind her.
In the ink-stained night she headed toward the nearest Mormon
farm, three miles away and on the other side of the Grand River.
With Agnes Charlotte strapped to her back and Sophronia in her
arms, she stepped into the waist-deep river with its floating chunks of
ice. She crossed the river safely and arrived at Lyman Wight's house
near midnight, telling the Wights that she had only "escaped by the
skin of her teeth."[11]

Agnes's story with the Mormons had begun in Boston six years
earlier. Twenty-three years old, Agnes Moulton Coolbrith moved to
Boston, Massachusetts, from Scarborough, Maine, her family home.
A photo of Agnes at the time shows a pretty and frail young woman
with a kind face, wide-set eyes, and capable large hands. She and her
best friend, Mary Bailey, joined the Church of Jesus Christ of Latter-day Saints after they heard two handsome missionaries, Samuel

Agnes Moulton Coolbrith Smith Pickett.

Smith and Orson Hyde, give testimony about the religious group. Two years earlier at twenty-four years of age, Joseph Smith Jr. had written *The Book of Mormon*, basing it on a set of golden plates he claimed to have found near his house in New York. Along with the plates he found two stones that helped him transcribe the plates when he put the stones and his head inside of a hat. *The Book of Mormon* was published to mixed reviews. A newspaper in Rochester,

New York, said it was "evidence of fraud, blasphemy, and credulity."[12] Others praised it as proof that Joseph Smith was connected to God.

Agnes and Mary believed the latter, and moved to Kirtland, Ohio, where Mary married Samuel H. Smith, the middle-born Smith brother, and Agnes married nineteen-year-old Don Carlos Smith, Joseph's youngest brother. Don Carlos was seven years younger than Agnes, and at six feet four, stood more than a foot taller. A year after Agnes gave birth to Agnes Charlotte, their first child, on August 7, 1836, the Mormons were driven from Kirtland when Joseph issued bad notes on his bank, the Kirtland Safety Society Anti-Banking Company. Many Mormons left the church at that point; those who did not moved to Far West, Missouri.

Several years earlier, Joseph had directed some of his followers to establish a "New Jerusalem" in Jackson County, Missouri, which he declared was the original site of the Garden of Eden. As Mormon converts poured into this lucrative outpost for westward migration, the settlers already living there resented the close-knit community and the influence they would have as a voting bloc. The Missourians were serious about wanting them out and expelled twelve hundred Mormons from Jackson County by setting fire to their houses and beating the occupants. An agreement was reached in which the Mormons were allowed to settle to the north in Caldwell County if they promised not to expand their territory. By the time Joseph arrived in Far West, the main settlement in Caldwell County, his followers had already built streets, a school, and the beginnings of a temple.

Don Carlos and family did not immediately move from Ohio to Missouri because Agnes was pregnant with their second child. Two weeks after Sophronia was born on April 23, 1838, Don Carlos took the family on a two-month journey by wagon to Millport, Missouri, north of Far West. They would not stay for long. The Missourians had renewed their campaign to flush the Mormons from the state, and Joseph ordered Don Carlos and his cousin George A. Smith to go out of state to raise funds so the Mormons could leave. Don Carlos was in Tennessee or Kentucky when marauders set fire to their house and forced his wife to flee.

Five days later, Don Carlos wrote Agnes a letter in the calm language of everyday family life, clearly ignorant of what had happened to his wife. "Be careful of your health ... See that the cow has sufficient to eat &c to charge you to be careful of the children is useless knowing you never neglected them."[13] He closed the letter with an original poem:

> I turn I gaze beyond the stream
> From whence I came propelled by steam
> There I behold by my fireside
> The choice of youth Agnes my bride.
>
> Her soft and tender voice I hear
> Which sounds delightful to my ear
> With her I find that pearl of price
> By some abused by some despised ...[14]

As Don Carlos's letter made its way toward Agnes, Missouri's Governor Lilburn Boggs issued Executive Order 44, later known as the Mormon Extermination Order. He declared, "Mormons must be treated as enemies, and must be exterminated, or driven from the state, if necessary, for the public peace."[15] Don Carlos was still a hundred miles from home when he learned what had happened to his family. He walked 110 miles in two days and two nights, and arrived at Far West on Christmas Day. As soon as he could arrange a carriage, Don Carlos took his wife, children, and parents out of Missouri. Joseph Smith chose Nauvoo, Illinois, as their next settlement, and Ina was born there two years later.

Ina's portrayal of Agnes's flight in the birthday ode is sentimental, lacks sensory detail, and doesn't convey the terror that Agnes must have felt. Ina didn't include the scent of the men's leather coats, the alcohol on their breath, or the cold snow beneath her mother's feet as she ran. Missing in the poem are the doubt, fear, anger, and resentment that her mother may have felt toward the Missourians, the

Mormon Church, or her husband for leaving her alone. In Ina's eyes her mother was not a bareheaded, barefoot, scared-to-death woman running for her life, but a "Night's proud Empress tread majestic / Down her regal path of stars!"[16] Ina's ode transformed the incident into a myth. A daughter's pride turned a horrific nightmare into a fairytale.

Three months after Ina wrote the poem for her mother, summer had turned to fall in Los Angeles and the birds feasted on unpicked pomegranates and figs. Everyone looked forward to the first rains, even though they would turn the streets into muddy rivers. The nation had plunged into war earlier that year, and Agnes and William Pickett lived next to a Union camp established by the federal government to discourage the secessionist sympathizers that dominated Los Angeles. Pickett had declared himself a Union man, even though his second cousin, George E. Pickett, was a devout Southerner. George Pickett had been in Los Angeles that summer, and on June 15 dined with fellow soldiers with whom he had fought in the US 6th Infantry during the Mexican War. Though devoted friends, the group had split and declared allegiance to opposite sides of the Civil War, and that night Lewis Armistead and George Pickett stole out of town to fight for the South.

Ina was busy fighting battles of her own. She could no longer live with Carsley and was living at her mother's house with William Pickett and the twins. Ina later told a judge that her husband drew weapons on her, treated her with cruelty, and caused her "extreme fear for her personal safety."[17] In early October, Carsley went to San Francisco with his acting troupe, and upon his return on October 12, 1861, banged on Agnes's door and demanded to see Ina. We know what happened next from the testimonies given during Ina's divorce trial, which was recorded by hand in lettering that looks as if it was written against a steady gust of wind.

During the trial, Agnes told the judge that Carsley claimed to have heard in San Francisco that Ina had received male visitors from the Union camp, and that proved her to be a "whore." Agnes told Carsley that she would hear "nothing derogatory to Ina's character." Carsley pushed his way into the house and found his wife. He told

33

Ina that he had had women in San Francisco and didn't intend to live with her again, but that she should come with him so that he could "torment her to death."

"He took his wife by the hand violently and [hauled] and pulled her from room to room," Agnes told the judge. Agnes and Ina begged Carsley to go away. Instead, he threw off his coat and brought out a knife. Ina coaxed it away from him. He grabbed scissors from the sewing table, which Agnes was able to take. When he brandished a carving knife, both women pleaded with him to give it up, along with a warning that Pickett would be home soon.

"I'll spill Mr. Pickett's blood as a pig's," he replied.

The fourteen-year-old twins returned from hunting, and Carsley took one of their guns. Agnes was able to take that from him as well. Carsley finally agreed to leave when he saw Pickett walking down the road. Before Carsley left, Agnes made him promise that he would not return until the next day when he had calmed down.

He did not keep his word. Thirty minutes later Carsley returned with a six-shooter. The house was locked against him. Agnes told him through a locked door that he had gone against his word. "I have only myself to satisfy," he replied while searching for an unlocked window. He found one and was climbing into the house when a family friend, Edward J. C. Kewen (who would later become California's first attorney general), rode by on horseback. Agnes and Ina called for his help. Kewen tried to talk to Carsley, but Carsley spewed so many swear words at the Southerner that Kewen had no other choice than to tell Carsley he would have to challenge him to a duel if he did not desist from swearing. Carsley stopped and Kewen rode off, confident that he had mollified the situation. Kewen was wrong.

The day grew dark. Carsley went around to the front of the house, waving his pistol and yelling for Ina to come out. When he went to the front of the house, Agnes ran out the back door and across the field toward the Union camp, screaming for help. Carsley warned her to stop. Terrified for her mother's safety, Ina ran after her. Carsley gave chase and grabbed Ina by the hair and dragged her toward the street.

Pickett came out with a loaded rifle fitted with a bayonet. He shot at Carsley and missed. He lunged at him and missed again. The distraction allowed Ina to escape Carsley's grip, and she ran for the camp and her mother in the gloaming.

Carsley raised his Colt revolver, used the sights to get a bead on his wife, and pulled the trigger. The .36-caliber lead ball shot through the air at a thousand feet per second. Agnes heard the bullet whiz by her head. When the smoke from the gun cleared, Carsley saw that he had missed. The bullet had gone astray and hit one of the tents in camp.

"If I had my rifle I would have better execution," he yelled.

Pickett fired at Carsley again, and this time the bullet smashed into Carsley's hand and ended the confrontation.

A week later, on October 19, the *Los Angeles Star* reported the incident as if Ina had not been there. "Wounded—On Saturday evening last, a difficulty arose between Messes Pickett and Carsley arising out of matters of a private character, in which the latter was wounded in the hand, causing the necessity of amputation."

With a bandaged stump for an arm, Carsley returned to the Pickett house to harass his estranged wife. He screamed at her through locked doors and windows, and was still outside the house when the deputy sheriff served him divorce papers. His reaction was so violent that the deputy arrested him and took him to jail.

Ina went before Judge Benjamin Hayes on December 26, 1861, to obtain a divorce. Agnes, William Pickett, Kewen, and the twins testified. Ina did not speak during the trial. When it was over, Judge Hayes read, "It is ordered, ajudged, and decreed, that the bonds of matrimony heretofore existing between Josephine D. Carsley and Robert B. Carsley, be and the same are hereby dissolved, annulled, rendered void and of no effect."[18] The judge told Ina that she was free to marry again, "as though the said Robert B. Carsley was dead."[19]

Ina never saw Carsley again. He left Los Angeles and returned to his home state of Massachusetts, where he remarried. After twenty years his second wife deserted him on grounds of extreme cruelty and public intoxication. On the day of his second divorce he married a third wife who was three months pregnant. He died at age seventy-two of a kidney infection.

There is no evidence to prove or disprove Carsley's claim that Union officers had called on Ina, or if she had been unfaithful. The enigma is deepened by several poems, including "In the Pouts" and "Pancho." "In the Pouts" described the lure of a young woman:

> Cheeks of an ominous crimson,
> Eyebrows arched to a frown,
> Pretty red lips a-quiver
> With holding their sweetness down ...
>
> And when, in despite her frowning,
> The scorn, the grief, and the rue,
> She looks so bewitchingly pretty,
> Why—what can a fellow do?[20]

In "Pancho," written sixty years after her divorce, Ina described a young woman who regretted her actions:

> Just to make Pancho jealous—*ay de mí!*—
> With Juan I flirted. I cared not for Juan,
> Yet talked, laughed, danced with him, just but
>   to see
> My Pancho's eyes grow flame as he looked on.
>
> *Padre*, it is the woman's way, you know—
> And I'm but woman: *Sí*, "with fire to play."
> What would you? Could I dream 'twould
>   madden so?
> Ah, God! The fires of hell are mine today![21]

Whether or not she had tried to make her husband jealous, Ina was a divorced woman by her twenty-first birthday. She buried her past in Los Angeles and for the rest of her life did not publicly acknowledge her marriage, her divorce, or her child. She also hid her Mormon ancestry and changed her name. She retained Ina, her pen name, and Donna, her middle name, and for her last name chose Coolbrith, her mother's family name. She boarded a steamer with her mother, Pickett, and twin half-brothers. Agnes Charlotte stayed

in Los Angeles with her husband and two children. Ina Donna Coolbrith was bound for San Francisco, a place she came to call home and
the "city of my love and my desire."[22]

Part II:

San Francisco

There is a poetic divinity,
Number one of the *Overland* Trinity,
Who uses the muses
Pretty much as she chooses,
This dark eyed, young Sapphic divinity.

—*Bret Harte, writer and editor*

4

Precious Metals and Gems

Ina's boots clicked on the planks of San Francisco's Broadway Wharf, but the sound of her arrival was lost in the din of masts clanking in the wind, horses and mules rolling carts across uneven boards, and men barking orders and unloading hay scows. Almost hidden beneath the industrious symphony was a sailor's sweet-noted aria sung while he swabbed the deck of a clipper ship. Much had changed in the seven years since Ina had left San Francisco in 1855, when the city still seemed brand new. San Francisco's alchemy from backwater to boomtown had begun in 1848 when Mormon apostate Samuel Brannan ran through the city to announce that gold had been discovered on the American River. Ina was still living in St. Louis when word spread and treasure seekers from around the world arrived in the port of San Francisco in such great numbers that entire ships were abandoned in the harbor after passengers and crews ferried up the Sacramento River and into the land of gold. Some found only enough gold to spend on oysters, champagne, and women before heading back home; others used their riches to erect a new city.

Between 1849 and 1851, six great fires consumed San Francisco, and each time the citizens built again. The first fire to take the expanding city broke out on Christmas Eve in 1849. The redwood planks laid down for streets and sidewalks served as wicks to carry the flames to theatres, dry good stores, saloons, and houses. Although there was much damage, the determined San Franciscans built again with cinders still swirling in the air. The fifth and greatest fire engulfed the city in May 1851. The San Francisco Directory for 1852–53 reported that the conflagration was "awfully grand, beyond the force of language to express. All night the fire continued to rage and to spread, until the morning sun rose on a city in ruins."[1] Ina and her family would leave St. Louis for California the following year.

Gold melts at 2,000 degrees Fahrenheit. The flames from the six great fires melted gold nuggets stashed in hotel rooms, gold flakes stored in glass vials, and gold dust that had settled between floorboards. At least some of the gold wrested from the mountains returned to the earth and seeded the city that eventually took hold.

San Francisco's population had doubled while Ina was in Los Angeles. In 1862, nearly ninety-two thousand people lived in San Francisco, with twice as many men as women. As gold became yesterday's commodity, the precious metal that fed the growth of the city in the 1860s was silver taken from Nevada's Comstock Lode. The 1862 city directory recorded that the city and county of San Francisco collected $885,000 in taxes and other revenues that year, nearly three times as much as it had a decade earlier. The city erected 1,228 buildings, installed two miles of brick sewers, and planked two miles of streets and three miles of sidewalks. Workers graded forty-seven blocks by removing 358,000 cubic yards of rock, dirt, and sand, which a steam locomotive dumped into the shallow harbor where more buildings were erected. Three grand hotels rose within a three-block radius downtown, including Russ House, billed as the largest hotel in the world. It was only three stories high, but its footprint on Montgomery Street splayed from Pine to Bush. All three hotels housed fashionable shops that served as promenades for wealthy women. One travel writer noted that the women in San Francisco were more beautiful than any in the world, and were "gregarious, laughing, stunningly dressed and self confident."[2]

Ina was far from rich, but was beautiful with her curly dark hair, gray eyes, and full figure. Josephine Clifford (later McCracken), a writer who came to San Francisco a few years later, described Ina as "beautiful in form and figure as she was brilliant in mind."[3]

Ina Coolbrith in 1871. Courtesy Oakland Public
Library, Oakland History Room.

Ina and her family moved into a house on Russian Hill from
which she looked east to the city's main harbor and across the bay
to Yerba Buena Island and the undeveloped East Bay hills. To the
north, she saw Alcatraz Island and the muscular hills on the other
side of the Golden Gate. Ina would live on Russian Hill on and off

for the rest of her life, and when she wasn't living there she longed to be. It was no wonder: the decade when she lived there after moving from Los Angeles would prove to be one of the most satisfying times of her life as an artist, and set the stage for her fifty-year reign as one of the West's most beloved poets. She associated Russian Hill with creative fulfillment, even later when the fog triggered her arthritis. Throughout her lifetime, hundreds of writers and artists would climb the hill to spend time in her parlor. One writer called the journey a "literary Mecca."[4] Another visitor told Ina, "Your house gives me a wonderful view of scenery, but *you* have given me a wonderful view of life."[5]

But poetry was not the priority when the family arrived—money was—and everyone went to work. Agnes sewed, Pickett took a job as a printer, and William worked as his apprentice. Don Carlos was a book clerk for Hubert Howe Bancroft, and Ina took a job teaching English at a language school.

The only literary person Ina knew when she arrived was Joseph Duncan, her former editor at *California Home Journal,* a publication that folded. Duncan loved poetry—he even wrote and published some—but after his printing press burned in a fire, he abandoned publishing and opened an import store that supplied art and furnishings for the new mansions on Rincon Hill. Duncan had a talent for making and losing fortunes, a skill that he perfected throughout his lifetime. Ina visited Duncan at his store and found him gentle and creative. He found her enchanting. Duncan was single because he had left his wife and four children, but his availability didn't tempt Ina. Her scars ran deep.

Ina's work at the school and at home helped distract her during the day, but at night she mourned her marriage and the loss of her child, and imagined death to be her only relief. One night as her family slept, Ina looked out the window to watch the wind push clouds across a night sky. A silvery moon slipped in and out of the clouds and a poem formed in her head. She looked down on the harbor to see "sail-reefed ships loom, ghost-like thro' the haze," and listened to "midnight winds go by / With slow sad wail, as of unuttered woe."[6] She formed the experience into a poem, which she titled "Unrest," and sent it to the *Los Angeles Star.* Ina suffered from insomnia, and when left alone with her thoughts she succumbed to a gloomy disposition that came with the regularity of San Francisco's fog. When the world slowed down and she settled into the dark night of her thoughts, the string of words she put on paper often communicated a deep melancholia, one that showed itself in her early poems and often colored her verse and days. This private melancholia, however, contrasted with the wit, intelligence, and humor she displayed in public. It was as if the clouds that blew across the moon also swirled inside of her and sometimes shadowed her light. "It is difficult for me to reconcile Ina Coolbrith's keen sense of humor with her rather un-optimistic disposition," said Ina's grandniece many years later. "Her sensitive, reticent nature seemed to close her in an isolation none could penetrate."[7]

Each long night did come to an end, but daylight brought nightmares of its own with the Civil War in full, bloody swing. Arguments for and against slavery and secession were as passionate in California as they were in the rest of the country, but the conflicts in the West were debated in newspapers, saloons, mining camps, and parlors instead of being waged on battlefields. Some men from California joined the ranks; others paid thousands of dollars for a surrogate fighter to go in their stead. Those who stayed behind read about the battles at Shiloh, Bull Run, and the bloodiest of them all, Antietam, where on September 17, 1862, twenty-three thousand soldiers were killed, wounded, or had gone missing.

On November 4, 1862, Ina paid the one-dollar entry fee to the Union Festival, an event held for the United States Sanitary Commission, an organization that raised money to feed, clothe, and care for Union soldiers. Inside Platt's Hall, red, white, and blue flags hung from the ceiling to declare Union allegiance; food-covered plank tables ran down the middle of the hall; and on the sides men and women posed in tableaux to recreate images from famous paintings.

The featured speaker at the event was Reverend Thomas Starr King, the popular minister who had come to San Francisco from Boston in 1860 to serve at the First Unitarian Church. Like most Californians, Ina knew of King, and may have first heard him lecture in Los Angeles. To those who supported the Union, King was a celebrated figure; to Southerners he was a "damned poodle-eyed Yankee." King was also the most accomplished writer in San Francisco. In New England he had written *The White Hills: Their Legends, Landscapes, & Poetry*, published in 1860. In California he wrote *A Vacation Among the Sierra: Yosemite in 1860*, published in 1862. He was a literary luminary to young writers like Ina.

King had been a minister at Boston's Hollis Street Church for more than a decade before he accepted an offer from San Francisco's Unitarian Church. He came to California because he believed that the new state needed him. When the Civil War started, most of California's populace and politicians were sympathetic to the Confederacy. To change their minds, King went on a lecture tour up and down California to thunder out the importance of saving the Union. He said he had not known the thrill of public speaking until standing in front of men armed with bowie knives and revolvers.

King's looks were deceiving. He stood less than five feet tall and had the complexion and stringy hair of a sick boy, but his passions and deep voice filled a room. "Though I weigh only 120 pounds, when I'm mad I weigh a ton," he said.[8] He didn't shy away from blending church and state, and felt it his duty to bring political issues to his parishioners. He campaigned for Abraham Lincoln's reelection, draped an American flag over his pulpit, and ended his sermons with "God Bless the President of the United States and all who serve with him and the cause of a common country."[9] Emperor Norton, a businessman who had lost his mind and crowned himself emperor of the United States and protector of Mexico, did not approve. Norton said, "The preacher must stop preaching politics. I will put a stop to it and issue a decree to that effect."[10] Though King preached about political issues, he had no interest in becoming a politician. When asked to run for United States senator he said, "I would swim to Australia before taking a political post. A dandy lives from one necktie to another, a fashionable woman from one wrinkle to another, and a politician from one election to another."[11]

Thanks to King's efforts on behalf of the United States Sanitary Commission, Californians contributed over one million dollars toward the welfare of Union soldiers, one-quarter of the total raised by the entire country. One of the ways King raised the money was to hold events such as the Union Festival at Platt's Hall. King had learned to lecture without a script since coming to California and his improvisational speechmaking was legendary. Charles Henry Webb, one of the most accomplished writers in San Francisco, described King's style best when he wrote in the *Golden Era*, "Straightening up his slight form and growing with his subject until you thought a giant stood on the platform, he spoke what was in him."[12]

At Platt's Hall, King praised Californians' service to the war and told the men in the crowd that it was not their fault that they were not fighting. The government needed them in the West to guard the frontier, fight the Indians, and keep an eye on Brigham Young—a dig that Ina was unlikely to miss. King read two patriotic poems by Francis Bret Harte, the most promising young writer in California. Ina had not yet met Harte. Little did she know that in a few years' time she, Harte, and writer Charles Warren Stoddard would form a bond so tight that others dubbed them the *Overland* Trinity.

Harte came to California from New York in 1854, the same year Ina lived in San Francisco for the first time at age thirteen. Harte bounced around as a tutor, an apothecary's assistant, and a stage-line express man. He toured the gold mines and wrote bad poetry. He moved to Union (now Arcata) to live with his sister, where he landed a job as a printer at a newspaper, the *Northern Californian*. He showed enough competence in writing the occasional article that the editor, going on vacation, left him in charge. During Harte's watch in February 1860, a group of local men slaughtered sixty Wiyot Indians, mostly women and children, in a nearby coastal village. The townspeople condoned the incident by not naming the perpetrators. Harte exposed the atrocity in an editorial titled "Indiscriminate Massacre of Indians: Women and Children Butchered," and in it called for those responsible to come forward. The townspeople responded by running him out of town.

Back in San Francisco at age twenty-three, Harte wrote for the *Golden Era*, San Francisco's most literary paper to date, and King and Jessie Ann Benton Frémont, wife of explorer and first-time Republican presidential candidate John C. Frémont, took notice. Jessie had a home on Black Point overlooking the Golden Gate where she hosted popular Sunday dinners and provided a quiet cottage for King to work. Under King and Frémont's tutelage, Harte wrote

Francis Bret Harte. Courtesy The Bancroft
Library, University of California, Berkeley.

at least thirty Civil War poems, many of which King included in
his speeches. King also asked editor James T. Fields to print one of
Harte's stories in the *Atlantic Monthly*. "I am sure there is a great deal
in Harte, and an acceptance of his piece would imprint him, and
help literature on this coast where we raise bigger trees and squashes
than literati and brains," wrote King.[13] Fields accepted "The Legend
of Monte del Diablo," a fictional tale set on one of the tallest peaks
in the Bay Area, which appeared in the October 1863 issue alongside

the work of John Greenleaf Whittier, Ralph Waldo Emerson, and Henry David Thoreau. In 1862, the same year that Ina left Los Angeles a divorced woman, Harte married Anna Griswold, a singer in King's church. With Frémont's connections, he landed a quiet government job at the United States Mint that paid well and allowed him time to write.

Harte was not the only writer whom King encouraged. One day, King walked into a bookstore where young Charles Warren Stoddard worked. Stoddard had explored San Francisco as a boy after he arrived in 1855, but in his teens grew nervous and quit school. He wanted nothing more than to write poetry, and at age seventeen took a part-time job at a bookstore where he had time to write. One day he drummed up the courage to submit a poem to the *Golden Era* under the pseudonym of Pip Pepperpod. The *Era* printed his poem, and each week thereafter Stoddard submitted a poem by Pip. His use of a *nom de plume* was not unusual. Webb went by Inago or John Paul; Harte signed some of his pieces "The Bohemian"; Prentice Mulford used Dogberry; and Samuel Clemens alternated between his given name and Mark Twain.

King entered the bookstore where Stoddard worked and said, "Charlie Stoddard, did you write this poem?" while pointing to the *Golden Era*.

"Yes, I did sir," replied Stoddard, a slight young man with soft curly hair who looked like Percy Bysshe Shelley, the English Romantic poet.

"It's a good poem and I hope you will write many more," said King, who told Stoddard to return to school and gave him complimentary tickets to a lecture series on American poets that King was giving at his church.[14] Ina also attended those lectures, but had not yet met Stoddard. Years later when Ina met John Greenleaf Whittier, she told Whittier how King had featured the Fireside Poet in the series. "He likened each of the group to some particular gem, and I supposed the pearl would fall to you, but he gave you the ruby, because, he explained, each line and word of yours came from a heart throbbing and full with the warm, rich, blood of humanity."[15]

At the Union Festival in Platt's Hall, King ended with another of Harte's poems and stepped down from the podium. The *Daily*

Alta California reported that the Presidio Band blasted the hall with music and the guests danced until late.

The casualties of the Civil War continued to pile up, and in July 1863 the news that fifty-one thousand American lives were lost in the Battle of Gettysburg hit hard, especially in Ina's household. On the battle's third day, Pickett's relative George E. Pickett, who had been promoted to general in the Confederacy, followed orders and led a charge resulting in the death of half of his troops. The blood of nearly seven thousand men soaked the field in less than one hour.

Half a year later, the war occupied Ina's thoughts. On Christmas Eve she watched the fire cast large shadows on the parlor walls while the family slept. The Christmas tree candles were out and the clock on the mantel kept time with her "midnight thought."[16] That night her personal melancholia made way for a broader pathos about the war in "Christmas Eve: 1863," a poem that seems influenced by King. These stanzas lie at the heart of the longer poem:

> Could the thousands of maimed and mangled,
> Of widowed and orphaned, be led
> To the rivers, and hills and valleys,
> That are drunk with the blood of their dead:
>
> How quickly would rage melt to sorrow,
> How silenced the cannon's roar;
> And the hands that are clenched in combat,
> Be clasped in love, once more![17]

The poem was her third to be published in the *Golden Era* that year.

King kept a frenetic pace during the four years he was in San Francisco, and on March 4, 1864, died of diphtheria at age forty. Webb wrote in the *Golden Era* that had King lived he could have single-handedly ended the war. "I am persuaded that could he have gone through the Southern States, shaking hands with secessionists, he would have won them back to their allegiance by the mere magnetism of his touch."[18]

On the day of King's funeral, Ina stood in line with twenty thousand others to pay her respects. Flags flew at half-mast and soldiers on Alcatraz fired guns at one-minute intervals. As she neared the metal coffin placed in front of King's pulpit, a poem formed in her head. By the time Ina's "Starr King" was published in the *Golden Era*, the paper had already published a eulogy by Stoddard and Harte's "Relieving Guard," the best of the three. In a few years' time, these three writers would be dubbed a literary trinity, but the bond that united them that year was their love for Starr King. According to the city directory, a heavy rain started ten days after King's death and did not stop for forty-seven days.

5

A Knack for Rhyme

Soon after King's death in 1874, Charles Henry Webb published the first issue of a new magazine. With himself as publisher, editor, and writer and Harte his main contributor, Webb declared his confidence in the *Californian* with a masthead that read, "Best Journal on the Pacific Coast, and the Equal of any on the Continent." Webb had arrived in San Francisco a year before, coming from New York where he had written for *Vanity Fair* and the *New York Times*. In San Francisco, he wrote for the *Golden Era*, the only literary magazine being published when he arrived, and within a year was ready to push San Francisco to a higher literary level.

Two months after the *Californian* launched, Ina went to the journal's office to see about a job for her brother. The fact that she, not Pickett or her brother, went on this errand says something about her share of financial responsibility for her family. She later told a friend that Pickett "was a victim of intemperance," which forced Ina "as a young girl to take his place in the chief maintenance of the family."[1]

Webb was out, so she left a note giving the reason for her errand. She also left a poem. Several days later, Webb came to Ina's house on Russian Hill. She described him as having hair so blonde it was almost white, and that although he wasn't handsome he was "rather pleasing" and had a "slight stammer that added to rather than detracted from the effect."[2]

She invited him into her parlor. He said he did need help and could hire her brother as an apprentice. "And now, a-about your p-poem," he said.[3] He liked it and asked if she had others to show him. He later explained that he did not believe she wrote "Cupid Kissed Me," and feared he would be accused of publishing a plagiarized poem. She showed him others that convinced him of her genuine talent, and he ran the poem in the August issue. She would publish twelve poems in the *Californian* over the next two years.

Webb visited her often and brought his work to her parlor. One day he asked her opinion on a poem-in-progress about a knight in love with a mermaid who combed her hair while sitting on a rock. "They are always combing their hair," Ina said in "Gossip," the lecture she gave in 1911.

Webb was stuck on a particular line and asked for Ina's help. He read aloud, "I led her as light as the seabirds flit / To the steed that stood chomping his silver bit."

He looked to Ina for the next line. She did not like the parody poems that were popular at the time, and offered a playful suggestion: "Tho' I hardly thought the saddle would fit?"[4]

Webb laughed and later told her that he would never think of the poem again without her line falling into place.

Webb sold his financial interest in the magazine a few months after launching it, but continued to serve as editor for two more years. During Webb's first vacation, he put Harte at the helm as interim editor. Before Webb left for Lake Tahoe, he and Ina were in front of the magazine's office on Montgomery Street when Harte approached. "Frank th-this is I-Ina. Ina, this is F-Frank. N-now you be good to her."[5]

Harte published two of Ina's poems during his editorial stint, and when he learned that the New York *Leader* had published "Cupid Kissed Me" without giving Ina credit, he suggested in the *Californian* that the *Leader* change its name to the *Misleader*. Harte also invited Mark Twain, known to his friends as Samuel Clemens, to write an article a week for the *Californian*. Clemens bragged to his family about his new position. "The *Californian* circulates among the highest class of the community, and it is the best weekly literary paper in the United States."[6]

Webb did not pay for poetry but did pay for prose. The fact that Ina's family needed money convinced her to write a column under the pseudonym of Meg Merrill. One of her columns took readers on a horse-drawn streetcar ride to Meigg's Wharf (near the foot of Powell Street) during the closing month of the Civil War. "Carefully, my friend … Don't you know [the drivers] never wait for one to be seated?" she said of the operator who nearly lurched her into the lap of a napping old man.[7] Once seated, Ina observed a young mother with a child on her lap, and judged her to be of better character than that of the sleeping gentleman. "Her fingers are less white and soft than those of our fat friend yonder—unlike his, also, in their total want of diamond hoops. She wears her diamonds, and they are of 'first water,' in her heart, my friend." She saw a man heading for the car "tripping daintily across the street, balancing his light walking stick in his gloved fingers" and dubbed him "the Dandy." More people got on at each stop, and the car became crowded.

"Ring, ring! What, still another passenger? Why, we are full now!" she wrote. "No, we are not, it's one of Uncle Sam's boys, and there is always room for our soldiers. Carefully conductor; don't you see the man is crippled?" As the soldier sat, the Dandy gathered up his coattails to keep them from contacting the soldier's soiled clothes.

"Why, you atrocious little jackanapes," wrote Ina. "Don't you know that one square inch of that old blue coat, worn and faded as it is, is worth ten times more—aye, a thousand times more—than the whole of your broadcloth suit, with the dummy which it contains thrown in!"[8]

Ina closed the column by telling her readers to call on Meg the next time they wanted a companion on the streetcars. But circumstances changed, and Ina no longer had time to write columns. Her sister was ill in Los Angeles and had sent for Agnes to come and help with the children. With Agnes gone, Ina was in charge of cooking and cleaning for a household of men that included Pickett, her two brothers, and two young Mexican boarders.

At last the Civil War ended on April 9, 1865. On the heels of that good news came bad. Six days later San Franciscans awoke to church bells ringing and flags flying at half-mast to announce the death of President Abraham Lincoln. In "Hereafter," published in the June 3 issue of the *Californian*, Ina wrote she was tired of losing "The treasured hopes which lie like precious gems / Scattered and lost amid the roadside dust."

That summer, Ina sent several poems to Bret Harte for consideration in a poetry anthology, California's first. Harte was editing the book published by Anton Roman, who had made a small fortune selling books to miners during the Gold Rush. Roman opened a bookstore in San Francisco in 1851, an enterprise that would eventually become Books, Inc., which is still in business today.

Of the poems Ina submitted, Harte accepted "Cupid Kissed Me," "In the Pouts," and "The Mother's Grief." She asked Harte why he had not chosen "Fragment from an Unfinished Poem," which she had also submitted. He replied, "To the general public, the evidence of genius is *completeness* ... Every man has sometime in his life said something good: It is the *habit* of being smart that makes the good writer, or poet, and the power of carrying a thought or fancy to completeness that makes the article or poem."[9]

Word about the anthology spread and amateur poets from all over the state sent in their verses. Harte did not like most of what he read, and kept his selections a secret. When *Outcroppings, Being Selections of California Verse* was released, hundreds of people waited in line outside Roman's bookstore to see whose poetry graced its pages. When they flipped through the gilt-edged book, they found forty poems by urban-bred transplants, and only a few by their favorite frontier poets. "The he-men among Pacific Coast poets were outraged," wrote Franklin Walker in *San Francisco's Literary Frontier*. "Here was a good subject for a real fight, one that they could all enjoy."[10] Newspapers throughout California attacked *Outcroppings*. Reviews from the gold country called the poetry "hogwash ladled from the slop-bucket" and a "quantity of slumgullion that would average about 33 ½ cents a ton."[11]

The criticism and controversy added to the book's interest and it sold out quickly. It also attracted attention in the East. Reviews in the *Boston Transcript*, *Boston Evening Courier*, and *Philadelphia Daily Evening Bulletin* were favorable. *The Nation*, however, expressed disappointment in the lack of regional voices that might have set the poetry apart. "[The] poets rarely make mention of [California's] climate and scenery; but sing, with an exile's fondness, of the seasons and landscapes known to us of the eastern shore of the continent."[12] The reviewer found exception in a few of the poems. "'Cupid Kissed Me' and 'In the Pouts,' by Ina D. Coolbrith, have a slight pathos and saucy charm quite their own; while 'The Mother's Grief,' by the same poet, is veritable and fine." After quoting a stanza from "The Mother's Grief," the reviewer added, "Miss Coolbrith is one of the *real* poets among the many poetic masqueraders in the volume."

It was Ina's first national notice, and perhaps gave her the courage to send several poems and a request for advice to Henry Wadsworth Longfellow. Longfellow, the most famous American poet of the time, replied, "One thing is evident, and that is that you possess a true instinct of versification, which is a prophecy of success.... I can give you no other advice than to look upon life with your own eyes, and to write always as simply and naturally as you have begun."[13] She had also asked him to say which poem he liked the best, to which he replied, "Fragment from an Unfinished Poem."

To appease those unhappy with *Outcroppings*, Samuel Brannan, who had become California's first millionaire, bankrolled another anthology. *The Poetry of the Pacific*, published by Hubert Howe Bancroft, included the work of seventy-five poets and included Ina's "Fragment from an Unfinished Poem."

In the spring of 1866 Webb returned to New York, and James F. Bowman edited the *Californian* until it folded at the end of that year. Webb and Ina corresponded until his death in 1905.

In May of 1866, editor and poet John Rollin Ridge called on Ina when he stopped in San Francisco on his way to Washington, DC. Ridge had published Ina's poems in the *Marysville Express* when she was just a teenager, and had encouraged her to keep writing. She described Ridge as her "first personal literary acquaintance" in her lecture "Gossip." During Ridge's visit to San Francisco, they decided to make a pilgrimage to Lone Mountain Cemetery, a 160-acre graveyard that sprawled across an area where the University of San Francisco stands today. There they hoped to find the unmarked grave of Edward Pollock, whose six-year literary career ended when he died young. Ridge had known Pollock when they were early contributors to the *Golden Era*, and for Ina, Pollock's poetry had been the first to demonstrate that poems could be written in and about California.

As Ina and Ridge walked through wind-dwarfed trees among the dead of Lone Mountain, Ridge did most of the talking. "He taught me more of poets and poetry than my ignorant, young, country-girl head had gathered in all its previous years," she said.[14] Ina described Ridge as "a man of splendid physique and character" who went hatless against the style of the day.[15] In his youth, Ridge was strikingly handsome, and at forty-one was still good-looking, though his once thick black hair had started to recede. He wore a goatee and looked at the world with deep-set, serious eyes.

Ridge had come to California in 1850 and made his living as an editor at several Northern California newspapers including the *Sacramento Bee*, where he was that paper's first editor. Ridge was also a poet and novelist, and the first writer to turn the oral tales of an infamous Mexican bandit into a novel, *The Life and Adventures of Joaquín Murieta, the Celebrated California Bandit.* His novel revealed the California goldfields as breeding grounds for prejudicial treatment of anybody who was not Anglo American, and marked the retaliation that followed. It was the first novel printed in California, and Ridge was the first known Native American novelist.

As Ina and Ridge walked the cemetery, they discussed the possibility of an afterlife. Ridge promised Ina that if it was possible his soul would visit her after his death. They left the cemetery without finding Pollock's grave.

The night before Ridge left for Washington, DC, where he was to serve as a Southern Cherokee negotiator for a postwar treaty, he joined Ina and her family for dinner. Ina said that during dinner Ridge "talked with quiet hopefulness of his plans for the betterment of his people."[16] Ridge's Cherokee name was Cheesquatalawny, or Yellow Bird. His father, John Ridge, and his grandfather, Major Ridge, were influential leaders in the Cherokee Nation in Georgia when John was born in 1827. Ridge's mother, Sarah Bird Northrup Ridge, was a Caucasian from New England. Although Anglo Americans had already taken two-thirds of the Cherokees' ancestral lands, the Cherokee people prospered as farmers and ranchers, like the Ridges who lived in large houses run like Southern plantations. John Ridge worked his 419 acres in Georgia with the help of eighteen slaves.

Major Ridge and John Ridge had fought Cherokee removal for years, but came to believe that assimilation was inevitable and wanted to gain recompense for the Cherokees before it was too late. Acting against the wishes of most Cherokee people and in defiance of John Ross, the principal chief of the Cherokee Nation, the Ridges signed the Treaty of New Echota to give the government the legal right to remove the Cherokees from their ancestral land. Three years later, US soldiers forced seventeen thousand Cherokees to Oklahoma on a march that is today known as the Trail of Tears. It is unknown whether Ina told Ridge that her father, Don Carlos Smith, had come upon thirteen hundred Cherokees on the Trail of Tears during his last mission. Don Carlos wrote in his journal that while waiting for a boat in Columbus, Kentucky, he spoke with several Cherokees who said they "felt deeply wounded at leaving their native country for the west."[17] Four thousand people died during the forced migration, and Ross and his followers held the Ridges accountable.

John Rollin Ridge was twelve years old when a mob of Cherokees dragged his father from their house in Honey Creek, Oklahoma, where they had resettled. At daybreak, young John watched from an upstairs window as several men held his father down while a third stabbed him twenty-nine times. John's grandmother told the boy that the responsibility of avenging his father's death was his.

John Rollin Ridge escaped to Fayetteville, Arkansas, with his mother, and later to Massachusetts, where he received a good education. Ridge married Elizabeth Wilson, and they had a daughter,

Alice. At twenty-three years old, Ridge went to California, and his wife and daughter followed later.

Ridge never forgot the night of his father's murder, nor did he forget that revenge for the deed fell to him. In *San Francisco's Literary Frontier*, Franklin Walker wrote that Ridge told a fellow editor in a San Francisco saloon that all but four of the thirty-six men responsible for killing his father were dead. Ridge stopped short of claiming responsibility, but knew how each had died.

After Ridge's visit with Ina in San Francisco, he left for the nation's capital, where he and others tried to negotiate a treaty to admit Cherokees into the Union. He returned to Grass Valley disappointed.

Two years later, Ina had a disturbing dream in which she walked through a small town where the walls of the buildings were draped in black. She entered a house filled with people and walked toward an open coffin in the middle of the room: it held Ridge. The next morning she wrote and mailed a letter to him in which she described her dream. That evening she read in the newspaper that Ridge had died the day before.

Perhaps at that time she recalled a story that Ridge had told her about a Choctaw Indian chief named Pushmataha who went to Washington, DC, to negotiate a treaty for his tribe. Pushmataha was dying by the time he arrived in DC and called his warriors to him. "You will return to my people, and you will see the grass springing, and hear the birds sing, but Pushmataha will see them and hear them no more. My people will say to you, 'Where is our Chief, where is Pushmataha?' and you will answer, 'He is no more.' It will strike upon their hearts like the fall of a mighty oak in the stillness of the forest."[18]

A few days after Ridge died, Ina received a letter from Lizzie Ridge saying that Ina's dream had accurately depicted the day of Ridge's funeral, and that the townspeople had accorded him the respect of the highest official of the land. It would seem that Ridge kept the promise he made to Ina at Lone Mountain when he told her that his spirit would visit her upon his death.

An undated article in Ina's scrapbook shows that she returned to Lone Mountain to search for Pollock's grave with poets Emilie

Lawson and Charles Warren Stoddard. They asked the caretaker if he knew where Pollock's grave was located. "Never heard of the man," he replied. The poets wandered the cemetery and came upon an old man who said he had helped dig the grave, and told them where to find it. The three young poets followed the old man's directions and found the site of Pollock's grave "sunken and utterly uncared for, without a stone nor even a rude head-board to identify the place."[19]

In a poem Ina wrote about their visit, she said she did not miss the tombstone. Far better, she said, that the Earth "clothes him with her grace,"[20] a line reminiscent of Ridge's own words from his poem "October Hills":

> What now to me the jars of life,
> Its petty cares, its harder throes?
> The hills are free from toil and strife
> And clasp me in their deep repose.[21]

6

Pearl of Her Tribe

San Francisco is known for its hills, but the hills of today are tame compared to the original topography. When the city was young, planners removed sandy hillocks at Mission and First streets, and on Market at Third and Fourth. Telegraph Hill was a perfect harbor lookout and picnic area for families of all nationalities on clear Sunday afternoons, even after the city dynamited huge chunks of rock from its sides and sold the pieces to outgoing ships for ballast. Rincon Hill was the neighborhood preferred by millionaires until the city cut a slab out of the hill at Second and Harrison. After the first good rain, the houses and trees began to slide into the slot they had created, and the millionaires fled to other quarters. Stoddard later described the abandoned house in which he squatted on Rincon Hill: "Every winter the rains beat upon it and drove through and through it, and undermined it, and made a mush of the rock and soil about it. Portions of that real estate deposited themselves, pudding fashion, in the yawning abyss below."[1]

The hills have always been a ripe subject for writers. "A cheerful resemblance to the knobs on an over-done meat pie, in which the vegetable predominates, is the utmost, I think, we can ask for them," wrote Harte of the sandy hills that stretched to the sea.[2] Reporter Adeline Knapp criticized those who did not recognize the health-giving aspects of the hills: "There is something absolutely pathetic in

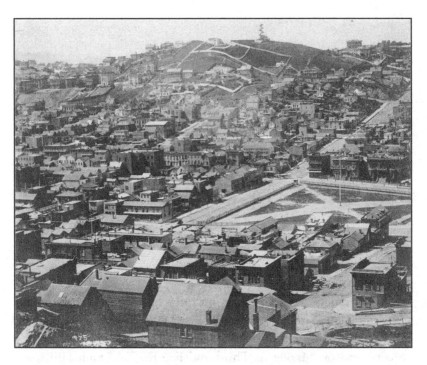

Russian Hill, 1865. Courtesy California Historical Society.

the sight of San Franciscans repairing to the quarters of the various athletic clubs for exercise when nature's own gymnasium is open to them day and night, free as the sunlight and the stars."[3] Ina wrote in "Longing" that she liked to climb the "grand hills, summer-crowned" with "limbs of steel, the heart of air."[4]

"We were all hillites," she later said. "There were no streetcars, only clumsy, lumbering omnibuses which jolted over the rock-paved streets most excruciatingly. The foot climb was preferable, and we were young."[5] Though she loved to climb all the hills of San Francisco, she always returned to Russian Hill, her sanctuary.

Ina continued to publish poetry after the *Californian* folded. In 1867 she published five poems in the *New York Galaxy*, a magazine containing work by Henry James, Walt Whitman, and Mark Twain. She had become one of the most talented writers in the city. "All her vitality seemed to center in her brain," said her niece. "When she was in her prime this mental vitality reacted upon her body [and] shone in the brilliance of her changeable eyes."[6] The other talents in the city—Stoddard, Twain, and Harte—agreed.

Charles Warren Stoddard lived with his family near Ina on Russian Hill. Charlie, as Ina and other friends called him, had kind eyes and gently sloping eyebrows that asked for acceptance. His nose was a bit large, but fit well on his face, and his thin lips seemed always to hold a gentle smile at their corners. His soft curly hair had already begun to recede, and his facial hair was barely visible except for neatly trimmed sideburns that skidded to a stop at the base of his ears. He dressed well, had a flair for the dramatic, and was told by friends that he would do well on the stage. He played the piano but could not sing. Ina said to him, "Charloway, don't you ever attempt to join the heavenly choir unless you wish to stampede the angels."[7]

After Thomas Starr King told Stoddard to return to school, he enrolled in courses at Oakland's Brayton Academy, but skipped his classes to roam the hills and write poetry. He became so nervous about his missed assignments that his parents sent him for an extended stay with his married sister in Hawaii, where he recuperated. The pace of an idle romantic fit his personality better than that of an industrious worker. Stoddard discovered the art of leaning gently into a day instead of pushing hard against it.

Ina found Stoddard's approach refreshing. The events in her life had forced her to grow up fast and left little room for a childhood, but with Charlie she could play. They explored the wild hills and fields west of the city and gathered ferns and flowers. Their favorite pastime was to go to the beach when the tides were low. They took a stagecoach or a one-horse car to Fort Point near the mouth of the bay, or to the Cliff House at the northern end of a beach that stretched for miles along the Pacific Ocean (today's Ocean Beach). On their excursions they combed the shore for treasures from the sea and cooked pork chops and coffee on driftwood fires.

Stoddard wrote about his early beachcombing days in his book *In the Footprints of the Padres*, and although he does not specifically refer to Ina, his descriptions in that book help us picture Ina and Stoddard at the ocean. "We could follow the beach for miles … And what sea treasures lay strewn there!... Such starfish and cloudy, starch-like jellyfish, and all the livelier creeping and crawling creatures that populate the shore!"[8]

Ina was proud of the varied collection of sea mosses and sea algae she gathered as they walked on the beach and ran from the waves. At the end of the day, they rode home over the sand dunes, and at dusk Stoddard deposited Ina at her front door, her cheeks flush and her pockets full of treasures that smelled of the sea.

Stoddard spent time in Ina's parlor, which he described as "a salon in the best sense of the word."[9] From her parlor window, Ina and Stoddard looked out on a nearby garden with a fountain and listened for a mockingbird that she called her "little poet." When Stoddard got the blues, which was often, he came to her parlor and laid his head in her lap while she comforted him. He described Ina as having an exotic air, and said she could have been mistaken for a daughter of Spain with her "dark eyes, the luxuriant dark hair, [and] the pure olive skin flushed with the ripe glow of the pomegranates ... Even the rich contralto voice, the mellifluous tongue and the well-worn guitar were hers—everything, in fact, save the stiletto and the cigarette."[10] On occasion, Ina may have been convinced to dance for Stoddard and other visitors. Her niece said that when Ina danced the Spanish fandango, "she was one of the prettiest sights I have ever seen, and most adorable."[11]

Stoddard had devoted himself to writing verse for years, and Harte convinced him that it was time to collect his poems into a book, also offering to help select the poems and edit the collection. Anton Roman agreed to publish it, and artist William Keith provided the illustrations. *Poems by Charles Warren Stoddard* came out to discouraging reviews, and Stoddard questioned his decision to be a poet. He sought solace in the Catholic Church and moved to Sacramento to give theater a try.

Ina missed him when he left. The day after her twenty-seventh birthday, and two days before Stoddard's opening night, she wrote him a letter. She teased him about wearing tights, and reminded him that she had spent her last two birthdays with him. She was "in the mists without and within" she said, and didn't like birthdays because they reminded her of time passing with nothing done.[12] She quoted

Charles Warren Stoddard. Courtesy The Bancroft Library, University of California, Berkeley.

Lord Byron, who on his thirty-third birthday said, "What have these years left to me? Nothing except thirty-three."[13]

When Stoddard did not write back for several weeks, Ina threatened to "box his ears" for not responding.[14] She chided him good-naturedly but was clearly upset by his inattention. She did not know what to make of his moods, which she said were "as variable as a San Francisco summer day."[15] She told him, "Charloway, if there were as many legs as there are sides to you, a centipede would not be in it."[16]

A butterfly, not a centipede, would have been a more apt description. Stoddard was undergoing a metamorphosis and it had little to do with Ina. On his first visit to Hawaii at age twenty-one, he had discovered that he was, as he put it, an "easy convert to the untrammeled delights of barbarianism."[17] On that trip he watched young native men swim at a local natural pool and met a boy named Kane-Aloha. The two young men rode naked on horseback by day, and by night slept in huts, where they "yielded to the seductions of the hour."[18] Stoddard was looking for opportunities that might provide him with similar satisfaction.

He also craved acceptance, and sent his book of poems to Walt Whitman along with a request for Whitman's thoughts on his work. While some people considered Whitman's *Leaves of Grass* obscene, Stoddard loved it and ranked Whitman as the greatest living poet. "His life was a poem and his poetry full of life itself," Stoddard later said. "Good people understand it and are better for it, and bad people misunderstand it and are the worse for their failure to comprehend."[19]

In spite of Stoddard's praise, Whitman did not respond to Stoddard's first attempt to communicate.

The birth of a magazine like the *Overland Monthly* was an inevitable next step for the bourgeoning literary community of San Francisco. Anton Roman envisioned a magazine to help boost the development of California and wanted Harte at its helm. Harte agreed to the venture with the stipulation that he be free to increase literary content, maintain editorial control, and hire two assistants. Roman agreed to those terms and to feature only local and original material and pay contributors fairly for their work. These were ambitious goals given that most newspapers and magazines survived by reprinting uncopyrighted material and paying little to nothing for original content.

Harte asked Ina and Stoddard to write poems for the maiden issue. He also asked Mark Twain to contribute a travel story based on his recent trip to Europe. Twain had come west in 1861 and lived in Nevada for several years, where he wrote for Virginia City's *Territorial Enterprise*. In 1864, he moved to San Francisco to work as a daily beat reporter for the *Morning Call*. Harte, who worked at the US Mint in the same building, recognized Twain's talent and helped him hone his skills. "[Harte] trimmed and trained and schooled me patiently until he changed me from an awkward utterer of coarse grotesqueness to a writer of paragraphs and chapters," said Twain.[20]

Twain gained national attention after he published "Jim Smiley and His Jumping Frog" in the *Saturday Press* in November 1865, and leaped from that success to being a correspondent in Hawaii for the Sacramento *Union*. From there he went on a five-month excursion to Europe and the Middle East with a group of ministers, and the stories he sent back to the states led to his first book, *Innocents Abroad*. Twain returned to San Francisco to acquire the rights of the stories he had sent to *Alta California*, and to solicit Harte's help with the book. In exchange for Harte's work, Twain gave him travel stories for the first few issues of the *Overland Monthly*.

The rumor that Twain visited Ina's parlor as a suitor has persisted for years. Author Margaret Duckett paid heed to the rumor in her 1964 book *Mark Twain and Bret Harte*, writing that it was tempting to believe the story because it provides a reason for the rancor that eventually developed between the two men. But without any real proof, she backed down from the argument. Nigey Lennon proposes in *The Sagebrush Bohemian: Mark Twain in California* that Twain and Harte vied for Ina's attention and came to verbal blows when Harte tried to protect Ina from Twain's philandering ways. The possibility of the triangle persists in contemporary San Francisco travel books, which claim that Twain wooed Coolbrith on the flowery paths of Macondray Lane, the model for Armistead Maupin's Barbary Lane in *Tales of the City*.

One of the early perpetuators of this rumor was author Raine Bennett who claimed in the November 1933 issue of *Touring Topics* that Ina told him directly about the romantic triangle when she was eighty-two years old. Bennett wrote that he frequented salons at Ina's Russian Hill parlor in the early 1920s when poet George Sterling commandeered the fireplace to roast marshmallows and pop corn. One night, Bennett was alone with Ina. He wrote that she wore a loose robe and her customary white lace mantilla, and that she sat in her favorite chair with a cane nearby. Her voice was low and musical with a frequent laugh that had a way of "echoing in your heart." On that occasion she showed him two packets of letters tied with colorful ribbons, telling him that one packet contained notes from Samuel Clemens but lacked his customary humor. Bennett asked why.

"Because he was in love, my dear; seriously in love. Besides there was another reason." She handed him a second packet, thicker than the first. Bennett suggested that based on the number of letters, the love affair with the second admirer must have been more ardent. "It was more serious," she said.

"Those notes are all from Francis Bret Harte, and Sammy didn't like him. His ties, among other things, inflamed him. So he tried to break up our little affair. That's why I stopped writing to Sammy, and his letters discontinued to me. I had no regrets, for they are not all pleasant reading. He forgot to laugh, and became a moralist. In fact, one day when he met Francis in the editorial offices of the *Overland Monthly* he called him a bad name."

"*Grand Dieu!*" replied Bennett. "But, did you really mind?"

"Of course not! Francis and I loved him; but then, we loved each other too."[21]

Ina showed Bennett a lock of Harte's hair, which she said she had clipped from his head as he worked. She had also cut a snippet of Stoddard's hair. These locks can still be found in the Bancroft Library at the University of California at Berkeley.

Although Bennett's story is entertaining, the truth of it has to be questioned since he told it after all three writers were dead and unable to refute or corroborate his tale. As for the letters he refers to, there are extant letters that Harte wrote to Ina, but there is nothing in them that proves an affair. There are no known letters between Twain and Ina. One of the few times she mentioned Twain at all was in a 1924 essay in which she included him with Harte, Stoddard, and Joaquin Miller as being "exceptionally fine-looking men."[22] It is curious that she did not include Twain in her "Gossip" lecture, in which she talked extensively about Harte and Stoddard. And there is no mention of Ina at all in Twain's memoirs, even though she was one of the most beautiful and talented women in the city. These omissions from both of their pens seem odd given the closeness of the group.

There is one more intriguing bit of evidence. In 1873, Stoddard, Harte, Joaquin Miller, and Ambrose Bierce were in Europe. Ina was supposed to be there too, but her sister and mother needed her at home. Later that year, Mark Twain, who by then had married Olivia Langdon, would perform his lecture in London and had arranged for Stoddard to serve as his temporary secretary, a job that required Stoddard to eat, drink, smoke cigars, and exchange stories about the good old days before and after Twain's performances.[23]

Ina wrote to Stoddard in New York before he left for Europe, "Why didn't I follow your advice and marry XXXXXXX [sic]? I might have entertained you in London this winter."[24] Of Ina's friends in Europe, only Twain had the means to entertain, and only Clemens, the name that Ina used for Twain, had seven letters to match her seven Xs.

On July 2, 1868, Twain delivered a lecture in San Francisco that coincided with the launch of the *Overland Monthly*. Ina was likely at the Mercantile Library lecture hall when Twain stepped onto the stage in front of the sold-out house. The *Daily Alta California* recorded his opening remarks in the morning newspaper the following day:

> Ladies and Gentlemen ... I appreciate your atten-
> dance here tonight all the more because there was
> such a widespread, such a furious, such a deter-
> mined opposition, to my lecturing upon this occa-
> sion. [Laughter.] Pretty much the entire community
> wrote petitions imploring me not to lecture—to
> forebear—to have compassion upon a persecuted
> people. [Laughter.] I never had such a unanimous
> call to—to—to leave, before [Great laughter].

His lecture was a success. It was also a send-off. The following Monday Twain left California forever. When asked later why he nev-er went west again, he said, "Those were the good old days, the old ones. They will come no more. Youth will come no more. They were so full to the brim with the wine of life; there have been no others like them. Would you like to have me come out there and cry?"[25]

Ina and Twain didn't meet again until fifteen years after he left San Francisco. During an event at the Authors Club in New York, a friend who didn't know that they knew each other introduced them.

"Mark, you are the handsomest man in the room," Ina said when he took her hand.

"As I remember you," Twain replied. "You are truthful as usual."[26]

The inaugural issue of the *Overland Monthly* contained Twain's "By Rail Through France," with Samuel Clemens's byline. It also featured an article by assistant editor Noah Brooks about a Sacramento diamond maker; an essay called "A Breeze from the Woods" by second assistant editor W. C. Bartlett; and a poem each from Harte, Stoddard, and Coolbrith. Although Ina's poem "Longing" came at the end of Bartlett's essay, it was her poem that brought fresh air to the issue. It begins:

> O foolish wisdom sought in books!
> O aimless fret of household tasks!
> O chains that bind the hand and mind
> A fuller life my spirit asks![27]

A young Ambrose Bierce reviewed the first issue of the *Overland Monthly* in the *San Francisco News Letter*. Overall he wasn't impressed, but did like Ina's poem. He reprinted "Longing" in its entirety with a comment that the "fifth stanza constitutes 'poetry with a great P.'"[28] It reads:

> And I could kiss, with longing wild,
> Earth's dear brown bosom, loved so much,
> A grass-blade fanned across my hand,
> Would thrill me like a lover's touch.[29]

His review didn't mention Ina by name because none of the contributors were listed. Harte insisted that contributors only be recognized in the final issue of the year, as was the *Atlantic Monthly's* practice. It is likely, however, that local people knew the author of each piece.

Two weeks after the launch of the *Overland Monthly*, a messenger knocked on Ina's door with a note from Harte. He wanted to know if she had revised the poem for the second issue. She had not and sent the messenger away.

She thought about Harte's suggestions but could only come up with a silly rhyme that she wrote on the back of Harte's note:

> O bliss of a patient heart
> To sit on a stool "to hum"
> And wait in a desperate sort of way
> For ideas that never come.
>
> Or to try for three long hours
> With temper and pulse serene
> To alter a line in a "pome" to shine
> In the *Overland* magazine.[30]

After she made the corrections she sent the revised poem to Harte by messenger and waited for a response. After waiting several days she wrote again and demanded to know why he had not yet replied. Several more days passed before she finally received a reply on *Overland* letterhead with the iconic grizzly bear from the front cover of the magazine growling at the top of the page:

> My dear Miss Ina,
>
> On my return to-day from Sta Cruz, where I have been staying for the last two weeks, I pried a vicious little note lying among my papers, like an asp. I do not know how long it had been there—not long I should say, for it was quite lively and venomous yet.
> Why, bless your heart, my dear young lady, "the poem was settled," as you call it, 8 days ago …

The poem is already in print in the first form of the *Overland*. It is the 1st poem.

Yours truly, F. Bret Harte[31]

Harte had been in Santa Cruz writing a short story for the new issue, a story that was nearly pulled. Ina and Stoddard visited Harte at the *Overland* office overlooking Portsmouth Square and found him in a rage and threatening to quit the magazine. The proofreader, Sarah B. Cooper, had found his story immoral and suggested that Roman pull it. Harte's story, "The Luck of Roaring Camp," is a tale about an illegitimate child born to a prostitute in a mining camp. When the mother dies in childbirth, the men in camp decide to raise the child collectively. Cooper suggested the tale would ruin the magazine, and Roman feared she was right. Harte was livid. He reminded Roman that he had been given full editorial control and threatened to quit if Roman sided with Cooper.

Ina later told an audience that Harte had paced the floor while swearing, and that she had tried to comfort and humor him but nothing worked. As a last resort, she decided to rhyme him and took a piece of paper from his desk. She began to write, and he demanded to know what she was doing.

"Composing an immortal poem of personal protest and consolation for the next issue of the mag," she said, and passed him what she had written.

> There was a young writer named Francis
> Who concocted such lurid romances
> That his publishers said,
> "You will strike this firm dead
> If you don't put a curb on your fancies."

"Any more?" he asked. "It seems hardly complete."
"If you will give me a moment," she said, and scribbled more.

> And they added, in terms most emphatic,
> That his wit was not always quite attic,

That his language, while terse,
Might be better, not worse,
And his characters were most erratic.

"Tu diablita," he said. "I am almost tempted to box your ears! But instead, like a good Christian, I'll proceed to heap coals upon your head."[32]

Ina found nothing offensive in Harte's stories. "Perhaps I lack the mental poise and refinement necessary to 'shock,'" she later said. "I am sorry. No I'm not ... At any rate, from some little life experience, I prefer the Sinner in the open to the Saint under cover."[33]

In the end, Roman backed Harte and "The Luck of Roaring Camp" ran as planned in the second issue. Scores of reviewers gave high praise to the magazine, and the *Atlantic Monthly* asked for more stories like Harte's. The popularity of the tale launched Harte and the *Overland Monthly* into that rarefied zone of receiving critical acclaim from the literary powers in the East.

As Harte had promised, Ina's poem "In Blossom Time" was the first poem in the issue. It springs off the page in its exuberance for the bees, birds, flowers, and wind that form a choir to sing God's praises. The first three stanzas express joy, something that had been missing from Ina's poems, and her life, for years. The last three stanzas demonstrate that although she had renounced polygamy and Mormonism, she had not renounced God:

For O but the world is fair, is fair —
And O but the world is sweet!
I will out in the gold of the blossoming mould,
And sit at the Master's feet.

And the love my heart would speak,
I will fold in the lily's rim,
That th' lips of the blossom, more pure and meek,
May offer it up to him.

Then sing in the hedgerow green, O thrush,
O skylark, sing in the blue;

Sing loud, sing clear, that the King may hear,
And my soul shall sing with you![34]

During her lifetime, "In Blossom Time" would be included in at least eight anthologies and set to music by five different composers.

For the third issue of the *Overland*, Ina wrote "Siesta," a lyrical poem that communicates her intimate connection to nature. While the subject of the poem reflects the Romantic literature popular at the time, the tone of it suggests that Ina was healing and finding her way as an artist. Things were going well: she was a star contributor in the West's most popular magazine, she belonged to a circle of artistic friends, and she had tapped into the saving grace of creativity.

Harte paid his contributors well and was responsible for Ina's first lucrative poem of occasion for the Corporate Society of Pioneers. They had asked Harte to write a poem for Admission Day, but he was too busy and recommended Ina. She told him she didn't think she could do it. Of course she could, he said, and reminded her that the Pioneers paid well. The money Ina earned for her poems was much needed by her household. Pickett had taken off again and funds were scarce.

Harte went to Ina's house a few days later to see how she was progressing. She said she had not finished and doubted she could. To show her how easy it was, he burlesqued some silly verse:

O listen while I sing a song
Of the Pioneers so nifty
Who came in the fall of '49
Likewise the spring of '50.[35]

"The result was so excruciatingly funny that it was impossible to resist the laughter evoked," she said. "He was a born actor of the subtlest, most refined type."[36]

When she finished the poem and delivered it to Harte, he said, "Well, little afraid to begin, you see it wasn't so hard after all. Most things are easier than we imagine once we knuckle down to them."[37] He handed her fifty dollars in freshly minted coins, the equivalent of nearly nine hundred dollars today.

Harte was married with two sons. Ina described him as a "family man, proud of and devotedly attached to his children."[38] Webb characterized Harte as a playful father who was eager to get on the floor and play with his sons, but that he stopped the game whenever Mrs. Harte came into the room. Anna Harte did not like foolishness, nor did she approve of Harte's writing career, and his friends knew it. Josephine Clifford McCracken, who served as Harte's secretary at the *Overland Monthly* for several years, said that Anna Harte ruled the house and would not let her husband write until she and the children went to bed, and even then complained about the light being on. "Mrs. Harte never seemed a lovable woman to me," wrote McCracken when reminiscing about Harte. "There was a morose, stubborn expression on her face which invited neither cordiality nor sympathy."[39] Ina described Anna Harte as "a very plain woman in appearance, but charming, never-the-less."[40]

Harte read his stories-in-progress in Ina's parlor. "He lived his story and was at once scene, plot, and character," she said, adding that it was a trait that bothered him. "I wonder what or who I am supposed to be, one of my own characters?" he asked Ina one day after an encounter with a fan.

"You're one and all of them by turns. I never know who I am to encounter when I come," she replied. "I sometimes surprise the whole crowd of them, and interesting as I find them, I sometimes would really enjoy meeting you alone."[41]

Harte continued to favor Ina's poetry. In fact, he rarely included any poetry other than hers, Stoddard's, or his own in the first six issues of the magazine. As a result, a critic in the *Dramatic Chronicle* (the precursor to the *San Francisco Chronicle*) complained of Harte's cronyism. "There may seem to be several meritorious versifiers in California outside of the *Overland*'s favored Triune," wrote the *Chronicle*, and from that day on, Harte, Stoddard, and Ina were dubbed the *Overland* Trinity.[42] Ina didn't like the term or the implication and suggested to Harte that he not include her poetry as frequently. "I edit the mag, Madam," he told her. "When better stuff comes to me than yours, never fear that I shall fail to take advantage of it."[43]

Harte gave Ina and Stoddard keys to the office, but there was never any doubt who held the editorial reins. Noah Brooks and

W. C. Bartlett were Harte's editorial assistants, though Brooks said his duties were more "nominal than actual."[44] Many sources claim that Ina was a coeditor, but that was not the case. When a reporter wrote decades later that Ina was a coeditor, Ina corrected her. To a long list of corrections, Ina added, "Nor did I ever state or imply that I was associated *editorially* with Mr. Harte. I was associated with his regular and *special corps* of contributors."[45]

Stoddard belonged to that special corps, and when he left for Hawaii in October as a paid correspondent for the *Evening Bulletin*, the *Overland* Trinity wobbled. Later that same month, on October 21, 1868, the largest earthquake yet recorded in California history hit at 7:53 a.m. It was known as the "great" San Francisco earthquake until the 1906 earthquake upended it. Furthermore, Ina and her mother had to move from the big house they were living in. Pickett and the twins came and went to pursue mining opportunities, and their two boarders had returned to Mexico.

Ina's mood darkened. As the anniversary of her divorce approached, "When the Grass Shall Cover Me" was published in the November issue. In her poem she fantasizes that after her death her beloved will finally realize her worth and say, "'Alas! / Now I know how true she was / Now I know how dear she was.'"[46] Harte placed the poem at the center of the magazine, where it throbbed with emotion. John Greenleaf Whittier included "When the Grass Shall Cover Me" in an anthology, *Songs of Three Centuries*, but since Harte did not list contributors until the year's final issue, Whittier attributed Ina's poem to "UNKNOWN."

Stoddard had promised to write from Hawaii but did not. After several months she wrote to him, "Of all your friends am I alone to be forgotten? I have waited so long for the promised letter that I write now with the thought that mine will be unwelcome, and but for the fulfillment of my word, it would be better to answer your silence by silence still." Perplexed by his silence she added, "I do not understand you."[47]

How could she? Stoddard did not tell her that Hawaii had introduced him to affairs of the flesh and heart, and that at twenty-four he wanted more. He did not share his experiences with Ina, but he did write to Walt Whitman, whom he saw as a kindred spirit, and with him shared his *modus operandi* for finding love on the islands:

> At dusk I reach some village—a few grass huts by the sea or in some valley. The native villagers gather about me, for strangers are not common in these parts … I mark one, a lad of eighteen or twenty years, who is regarding me. I call him to me, ask his name, giving mine in return … I go to his grass house, eat with him his simple food, sleep with him upon his mats, and at night sometimes waken to find him watching me with earnest, patient looks, his arm over my breast and around me. In the morning he hates to have me go … You will easily imagine, my dear sir, how delightful I find this life. I read your poems with a new spirit, to understand them as few may be able to. And I wish more than ever that I might possess a few lines from your pen. I want your personal magnetism to quicken mine.[48]

Whitman responded with a short note: "I cordially accept your appreciation, & reciprocate your friendship."[49]

Ina did not let up on Stoddard. "I have never given more, or as much expression to any friendship," she wrote. "And yet I am compelled to believe that the real depth and sincerity of it was confined to my own heart." She went to a fortuneteller who predicted that her future wouldn't "amount to a row of pins," but Ina knew better than to listen to a fortuneteller. "I shall fight fate, and you too if you don't treat me better. On second thought, you needn't treat me better—I don't want you to."[50]

7

Unraveling

Harte knocked on Ina's door on Saturday, May 8, 1869, the day San Franciscans celebrated the completion of the Transcontinental Railroad. The city had long planned a celebration on that day, and even though word came on Friday that the hammering of the final spike had been delayed until Monday, San Franciscans decided to stick with their plans.

Harte knocked again. After waiting some more, he let himself in and found Ina doing chores. Agnes had always been frail, and at fifty-nine she was ill so often she was nearly an invalid. As a consequence, it was Ina who scoured the floors and scrubbed, rubbed, and dunked clothes in washtubs. She started the morning fire, salted and cured meat, peeled potatoes, and washed the dishes after each meal. "Dishes are alright for awhile," she later told a reporter, "but did you ever stop to think how many dishes a woman has to wash in the course of a lifetime?... I would like to have the men change occupations with the women for a time. Then we'd see some improvements."[1]

There are no photographs of Ina's early San Francisco parlor, but later photographs show a meticulously kept room. Stoddard described it as having "a cozy interior [where] there was always a kind of twilight ... a faint odor of fresh violets, and an atmosphere of peace."[2] Catharine Beecher, sister to well-known author Harriet Beecher Stowe, advised Victorian women how to obtain a cozy, peaceful parlor in *Miss Beecher's Housekeeper and Healthkeeper*. Stowe recommends women cover the furniture, books, and mantel-piece with old cloths. Then remove and shake the rugs, and sweep the room. Use a brush to dust varnished furniture and finish with a piece of old silk. Use a feather brush for the ornaments and books. Wipe the lamp chimneys, admonishes Beecher, and if wiping doesn't clean them, dismantle them completely and wash in warm water and soda. Finish by trimming the wicks.[3]

And that's just the parlor.

When Harte found Ina, he insisted that she join him for an event on Telegraph Hill, where Governor Leland Stanford was to give a speech and read a poem Harte wrote for the occassion. Ina said she had too many chores and could not go. Harte promised to help her when they returned, so she grabbed her coat and hat.

Most San Franciscans were excited for the rail to connect California with the rest of the country. They were optimistic that the train would increase commerce and that California would experience another El Dorado. While Chinese laborers built the rail lines at six miles a day, real estate developers parceled out land for sale. Historian John Hittell reported that land sales jumped by ten million dollars from 1867 to 1868, with speculators reselling the land at two to three times its purchase price. Not everyone was on board with that optimism. In October 1868, Harte published an essay by economist Henry George that predicted San Francisco would experience the opposite of an El Dorado. George foresaw an economic downturn and argued in "What the Railroad Will Bring Us" that the unique charm of California culture had developed because of a level playing field. "The truth is, that the completion of the railroad and the consequent great increase of business and population, will not be a benefit to all of us, but only to a portion. As a general rule, those who *have*, it will make wealthier; for those who *have not*, it will make it more difficult to get," he wrote.[4] George's predications would prove true when the expected boom turned into an economic bust.

Ina joined Harte on Telegraph Hill, where Governor Stanford promised good times ahead and then read "What the Engines Said," Harte's poem of occasion challenging the entitled superiority of the East, which included these lines:

You brag of your East. You do?
Why, I bring the East to you!
All the Orient, all Cathay,
Find through me the shortest way;
And the sun you follow here
Rises in my hemisphere.
Really,—if one must be rude,—
Length, my friend, ain't longitude.[5]

The highlight of the event was the dynamiting of Blossom Rock, a 195-foot-wide chunk of sandstone submerged five feet below the surface near the harbor; it had been the bane of ship captains for years. When the time came to blow up the rock, whistles blew, bells rang, and word was sent to light the fuse. Viewers expected a large explosion, but the blast delivered little more than a splash.

"Just the flash of a dolphin's tail," said Harte.[6] "Let's go home. It wasn't worth the climb."[7] They returned to Ina's house, where Harte donned an apron and helped Ina shell peas, hull strawberries, and put on dinner.

Stoddard returned from Hawaii that summer and wrote a travel story called "A South-Sea Idyl." The story featured Kana-ana, a sixteen-year-old native Hawaiian boy whom Stoddard, then twenty-five, described as having "ripe and expressive" lips and almond-shaped eyes with "mythical lashes that sweep."[8] Stoddard described how Kana-ana spoiled him: "Again and again he would come with a delicious banana to the bed where I was lying and insist upon my gorging myself, when I had but barely recovered from a late orgie [sic] of fruit, flesh, or fowl. He would mesmerize me into a most refreshing sleep with a prolonged and pleasing manipulation."[9] Harte accepted Stoddard's story for the September issue, writing, "Now you have struck it. Keep on this vein and presently you will have enough to fill a volume."[10] Stoddard would follow Harte's advice and build a career writing travel stories.

In San Francisco, Stoddard missed his island boy and arranged for a friend to put Kana-ana on a boat. When Kana-ana arrived he seemed happy to see Stoddard, but when Stoddard found the boy naked in a dark corner of his house fingering a necklace made of bird feathers, he knew his attempt to convert the boy would fail. On an-other occasion, Kana-ana came upon a life-sized wooden sculpture of a Native American on the street and knelt down to pray, and every day thereafter the boy brought offerings to the statue. To his credit, Stoddard understood that by transplanting his tropical flower he was killing him, and sent the boy home on the next available ship. Back in Hawaii, Kana-ana launched an outrigger into the Pacific Ocean and was never seen again.[11]

Ina continued to contribute to the Overland, but gone was the lilt-ing cheerfulness of "Longing," "In Blossom Time," and "Siesta." Her newer poems revealed a darker side. In "Rebuke" she called the world "heartless." In "My 'Cloth of Gold'" she empathized with the leaves battered by storms, and imagined that it would be less painful to be silenced by snow than beaten by rain. Broken blossoms and tattered leaves were also a theme in "Ungathered," a poem in which blossoms carried unspoken love to their withering.

Her soul was a battlefield in "The Coming," a poem that re-vealed her struggle between her religious indoctrination and her love of poetry. It's clear that while she loved to daydream and make poems on a sunny day, she also feared there would be a price to pay for her enjoyment. She felt guilty for collecting flowers and writing poetry when practicing Mormons were working the fields and toiling in their homes in preparation for the Second Coming. She worried that when "the Master" arrived, those who had prepared would be able to offer the fruits of their labors in "garments white," while she, in garments "stained and dim," would have nothing but "these with-ered leaves / And these poor, foolish songs!"[12] She prayed for courage when she would have to stand before God in atonement to account "for wasted days / For all His broken laws."[13]

She also wove threads of another kind of guilt into her poems. She wrote that death would not be so bitter if she could hear the voice of her love upon dying, even if he "shouldst stand / With cold, unreaching hand."[14] In another she gave a simple field flower a "sinless face," and in another asked to be rid "of wrongs, of sins, of heavy tears."[15]

Whatever her turbulent feelings, she was unable to share them with Stoddard; he was on the move again. This time it was Tahiti. Stoddard explained why in a letter to Walt Whitman: "I am numbed with the frigid manners of the Christians; barbarism has given me the fullest joy of my life and I long to return to it and be satisfied."[16] Whitman replied that he approved of Stoddard's "emotional and adhesive nature," but suggested that Stoddard need not travel around the world for love, as America might supply it in a less sentimental way.[17]

The day before Stoddard sailed for Tahiti in July 1870, he went to the docks to meet Oregonian poet Cincinnatus Hiner Miller, who had lived in San Francisco once before and was on his way to Europe. "He was en route to London with a large package of manuscripts," Ina later said, "and a larger one of ambition, with the modest intention to conquer that small citadel of letters or be conquered."[18] A year earlier, Harte had reviewed Miller's collection of poems, *Joaquin et al*, and said that Miller had a "true poetic instinct." Harte also said that Miller was "not entirely easy in harness, but is given to pawing and curvetting; and at such times his neck is generally clothed with thunder and the glory of his nostrils is terrible."[19] Ina liked Miller's poems and Harte gave her the book to take home.

Miller was tall and blond, and had the sinewy body of one who spent his time outdoors. Stoddard liked him immediately and later said, "Never had a breezier bit of human nature dawned upon me this side of the South Seas than that Poet of the Sierra when he came to San Francisco in 1870."[20] Miller asked Stoddard to take him around to meet the poets of San Francisco, which Miller had characterized in a poem as cavorting on "brown bent hills" where the "full moon spills."[21] Stoddard suggested that Ina play literary hostess, and took Miller to meet her. She opened the door to a man she described as a "fine-looking gentleman."[22] For Miller's part, he was inspired to quote Alfred Lord Tennyson upon meeting Ina: "A daughter of the gods / Divinely tall and most divinely fair."[23]

Miller stayed in San Francisco for a month. Ina introduced him

Joaquin Miller in 1872. Courtesy Oakland Public
Library, Oakland History Room.

to the editors at the *Daily Alta California* and the *Daily Evening Bulletin*, who agreed to publish any articles he sent from Europe. (The stories he did send were tossed in the garbage because nobody could read his handwriting.) In Ina's parlor, she and Miller read Christina and Dante Gabriel Rossetti, Percy Bysshe Shelley, and Lord Byron.

Byron's name was on everyone's lips due to the recent publication of *Lady Byron Vindicated* by Harriet Beecher Stowe, the bestselling author of *Uncle Tom's Cabin*. Stowe had been friends with Lady Byron, and after Lady Byron died, Stowe wrote a book that accused Lord Byron of incest and homosexuality. In an *Overland Monthly* review, Harte skewered Stowe's book for its "solemnly ridiculous mingling of great moral principles with narrow methods and small applications."[24]

"I don't know of anything that was not my business that ever made me more indignant," Ina said of Stowe's attack on Byron. She adored the Romantic bard, author of *Don Juan* and *Childe Harold's Pilgrimage*, and was angry with Stowe for having "dragged the name of Byron from the grave to befoul it with a new scandal."[25] Miller, whom his friends called "a second Byron," idolized the bard too.

Ina had an idea to counter Stowe's attack and demonstrate that not all American writers were critical of Byron. She would make a crown of California laurel leaves and entrust Miller to carry it to Byron's gravesite in England. The day before Miller left San Francisco, he and Ina boarded a side-wheel ferry at Meigg's Wharf (near today's Fisherman's Wharf). The Princess plied six miles across the mouth of the bay to Sausalito (spelled Saucalito at the time), which was nothing more than a building or two at water's edge. The poets climbed the steep hill above the pier until they reached a mixed hardwood forest of coast live oaks, tanoaks, and California bay laurel.

As she collected the fragrant leaves, a poem wove through her head:

> O winds, that ripple the long grass!
> O winds, that kiss the jeweled sea!
> Grow still and lingering as you pass
> About this laurel tree.[26]

She willed the birds to sing softly and sweetly as she lamented that Byron's tomb was unblessed by wife or child, and entreated the leaves to carry the wind, sun, and light of the West to England.

She finished the wreath that night and stitched it, along with her poem, into Miller's valise lining. She also asked Miller how he expected to climb the heights of Parnassus with a name like Cincinnatus Hiner, and suggested he change it to Joaquin, the namesake of his most recent book of poems. Miller heeded her suggestion and boarded his steamer. As promised, Miller delivered the crown to Byron's dilapidated gravesite in Hucknall Torkard where he read Ina's poem aloud with dramatic flair. He also paid the caretaker to nail the crown above the tomb. But the parish priest called for its removal, and when word of the crown and the controversy reached King George in Greece, where Byron was revered as a fallen hero, King George sent a wreath of his own along with a glass dome to protect both crowns. The entire incident brought attention to the shabby gravesite and church, and led to its restoration. Harte published Ina's poem "With a Wreath of Laurel" in the September issue, but the story behind the poem was unknown until Miller told it twenty years later.

The only known extant letters that Harte wrote to Ina suggest an evolving relationship. His early notes are businesslike: in one, he asks if she can come by his office and view the proof of her poem in first form; in another he asks if she has finished her poem, or "is the weather unpropitious for your muse?"[27] The notes became friendlier, such as when he wrote, "I called at your home Sat. P.M. and rang and rang and rang."[28] Another shows how they teased each other. "'The King' isn't ready yet but you should have a proof of his Majesty by Thursday if not to-morrow."[29] At first he signed his notes, "Truly, F. B. Harte." Within a year he wrote, "Yours, H."

The thing Ina loved most about Harte was his humor. Nothing escaped his barbs or burlesque. He wrote limericks for and about his children and performed them for Ina and Stoddard, who would "shout with laughter" when he acted them out in the *Overland* office or Ina's parlor.[30]

Harte mined the goldfields for more stories like "The Luck of Roaring Camp" and came up with "The Outcasts of Poker Flat" and "Tennessee's Partner." His were the first popular short stories set during the Gold Rush and readers across the country gobbled them up.

His acclaim exploded after he wrote and published "Plain Language from Truthful James," a poem about a Chinese man who bested a couple of gamblers. He intended for it to be satirical, but when another editor renamed it "The Heathen Chinee" it was used to flame the anti-Chinese sentiment that prevailed at the time, and to Harte's disgust the poem made him more famous than anything else he had written. When publishers tried to lure him east in 1870, John Carmany, the publisher who had taken over the *Overland Monthly* in 1869, countered with an offer of five thousand a year, one hundred dollars for each short story, and an interest in the magazine. The University of California also tried to keep Harte in California by offering him the post of professor and curator of the library and museum, with a monthly salary equivalent to more than five thousand dollars today.

The offers from the East interested Harte more. A proposition to name him editor of the *Lakeside Monthly* in Chicago attracted him, as did another from the editor at the *Atlantic Monthly*, who offered ten thousand dollars a year for Harte to write short stories exclusively for its pages. After two and a half years of editing the *Overland Monthly*, Harte started packing without having accepted either offer. He would decide once he got there.

When Harte told Ina he was leaving, he told her to prepare a packet of her best poems, which he promised to hand deliver to James Osgood, the publisher of *Atlantic Monthly*. He also told her that she and Stoddard should follow him east.

"What kind of an instrument would a triangle be with only one angle?" he asked.[31]

She said she would never leave her invalid mother.

"Bring her with you," he countered.

She would never leave her boys, said Ina.

"Well then. I see no other way than to marry the whole family," he replied.[32]

Harte left in February 1871 with his wife and children. His first stop was Chicago, where he received an invitation to a dinner party from the local literati. Since the invitation did not include Mrs. Harte's cousin, with whom they were staying, Mrs. Harte refused to go and convinced Harte not to go as well. Harte later learned that financial backers had placed a fourteen-thousand-dollar check beneath his plate for him to purchase the *Lakeside Monthly*. Having been snubbed, the backers did not offer the money again. Harte accepted the offer from the *Atlantic Monthly* but in the end did not fulfill his contract, and within a year he was out. Harte never again rose to the level of celebrity and achievement he had attained in California. He eventually moved to Europe without his wife and children and lived out his days as a short story hack. He and Ina never communicated again, and she believed she knew why.

"The spell was never broken," Ina wrote when she was in her eighties. "I know, though he never from the time of his departure broke the silence between. From that very token do I know the love and longing too keen to permit him to remember—or forget."[33] She never criticized Harte for leaving California, though many others did. When a reporter accused Harte years later of having a "Herculean vanity," Ina defended him. "My dear Mrs. Martin, do you not suppose I knew something of the nature and circumstances of the man whom I knew almost as well as the members of my own family?... I bear witness that he was one of the most genial, unselfish, kind, unaffected and *non*-conceited of all the writers I have known."[34]

The month Harte left, Ina published a poem in the *Overland Monthly* called "An Emblem" in which she lamented how she had tended one flower while she turned away others that offered their blooms to her. She assumed that the flower she nourished would be sweet, but it ended up a "sickly, dwarfed, and scentless thing."[35] She did not name the flower.

More bad news came when Ina learned that another one of her sister's children had died. Poor Agnes Charlotte had seen enough death already. Her first child died the day it was born in 1858. She had five more children, but her youngest had died at seven months old. Then her husband, William Peterson, died suddenly in May 1868, and a few months after that, Mary Charlotte, their third child, died. And now William had died six days after his fifth birthday. Only two of Agnes Charlotte's six children had survived: Henry Frank, eleven, and Ina Lillian, seven.

That spring Ina wrote "Oblivion," an agnostic and enigmatic poem, the catalyst for which could have either been the deaths in her sister's family or the disappointments in her own life. Here are the last two stanzas:

> Pale leaves of poppies shed
> About the brows and head,
> From whence the laurel, dead,
> Is dropped to dust.
> Strength laid in armor down
> To mould, and on the gown
> The mould, and on the crown
> The mould and rust.
>
> So evermore they lie:
> The ages pass them by;
> Them doth the Earth deny,
> And Time forget;
> Void in the years, the ways,
> As a star loosed from space,
> Upon whose vacant place
> The sun is set.[36]

The *Overland Limited* published "Oblivion" in May 1871. She considered it to be one of her best and submitted the poem to the *Atlantic Monthly*. The magazine rejected it.

8

Loss of Love and Poetry

Ina boarded the Oakland-bound ferry at the San Francisco Ferry Building on July 19, 1871, with dignitaries, speakers, and guests to attend a graduation ceremony at the University of California where five men would receive diplomas. Female students had been admitted that year, and Ina had been chosen to write the commencement ode. The university was founded in 1869 as an amalgamation of the private College of California and the new Agricultural, Mining and Mechanical Arts College. Construction of a new campus in Berkeley was under way, but its buildings and grounds were not yet ready, and classes took place at the old College of California campus at Fourteenth and Franklin in Oakland.

Ina and the other attendees crossed the bay in good spirits and arrived at the Oakland Long Wharf, where a parade of university and military cadets and fire companies greeted and escorted them to the campus. A reporter noted that women were not required to take seats along the wall as they had been in the past, but were invited to sit among the men, an event that was likely a result of the commencement ode being written by a woman.

Ina chose not to read the 161-line commencement ode she had written, and instead asked Reverend Horatio Stebbins of San Francisco's First Unitarian Church to read it. Although it was customary at the time for someone other than the poet to read a poem of occasion, Ina had been asked to read the ode and chose not to. An article in the *San Francisco Call* on July 20, 1871, reported that Stebbins's preamble reflected his wish that she had: "The University is now open to your sons and daughters alike, and soon the woman who writes the poem will herself read it, and then the wind from her rustling garments, as she comes on the stage, will brush away the insignificant insects who now people it."[1]

Ina titled her ode "California," a work that urged poets to write about the natural beauty of the state. In her ode she gave the land a voice:

> Are not the fruit and vine
> Fair on my hills, and in my vales the rose?
> The palm-tree and the pine
> Strike hands together under the same skies
> In every wind that blows.[2]

California was her muse, a belief that lasted her lifetime. Years later she wrote:

> For California is a poem! The land of romance, of
> mystery, of worship, of beauty and of song. It chants
> from her snow-crested, cloud-bannered mountain
> ranges; it hymns thro' her forests of sky-reaching
> pine and sequoia; it ripples in her flowered and
> fruited valleys; it thunders from her fountains pour-
> ing, as it were, from the very waters above the fir-
> mament; it anthems from the deeps of the mightiest
> ocean of the world; and echoes ever in the syllables
> of her own strangely beautiful name, California.[3]

The land had been waiting for poets, she said, for what use is beauty if poets do not gather its fruit? Poets are the reapers of life; without them "legends fade away."[4] California was the Parnassus of America, and "it is here that the coming generation is to be dreamed, for here, you know, one has the blessed privilege of communing with God as expressed in the ocean, the trees, the rocks, everything that has form and color. It is here that the soul expands, and in the expansion produces music."[5]

She set an example in "California" with her rendering of a sunset seen from Russian Hill:

> Was it the wind, or the soft sigh of leaves,
> Or sound of singing waters? Lo, I looked,
> And saw the silvery ripples of the brook,
> The fruit upon the hills, the waving trees,
> And mellow fields of harvest; saw the Gate
> Burn in the sunset; the thin thread of mist
> Creep white across the Saucelito hills;
> Till the day darkened down the ocean rim,
> The sunset purple slipped from Tamalpais,
> And bay and sky were bright with sudden stars.[6]

The poem would not be published for a decade. Nonetheless, Ambrose Bierce read and reviewed it. "It is one of the very best 'occasion' pomes [sic] we have ever read ...There is not another person west of the Rocky Mountains—now that Joaquin Miller is gone away—that could have done better; but they are men, and Ina Coolbrith is a woman."[7]

Ina had written the ode late at night while her family slept. She rarely had time to write during the day. When Stoddard suggested that she write prose as she had for the *Californian*, she replied, "Write prose, yes, with all my duties that leave me no time to scribble my little verses, except what I steal from sleep. I have written nothing by daylight for over a year."[8] The poems she did manage to write reflected her fear that opportunities were slipping away. In "At the Hill's Base" she appealed to the poetry gods to find "a little room" for her, even if "low at your feet."[9] In "An Ending" she wrote, "I dreamed a dream exceeding fair / They woke me rudely from my sleep: I toil my task I nothing ask / I neither laugh nor weep."[10]

In early 1872, Miller returned from England triumphant. He had changed his name from Cincinnatus Hiner to Joaquin as Ina had suggested. He also donned a sombrero, wore his hair long, and told stories about the Wild West. Stoddard, who was in England at the time, approved of Miller's new look. "I believe it the duty of everyone to look as picturesque as possible," he said.[11] Eventually, Miller found a London publisher for his new book of poems, *Songs of the Sierras*. It received positive reviews, and he became a social darling of London's literary circles. Several months after Miller's launch, he learned that his sister had died and his brother was seriously ill in Oregon. He got on a boat for America.

The death of Miller's sister introduced a problem. Miller's half-Indian, fourteen-year-old daughter, Calla Shasta, had been living with his sister, and now Miller needed to find his daughter a home. When Miller was around twenty years old, he had lived in a cabin in the Siskiyou Mountains with his common-law, Wintu-McCloud Indian wife, Sutatot, who wore three blue points on her chin. Miller and Sutatot named their daughter Calla Shasta because she was born "under the shadows of Mount Shasta."[12] In time Miller tired of his domestic life in the mountains and left Sutatot and Calla Shasta. They were kidnapped by Modoc Indians and used as slaves until Miller's friend Jim Brock rescued them. Sutatot married Brock and changed her name to Amanda. It is unknown why Calla Shasta lived with Miller's sister and not her own mother, Amanda Brock.

Miller took Calla Shasta to Ina's house and asked if she could stay there until he figured out a permanent solution. Ina said yes and put the girl in school. Calla Shasta had been given the Anglo name of Carrie, the name that Ina used for her, but Calla Shasta preferred the name she had been given and used it to sign her letters once she learned how to write them.

Miller finished his book *Life Amongst the Modocs: Unwritten History* while in San Francisco and asked Ina to copy the manuscript so a publisher could read it. When she finished, she wrote Stoddard, "[Miller's] novel is finished, and the same is an abomination in my sight! I had to copy it, 358 pages—foolscap, every last one of them! I finished it Monday, and feel as though I had just graduated in the dead languages."[13]

In *Life Amongst the Modocs*, Miller wrote that Calla Shasta could "ride, shoot, hunt, and track the deer, and take the salmon!"[14] He closed the book with a sentimental thought for her welfare: "Poor little lady, she will never hear the voices of her childhood any more.

There is no one living now to speak her language. Touch her gently, O Fate, for she is so alone! She is the last of the children of Shasta."[15] His sentiment did not extend to responsibility, and he never came back for Calla Shasta, who lived with Ina for more than a decade.

Stoddard's career progressed apace with his South Sea stories, and he was bound for Samoa on another adventure when bad weather sent him back to Hawaii. He wrote Ina a letter but did not receive a reply for months. When Ina did reply, she explained that she was only able to do so because she had imbibed some wine. She said it helped her to feel "as if there were something in the world beside sorrow, and that even sorrow—a little—is sweet, in its uses."[16]

"Who is your Eve?" asked Ina, who had come to accept Stoddard's promiscuity. A year earlier Stoddard had asked Ina to reform him. She replied that she would just as soon try the impossible.

> You will continue to be yourself and none other
> to the day of your death; and I don't know that I
> would wish to have you any "other" ... You'll come
> home when you have grown weary with the recent
> chase and have caught and brushed the golden dust
> from the wing of your last butterfly. Come creeping
> back, with your head on one side, and just enough
> of a smile to make "the dimples" look coaxing and
> beg your "old faithful" for a sugar-plum and a caress,
> and a quiet hour of rest by the side of her who
> never forgets her friendships, even for a moment. Is
> the picture true, Charlie?

She ended the letter with a bite: "*Adios, queridisimo mio.* Of course, I love you always, as you do me—on paper."[17]

Ina was in Los Angeles when she turned thirty-two on March 10, 1873. It was not a joyous birthday. Her mother had gone to Los Angeles to help Agnes Charlotte, who was ill, and when Agnes became ill too, she sent for Ina. Ina arrived and took charge of the household chores including several weeks' worth of laundry. Her body still ached the following night when she folded a piece of transparent paper in half, dipped her pen in brown ink, and wrote on the top right corner of the first page, "City of Sorrows (mistakenly called 'of Angels')," and continued:

> I wish I could tap you on the shoulder tonight in
> the midst of your friends with whom you may be
> passing pleasantly the hours, and transport you just
> for a moment to the dingy little room in the gloomy
> old house wherein I pen you this. I am certain you
> would not growl for a month, so heavenly would
> seem your lot in comparison.

Ina said her sister looked fifty, not thirty-six, and it was no wonder. On this visit Ina learned of the circumstances of her nephew William's death. "Mother tells me that in his final convulsions, which lasted *five hours*, he was drawn back nearly double, and the blood came from mouth and nostrils and eyes. They could not straighten his poor little hands and feet even after death. And Aggie never left his side for a day and night for one moment, someone being required to keep hold of him, nor would she allow any hands but her own to prepare him for his grave."

Ina dipped her pen in the ink and continued, "O Charlie! What do *we* know of sorrow?"

Agnes convinced Agnes Charlotte to move to San Francisco with her children, and Ina knew that the bulk of the move would fall to her. "Now I have work to do indeed, in getting them off, and after I get them there to take care of them. God only knows how I am to do it," she said. "If I were only a man! I could do so much more ... but a woman must fight till she dies and it's astonishing how some of them hold out. If you could see the washing I did yesterday you would say so, and if you could have the sensation of my back and arms today, you would say so again, with emphasis."

Ina reached the bottom of the last page and still had more to say. She turned the folded letter sideways to write on top of what she had already written. "One more thing and I'm done. This house is haunted if ever one was. I'm not a coward. I can face about anything living, but I have a horror upon me in this house for which there are reasons, and tho' you may laugh, unaccountable ones."[18] Ina did not explain her mysterious reference.

Back in San Francisco, Ina published "Marah" in the June issue of the *Overland Monthly*. The title refers to a place in Ancient Egypt where Israelite slaves stopped for water after walking in the desert for three days, and found the water too bitter to drink. "Marah" is a fierce poem that defends a poet's right and obligation to write about hardship and suffering. She ended with this:

> To the weary in life's wildernesses
> To soul of the singer belongs:
> Small need, in your green, sunny places,
> Glad dwellers, have you of my songs.
> For you the blithe birds of the meadow
> Trill silvery sweet, every one,
> But I cannot sit in the shadow
> Forever, and sing of the sun.[19]

Ina's family had grown by four people. Pickett was gone and they were broke. The Bohemian Club knew of her need and hosted an event to raise money for her and her family. Ina would be named an honorary member of the all-male club later that year, making her one of the few women members in the club's history. Hundreds bought tickets in advance for the event at Platt's Hall on January 15, 1874. Celia Logan of New York's *Graphic* wrote, "Miss Coolbrith is called 'California's peerless poetess.' On the occasion of her benefit they read poetry by the yard, except hers." The benefit yielded over six hundred dollars, equal to about twelve thousand today. The event marked the first time the Bohemian Club raised money for Ina, and it would not be the last. Their support flowed to her intermittently for the rest of her life.

Before Agnes Charlotte died on January 30, 1874, she extracted a promise from Ina to care for her two surviving children. There was no question whether Ina would fulfill the promise. As a woman in the Victorian age raised in a religious family, she put duty first.

Agnes Charlotte had also asked Ina to continue to hide her children's heritage. Ina later told her relative John Smith that their Mormon past was a "large factor in the troubles of my poor sister's married life—troubles which helped to shorten that life—and she made me promise before she died that, insofar as I could, I would shield her children from the sufferings we had experienced."[20]

It is likely that Ina wrote "Beside My Dead" as she and her mother prepared Agnes Charlotte's body for burial. In her poem Ina expressed empathy for the relief her sister must have found in death:

> It must be sweet, O thou, my dead, to lie
> With hands that folded are from every task;
> Sealed with the seal of the great mystery
> The lips that nothing answer, nothing ask.[21]

Alone, Ina took Agnes Charlotte's body to Los Angeles to bury her alongside her husband and four children. When Ina left San Francisco, her mother was ill, and when she returned she found her mother still in bed. Ina could no longer entertain the hope of furthering her literary career. She had been invited to Europe with a wealthy friend but had to cancel the trip. All of her colleagues were there. "Swallow, swallow, O brother swallows! Now that all are flown over the seas and away, how gladly I would follow you if my wings were not clipped so closely, and so heavy a burden about the poor little throat, that has grown too tired even to sing," she wrote Stoddard. "Do me a favor," she added. "You cannot avoid meeting Harte. Don't mention me to him please, and if he should ask of me, which is not probable, say nothing of my poems. Of these I would prefer you to speak to no one. The subject ceases to be other than ridiculous."[22]

It is difficult to understand why she thought that Harte would not ask about her. She, Stoddard, and Harte were the *Overland* Trinity, and Harte was her editor and friend. Why wouldn't he care about her career and well-being? Was it her low self-esteem talking, or did something more complicated occur at their parting?

Stoddard complained from Europe that he was blue and short on funds. "Come now," Ina wrote. "Lie down a little on the old lounge, let me pass my hand over your forehead and send away the evil spirit that troubles you."[23] In reality it was Ina who needed comforting. Her doctor told her that she would not last the year unless she rested. But rest was impossible. She needed a steady job. Carmany was looking for a new editor for the *Overland Monthly* and Ina applied. He did not hire her. Instead, she took a position at the Oakland Library Association, a private library open to dues-paying members. The outgoing librarian told Ina that her hours would be from 6 a.m. to 11 p.m., and that her duties would include janitor, dues collector, and secretary. Ina was offered a salary of seventy dollars a month, an amount that would be stretched to support five people. "In my tired, burdened heart, no one holds a dearer place than do you," she wrote Stoddard in her next letter. "Remember that when I shall be only a memory."[24]

By the time Stoddard received her letter, his situation had improved. He was living in Venice with American writer and painter Francis Davis Millet, who later died in the sinking of the *Titanic*. For a time, Stoddard and Millet lived a happy Bohemian life in an apartment overlooking the Grand Canal, where Millet painted and Stoddard wrote letters for the *San Francisco Chronicle*. When Ina learned that Stoddard was romantically involved, she told him he should settle down. "There is nothing in life but love, anyway. Life is nothing worse than nothing without it!"[25]

She preached love but made a sorry practice of it. Like Stoddard, she was adept at affairs of the heart without lasting commitments. Based on evidence found in her poems "A Prayer for Strength" and "Freedom," she had a short-lived tryst the summer before she started at the Oakland Library. "A Prayer for Strength" seems to be about her decision not to pursue a relationship with a married man. In the poem she vows to turn from love if she must win it "by treachery or art" or "wrong one other heart."[26] If finding love meant that she must use "a footstool for that sake," she wrote, "Grant me to turn aside."[27]

While there is no definitive proof of who her lover was that summer, the evidence points to Joseph Duncan, her former editor who had become one of the most respected and wealthy businessmen in San Francisco. The evidence of their affair comes from radio reporter Samuel Dickson, who met Ina at a San Francisco soirée a year before her death. He sat at her feet while the rest of the guests gathered around the piano on the other side of the room. Ina told Dickson that she was the one great love of Duncan's life. "He was a poet, a dreamer, a musician, and a connoisseur of the arts. Joseph Duncan! He had been so gentle, so great an idealist, and so fine a poet. What if he was a cashier in a bank? Even a bank cashier could dream of sonnets."[28] Duncan was a banker for only a short period, and during that time he was married to Mary Dora Gray, whom he wed in 1871. Several years later he built a five-story building on California and Montgomery streets valued at two million dollars. On the first floor, he opened the Pioneer Land and Loan Bank of San Francisco, which closed in 1877, the same year Isadora Duncan, his daughter with Mary Dora, was born.

If Ina's poetry can be counted on for clues, a poem she wrote the following year suggests that her affair lasted only one summer. One stanza explains why she ended it:

> ... One tires at times
> Of even one's favorite rhymes;
> Of roses, oversweet,
> Of joys that are too complete,
> Of all things in one's reach;
> And just to be alone
> With silence sweeter than speech,
> Seems best of all known things.[29]

She sent the poem to the *Overland Monthly* and told the new editor she could not decide whether to call it "Wisdom," "Folly," or "Regret." He chose "Regret" when he took it for the November 1875 issue. When Ina later included the poem in her first poetry collection, she changed the title to "Freedom."

But Ina was not free. On Monday mornings she boarded a ferry bound for Oakland, where she worked fourteen hours a day and slept on a cot in the library. She returned to San Francisco on Saturday nights to spend Sundays with her mother.

Part III:

Oakland

Down the long room, grown weird and grim,
Strange shadows hover, waveringly;
I move among the folios dim,
And count the hours till I am free.

—Ina D. Coolbrith, "A Night of Storm," 1881

9

The Inferno

Paddles churned and smoke spewed from the Oakland-bound ferryboat that carried Ina away from San Francisco on a Monday morning in September 1874 with the sun still low over the East Bay hills. Twenty years earlier, Ina would have looked to the same hills and seen the last of the "navigation trees" in the San Antonio Redwood Grove, a stand of *sequoia sempervirens* that had once been a five-square-mile grove tall enough to serve as markers for captains navigating into the mouth of the bay sixteen miles away. At first, only the occasional tree was taken from the grove because they were hard to reach and only yielded thirty dollars per thousand board feet. After the Gold Rush, however, a tree brought ten times that amount, and by 1850 hundreds of men worked the grove and sent the lumber across the bay to San Francisco. Each time the city burned more lumber was needed, and within a decade the thousand-year-old giants were gone.

San Francisco was not the only city that was growing. Oakland's pastoral beauty, climate, and easy commute to San Francisco contributed to its favor, and after Oakland became the western terminus of the Transcontinental Railroad, the population tripled to thirty thousand and the city became the second largest on the Pacific Coast.

Ina's ferry entered the mouth of San Antonio Creek for its three-mile chug to the Broadway Wharf. From the wharf she walked seven blocks to the library, next to City Hall at the top of Washington Street. The building that housed the library had once been a two-story building, but the Oakland Library Association had sliced it in half and moved the top half to this location, selling the bottom half and the land it stood on to pay an outstanding debt. The members-only library was several years from becoming public.

From the start, Ina called the place her "Inferno." Once she entered it on Monday mornings she rarely left for six days. Ina wrote Stoddard that she worked fourteen-hour days, "lived nowhere," and slept on a cot in "the great barn of a library."[1] Board minutes show that book circulation was seventeen thousand annually, which equals about fifty books a day. She also organized daily newspapers in the reading room. On occasion, Jeanne Carr, a library trustee, sat at the desk so Ina could run errands or get dinner. During the day Ina smiled and hid her feelings, but at night cried to the unsympathetic walls that creaked in the darkness. "The tears I have shed, the prayers I have prayed, thro' the long hours of the nights in that library, it seems to me, would have moved the heart of a God of stone!" she told Stoddard.[2]

Her family lived in San Francisco, including her brothers, who were nearly thirty. Ina had invested in a mine her brothers claimed, but when they couldn't get other investors her outlay was lost and Don Carlos and Will returned to San Francisco broke. Will found a job and promised to give Ina twenty-four dollars a month for food and board, but rarely paid. Don Carlos was out of work for a year and Ina fed and clothed him. She resented her brothers' dependence on her, and told Stoddard that her brothers "sat at home at ease, and happy on the money I was selling my life for."[3]

On occasion, Fred Henshaw, a young friend of Stoddard's, visited Ina at the library. Before Stoddard left for Europe, he brought his "chum" to meet her. After Stoddard left, Henshaw brought Stoddard's letters to the library to share with Ina. Ina had come to understand what Stoddard meant when he called certain friends "chums," and accepted it. In one letter she said, "I sleep in that great barn of a Library, *alone*, (you see how much I need a *chum!*)." In the same she said, "If I could only change sex and be Charlie's 'chum' —but then, there's Fred, I wouldn't rob him the dear little wretch!"[4]

Ina told Stoddard that she had a "sweetheart" too:

> A Mrs. Flint of Oakland, wife of one of the trustees
> of the library, has taken the greatest fancy for me
> you can conceive of. In fact, tho' this is strictly and
> earnestly *entre nous*, she is too fond of me, altogether
> … She is as fond of me, I verily believe, as you are
> of Fred. Indeed, I proposed to Fred one evening that
> she should obtain a divorce and on your return we
> should have a double wedding: Fred and yourself,
> and Mrs. F and Ina. She is rich, and I could use her
> money to help you boys in your housekeeping![5]

Ina's acceptance of Stoddard's homosexuality did not diminish
her love for him. In one letter she addressed him as "My best-beloved
Friend," and in the same closed with, "I put my arms about you and
kiss you on [the] forehead and eyelids and mouth; and pray God to
keep you in safety, body and soul."[6]

It made economic and practical sense for Ina to move to Oakland, and she found a cottage on Fifteenth Street a few short blocks
from the library, a place large enough for her mother, Henry, Ina Lillian, and Calla Shasta. Her brothers stayed in San Francisco. Henry
helped Ina in the library, and Ina told Stoddard that she didn't know
what she would do without his help. She intimated that the relationship was far from perfect, though, when she said, "O how he hurts me
in some respects!"[7]

Most women in Ina's position would have remarried, but she did
not. Ina Lillian later said that many men came to call with matrimony in mind, but Ina turned them down. In a letter to Stoddard
Ina said, "Why doesn't some rich man fall in love with me and give
me a chance to refuse him!"[8] One such eligible bachelor who frequented her new parlor in Oakland was John Carmany, publisher
of the *Overland Monthly*. When Stoddard asked if Carmany came
"awooing," Ina replied that if he did it would do no good; Carmany
was too prudish. One day Ina told Carmany that she had a poem in
her head that she hadn't been able to write down because she didn't
have the time. He offered to write if she dictated. She agreed and

recited "The Poet," a poem that describes how nature reveals herself to poets. After Ina gave him the last two lines, "Unclad before his eyes she stands / And gives her secrets to his hands," he suggested that she change "unclad" to "unveiled" for propriety's sake. She argued with him but eventually gave in and changed the word as requested.[9]

John Muir, the naturalist, also visited Ina's parlor. One day he brought pine tassels and lilies after a day hiking in the hills, but Ina knew it wasn't a romantic gesture. He had delivered the same gifts to his friend and mentor Jeanne Carr. Besides, Muir, her lanky, blue-eyed Scottish friend, who was then thirty-six, was courting Louisiana (Louie) Strentzel, the woman he would marry. Muir thought that Ina should marry too, and tried to set her up with Mr. Brown, a schoolteacher. Ina wanted no part of the match and told Muir as much by "rhyming him." A typeset, unpublished poem pasted in Ina's scrapbook is titled "To John Muir: Self-Explanatory." It starts:

> *Up from her catalogues she sprung,*
> And this the song she wildly sung:
> O Johnny Muir! O Johnny Muir!
> How could you leave your mountains pure,
> Your meadow breadths, and forests free,
> A wily matchmaker to be?

Muir had brought Brown to Ina's parlor one Sunday, and Ina was put off by Brown's pompous display of knowledge. She ended her poem to Muir:

> A *resume*. 'Tis understood
> That he is wise, and RICH, and good,
> And fair in all things but in name;
> But still the fact remains the same,
> I do not want him Mr. Muir!
>
> Sail him across the placid Bay
> And sun him in the smiles of May;

Or tow him up to Martin-ez,
There to abide with fair Louise;
Or lure him to some lonely shore
Where sages die—and live no more;
Or clasp him to your pitying breast,
And bear him to some glacier nest,
There tuck him in, and let him rest.
But O of this 'I pray there be
No more, John, an' thou lovest me!'
The earth may quake, the heaven fall,
The ocean fail, or (thought appalling)
I may never wed at all!
But this is certain—write it down—
Or if you smile, or if you frown,
I do not want your Mr. Brown.[10]

Ina never explained why she chose not to marry again. It could be that her first marriage tainted her ability to trust. It is also true that her ideas about the institution had evolved beyond traditional mores. When a reporter later asked what she thought about marriage, she replied that a union should be an equal partnership. A woman should be educated to the furthest degree possible, be able to retain her chosen religion, and have a say in where she and her husband lived.

Ina's rebuke of Muir's matchmaking attempt did not mar their lifelong friendship. Muir had arrived in San Francisco in 1868 on foot, and walked to Yosemite almost immediately thereafter. He climbed mountains and studied glaciers in the summer, and in winter returned to San Francisco or Oakland to give lectures and write about his explorations. It is easy to see why Muir and Ina liked each other. For them, nature and poetry commingled in form. Muir communicated his poetic take on nature in articles and letters, such as in the one he wrote to Jeanne Carr about the "ancient river drift" in the Sacramento River. "In every pebble I could hear the sound of running water. The whole deposit is a poem whose many books and chapters form the geological Vedas of our glorious state."[11]

One day, Muir and William Keith took Ina out for a Sunday

John Muir, c. 1875. Courtesy Holt-
Atherton Special Collections, University
of the Pacific Library.

carriage ride. She wrote Stoddard, "I had a most delightful time, for
the day was superb, and Keith in one of his wildest moods."[12] California landscape artist William Keith and Muir had met a few years earlier in Yosemite, and formed a bond that lasted a lifetime. Keith, who
was married to painter Elizabeth Emerson, cousin to Ralph Waldo
Emerson, was born in Scotland the same year as Muir. He frequently
painted the East Bay hills, where cows sloshed through streams flowing near large sycamore trees, horses traversed trails near large oaks,
and friends reposed on a grassy meadow for a picnic.

It is not known where Ina, Muir, and Keith stopped for a picnic

William Keith. Courtesy The Bancroft Library,
University of California, Berkeley.

or what they ate that day, but their repast can be gleaned from a
recipe for a meal that Ina later contributed to a cookbook. When
asked in 1913 to contribute a recipe to the book, Ina responded that
all of her family recipes had burned in the 1906 earthquake, but that
she could supply a suggestion for a picnic from one she would never
forget. The setting should be "a nook under the trees," and the meal
should be eaten with a "sauce of appetite acquired by a long tramp
in the fields." The menu should include "old-fashioned, home-made
salt rising bread; fresh butter; young green onions just pulled from
the soil; [and] water-cresses fresh from any washed in the brook."
For the beverage, she suggested "vintage of Adam, cold, clear and

sparkling from brook that grew the cresses." At the end of the recipe, she added, "Good anywhere, but best in California."[13]

One month after their carriage ride, Muir was the guest speaker at a fundraiser for the Oakland Library Association and Ina likely greeted those who came to hear his talk about glaciers. Ina appreciated that Muir studied glaciers as a scientist and wrote about them like a poet. In a December 5, 1871, article in the *New York Tribune*, he contrasted glaciers to rivers:

> Water rivers work openly, but glaciers work apart from men, exerting their tremendous energies in silence and darkness, outspread, spirit-like, brooding above predestined rocks unknown to light, unborn, working on unwearied through unmeasured times, unhalting as the stars, until at length, their creations complete, their mountains brought forth, homes made for the meadows and the lakes, and fields for waiting forests, earnest, calm as when they came as crystals from the sky, they depart.

Muir's lecture for the library had low attendance, but the association board was pleased with Muir's talk and voted to give him half the receipts. Ina likely read many of Muir's articles as she spread out the various newspapers in the reading room of the library. She would have had a special interest in an article he wrote for the San Francisco *Bulletin* while on a trip to Utah in the spring of 1877. Several months before Muir went to Utah, John D. Lee had been executed for the crimes of the Mountain Meadows Massacre. He was the only Mormon tried and convicted for the massacre, and just before execution named Brigham Young as an accomplice. Young denied it, and tensions were high in Utah. Many newspapers sent reporters to cover the confrontation expected between the Mormons and the federal government. It's unknown if Muir went on assignment or if he had gone for other reasons. Regardless, the articles he wrote captured the natural beauty of the area. In a May 22 article for the *Bulletin*, he found the city "barely viable" in the presence of such grand mountains. He anchored the description of the area in terms of the glacial landscape, and even compared the houses to a field of glacier boulders seen from a distance.

In the end there was no confrontation to write about, nor did Muir write anything about the Mountain Meadows Massacre. In the same May 22 article, he shared his impressions of the people. The women looked tired and repressed when alone, he said, but had a different countenance when in a group of fellow wives. "Strange as it must seem to Gentiles, the many wives of one man, instead of being repelled from one another by natural jealousy, appear to be drawn all the closer together, as if the real marriage existed between the wives only." It was the men, he said, who seemed to pay the price of polygamy, and looked "incapable of pure love of anything." In his personal journal, Muir noted that he didn't like how the Mormons called themselves Saints. "The sun is a saint, so is the snow & the gl[aciers] & every virgin river."[14]

As expected, Muir married Louie Strentzel. Ina sent a note of congratulations: "God bless you both always! I can say no more than that, if I were to write forever."[15] Muir and Louie sent Ina fresh cherries from their orchard each spring, and Ina continued to correspond with Muir. She kept all of his letters and planned to write a biography of him until all her letters burned in the 1906 earthquake and fire.

During the first year Ina shelved, dusted, and checked out books, she managed to publish eight poems in the *Overland Monthly*. But she couldn't keep up the momentum, nor could the *Overland Monthly* keep up without Harte, and the magazine folded after the December 1875 issue. In 1876 Ina wrote only two poems. One was "From Living Waters," a University of California commencement ode given to thirty graduates, including two women.

In the fall of 1876, Ina wrote Muir that her mother was failing. To Jeanne Carr she wrote, "The days wherein I shall have my mother with me are passing, passing! And the agony of even the thought of the approaching separation is more than I can bear."[16]

Ina missed her friends and told Carr:

In all honesty, I believe I shall go mad with the horrible monotony and loneliness of my life. All my old "familiars" seem to have vanished away, and I wish myself with them, whether to other parts of the world, or out of it, altogether. I don't believe in separation and absence. Absence is deaf, is dumb and blind and cold. I want the warm, bodily presence of my friends; that I may hear them, see them, touch them—know that I have them, that they are, and are mine beyond a doubt![17]

Agnes Moulton Coolbrith Smith Pickett died at sixty-five years old the day after Christmas in 1876. Ina was thirty-five. She held the memorial service at her rented Oakland cottage, where she pinned winter leaves on the curtain edges. John Muir, William Keith, and John Carmany served as pallbearers, and Reverend Hamilton spoke. "True heroism of life is not confined to the battlefield or the forum, nor are the names of all the saints recorded in the calendar," he said to the crowd that filled the small house. "I can point you to no better guide in life than the worthy example left by the still form before you."[18]

In two years, Ina had lost everything she cherished: time, poetry, friends, and her mother. She wailed to Carr, "O God! O God! If there be a God."[19]

10

"A Perfect Day"

In 1878 the California legislature passed the Rogers Free Library Act to establish free public libraries. The Oakland Library Association donated its building and books to the City of Oakland, making Oakland the second city in the state, after Eureka, to open a free library. To improve the library before handing it over to the city, the association raised the one-story building and added a lower floor to serve as a reading room. It bought new furniture, carpeted the rooms, acquired new books, and opened two reading rooms in West and East Oakland. The board determined that the main library would be open from nine to nine every day except Sundays and holidays, with the downstairs reading room open from eight to ten.

Ina was retained as chief librarian and worked twelve hours a day, six days a week. Mr. Snyder, the new janitor, opened and closed the downstairs reading room before and after regular library hours. Ina's salary was raised to eighty-five dollars a month, about seventeen hundred today. It was more than a female teacher earned. In 1873, male teachers in Alameda County earned a hundred dollars a month, when females made sixty dollars for the same work. Though Ina's experience of the work was as a drudgery that took her away from her literary work, at least it paid better and was less grueling than what other working-class women in Oakland endured in canneries or cotton and woolen mills.

The Oakland Public Library. Courtesy Oakland Public Library, Oakland History Room.

The new library opened to the public in November. On the first floor of the square Georgian-style library, patrons read newspapers and magazines and men played checkers and chess. When the weather was cold and rainy, patrons dried their wet socks near the heat of the potbellied stove. At the top of the creaking wooden stairs, a rail surrounded the librarian's desk, where business was brisk. Two months after the library went public, Ina checked out about 250 books a day, which added up to 6,483 books a month and about 78,000 books a year. To check out a book, a patron looked through a printed catalogue and requested the desired book from the librarian, who retrieved it from the closed shelves. Patrons returned the books, and she replaced them in their proper places on the shelves.

The board had voted to allow each user to borrow two books at a time, but after several months Ina concluded that she had to limit borrowing to one at a time. She was buried in books, and as circulation increased, the board admonished her not to allow books to pile up on the railing that surrounded her desk. They also voted to redo the catalogue, and six months later praised Ina for accomplishing the task on top of her regular duties.

It was clear that Ina needed paid assistance, and her nephew Henry, now nineteen, and niece Ina Lillian, fifteen, were hired; they had helped Ina unofficially and without pay since she took the job and already knew the system. Henry received forty dollars a month as the first assistant, and Ina Lillian received thirty as the second.

At the end of 1879, the library board fired the janitor, due to an undisclosed problem. On March 30, 1880, the *Oakland Evening Tribune* printed an anonymous letter by a "Taxpayer" who claimed that Mr. Snyder should not have been fired. The letter writer claimed that it was Miss Coolbrith who was "unpleasant and almost unbearable" and didn't show up to work for weeks or months at a time due to intemperance. The accusation was certainly a stretch, though admittedly Ina did occasionally imbibe. Americans have always liked their alcohol; our founding fathers took alcohol breaks before noon. Even though Ina was raised in the Mormon faith, which admonishes its followers to avoid coffee and alcohol, she liked both. Kona was her favorite coffee, and it is clear that she drank alcohol on occasion. In a letter to Stoddard she said that she was feeling mellow after drinking claret with Carmany. In another she admitted she'd had one too many the night before. "Do you know what it is to feel like a stewed witch? Because I have heard of such a feeling, and believe I am experiencing it today."[1]

Ina didn't think much of the temperance movement either. When told by the board to compile a list of books on the subject a few years later, she suggested six volumes would be plenty. The wife of another board member handed her a list of twenty-two, which Ina pared down to nine. When the board member ordered Ina to order all twenty-two books on the list, Ina complained to another board member, "All right! I did it: but I'm mad! If it would do any good ... I should say fill the shelves with these books. But it doesn't. It is such a namby-pamby, boshy, imbecile, Sunday school method of doing nothing."[2]

If Ina was negligent of her duties, or if the board gave any credence to the accusation that Ina had a drinking problem, the board minutes did not reflect it. They refuted the charges against the librarian as "malicious insinuation."[3]

In 1880 the California legislature passed a law that required small cities to elect a five-member board of directors to run their public libraries. Prior to this law being passed, the library boards had been made up of men who were passionate about literature and education, but after the law's passage, many who ran for the post did so for political or business reasons. These publicly elected boards would prove to be trouble for Ina. The first sign of this came from a committee appointed to establish the powers of the board. One of the first questions the committee addressed was whether or not it was legal to employ a woman. They consulted lawyers and judges, all of whom had different opinions. The matter was finally settled by the city attorney who decreed, "sex is no test of citizenship."[4] Six years into her job, Ina was allowed to keep it.

Stoddard returned to San Francisco in 1878 after having been gone for five years. He had left as a wispy young man and returned as a portly gentleman. He continued to write for the *San Francisco Chronicle*, frequented the theater, and lived in a crumbling mansion on Rincon Hill. One day Stoddard looked out his window and saw a frail man sketching his house. He went outside, where the younger man introduced himself as Robert Lewis Stevenson. Stoddard invited Stevenson inside and showed him treasures from his South Sea travels. The two men became friends, and Stevenson later said that it was Stoddard's home, friendship, and stories that planted the desire for his own South Seas adventures and led him to write *Treasure Island* and other classics.[5]

Ina did not see much of Stoddard. She told him by letter that she had seen him at a bookstore but didn't say hello because she felt too frazzled and shabby. He offered to submit some of her poems to national publications and she sent him several. He reported back that the magazines had rejected them, and he would try other markets.

No, she said, she had learned long ago that the Eastern magazines didn't want her.

Ina had lost confidence in her work, but her popularity among readers had not diminished. She had published more than sixty poems in the *Overland Monthly* during its reign, and had not yet published a collection of her work. Her reading public clamored for one and Carmany offered to publish it. The vast majority of the poems would be those she had written for the *Overland Monthly*. The collection would also include her two University of California commencement odes and the few new poems she had written since starting work at the library.

In preparation for the book, Carmany wrote to Bret Harte in Germany about the packet of poems Ina had given him to take east. Harte replied that he did not have Ina's packet of poems, and couldn't recall what had happened to it. He said that he had shown the poems to Osgood of Houghton, Osgood, and Co., and that the publisher had rejected them. If the packet had contained any original material, as Carmany suggested, Harte said he would feel more obliged to track the package's whereabouts, but as far as he could remember it only contained clippings from the *Overland Monthly*. "I need only say that the personal regard I have for Miss Coolbrith and the high value I set upon her talents would impel me to do anything I could to assist her," wrote Harte.[6]

One year later, unbeknownst to Ina, Harte wrote a letter to his wife that contradicted this assertion. Apparently, Anne Harte had written her estranged husband that she found some of his papers, and Harte replied in July 1879 that he was anxious to see them. "If all the papers—including Miss Coolbrith's packet—do not make too large a bundle, you might send them to the State Department addressed to me."[7] If Harte's wife had found Ina's packet, why did Harte instruct her to send it to Germany instead of directly to Ina? Ina never knew that Harte or his wife had the packet until many decades later when a friend came across Harte's 1879 letter in a library collection and shared it with Ina.

Carmany gathered Ina's poems from his *Overland Monthly* files, her scrapbook, and the unpublished poems in her desk. She told

Stoddard that she did not have time to make revisions or think of a title. "I think I shall name my book simply, 'Drift,' or 'Driftwood,' for that is what my verses are," she said.[8] Stoddard helped her come up with a more appropriate title, and A *Perfect Day and Other Poems* came out in March 1881, the month of her fortieth birthday. Carmany printed five hundred copies of a "special subscription edition," which sold for two dollars. He also printed fifty copies in a large format that sold for ten dollars. Both versions sold out quickly.

Friends sent notes of praise and congratulations. Stoddard wrote, "I know of no living poetess in either England or America who is your superior and but few who approach you in beauty of sentiment, richness of melody and delicacy of expression … You are mistress of your art."[9] Edward Rowland Sill, a poet and literature professor at the University of California, said that he had sent a review to the *Atlantic Monthly*, but they did not pick it up. "Keep up good courage," he said. "Anyone who can write genuine poetry ought to be so glad that nothing else would matter much—for I tell you the number of them is very small indeed."[10] She sent a copy of her book to John Greenleaf Whittier, who replied, "Now Bret Harte has left, there is no verse on the Pacific Slope which has the fine quality of thine."[11]

A *Perfect Day and Other Poems* was reviewed widely. Ambrose Bierce said, "[It] contains nearly all the verses written by woman's hand in California that have been true in feeling and correct in art."[12] The *San Francisco Chronicle* claimed her as "one of the few women on this coast who have genuine poetic ability," though it added it didn't like her "fancy for the funereal element in life."[13] A critic at the *Oakland Tribune* complained that she "loves her mother and some others, and man last and least."[14]

As testament to her prominence, newspapers in the East also reviewed her book. The *Boston Courier* said her poems "contain no striking truths or startlingly original conceits, but are nevertheless the utterances of a true poet who, like the robin, sings because she must."[15] The *Boston Saturday Gazette* said that the "prevailing sentiment of the volume is one of sadness, which gives a tone of monotony to it; but the versification is spirited, fresh and flowing."[16]

Others were not so generous. *Vanity Fair* charged that the poet's job is to elevate a reader's understanding, to soar, not walk, among us. The reviewer pointed out several poems and passages that he liked, but concluded that as a whole, "There is an intense consciousness of pain, but it is a consciousness of one's own, rather than a beating with that of the world's. The book therefore recommends itself generally to admiration, rather than fellowship."[17] *Century Magazine* also complained about her inability to inspire. "She seldom clears for us the moral atmosphere, or lifts us up to the heights where we can see broadly what is below, or serenely what is above in the heavens."[18]

The publication of her first book did little to change Ina's life and did not help to get her out of the library. The reviews, good and bad, increased her growing despondency. So did the book's receipts. She told Stoddard that Carmany had cheated her on the book. "It was infamous-infamous-infamous!... I could murder him for it, without remorse, I do believe."[19] She was so miserable that she even entertained marriage. "Find me someone to marry, no matter how old, or black, or imbecile, so long as he has money," she told Stoddard.[20]

Circulation at the library increased to about 280 books a day. Henry was elected as assistant secretary of the board, and in that role took minutes of the monthly meetings in careful cursive lettering. The trustees raised his salary to forty-five dollars a month, and Ina's to one hundred.

The *Overland Monthly* was resuscitated in January 1883. A new publisher, Warren Cheney, got the rights to use the name and began the magazine with Volume One, Number One. He hired Millicent Shinn, a recent graduate of the University of California, to be its editor. Ina contributed "Unattained" to the inaugural issue, a poem that expressed her frustration at not finding peace or creative satisfaction. Ambrose Bierce reviewed the new magazine, which he dubbed *The Warmed Overland Monthly*, and took a jab at Ina's poem. "Having in mind the whole body of Miss Coolbrith's works for the last fifteen years, we are compelled to ask—when is she going to 'attain'? If never, is it not about time for her to remove her pretty lace handkerchief from her pretty brown eyes and put it comfortably in her pocket?"[21]

Ina pasted Bierce's review in her scrapbook, as she did all of her reviews, good and bad. She was not overly fond of critics. Years ear-lier she had told Jeanne Carr that they "must be selected from the doctors' lists of incurable dyspeptics."[22]

11

A Strategic Move

The first-floor addition to the Oakland Free Library building rendered the building unsafe for public use. If too many people tried to use the stairs at the same time, the building shuddered. In the early 1880s, the local fire department installed a tower with a fire bell just outside the rear wall of the library, and whenever the bell pealed the unstable building quivered and frayed the nerves of everyone inside. The ringing fire bell only served to exacerbate the librarian's problems with the new library board that had assembled in April 1883. Two years earlier, the city had shrunk appropriations for the library but the previous board had done little in the way of cuts. In contrast, the actions of the new board were draconian. Worse than that, several of them seemed intent on ousting Ina. The two incumbents, O. H. Burnham and Charles W. Kellogg, were reasonable and civic minded, though they were not literary men. The three newcomers were neither reasonable nor literary. Wilbur Walker, a lumberyard salesman, and Amory M. Long and Eugene A. Trefethen, both railroad clerks, were trouble.

The difficulties began at the June 1883 board meeting, the minutes of which were recorded by assistant secretary Henry Peterson in a large red and black leather ledger. Trefethen moved that the second assistant position, held by Ina Lillian Peterson, be declared vacant. Henry must have looked up from his minute taking with the

123

mention of his sister being fired. When Burnham asked for a reason, Trefethen replied that the library staff was all from one family and there should be a change. Trefethen proposed a vote, which was seconded. Burnham voted no. Kellogg said that he didn't intend to fire anyone without cause and refused to vote. Trefethen, Long, and Walker voted aye and the motion passed.

Trefethen then moved to nominate a replacement and nominated Mrs. J. L. Plummer.

"Who is she?" asked Burnham.

"A widow, and my sister," said Trefethen.[1]

The motion for the vote was seconded and taken. Burnham voted no. Kellogg refused to vote. Trefethen, Walker, and Long voted aye, and the motion passed. By the end of the meeting, Ina Lillian had been replaced by Trefethen's sister and Kellogg had resigned. He said he had never been on a board run by "a ring" and didn't intend to be on one now.

The next month's meeting was moved to a larger room of the library to accommodate the crowd that showed up to protest Ina Lillian's dismissal. Henry Peterson read three letters of protest aloud. One was from the mayor, and the others were signed by hundreds of citizens. Burnham moved that a vote be taken to reinstate Ina Lillian to her position, but Kellogg was not there to second the motion and the meeting was adjourned. Ina Lillian did not get her job back and Mrs. Plummer remained. Ina complained to Stoddard that Mrs. Plummer was the most ignorant person she had ever met; one day she asked Ina who wrote *Hamlet*. Ina added that the work had been hard enough when there were three who knew what they were doing, and unless something changed, she and Henry would resign. "I did not starve before I came here. I don't anticipate I shall when I leave."[2]

But Ina could not easily resign because she had recently bought an eight-room house at 1261 Webster Street. "A pretty place, but unfortunately in Oakland," she told Stoddard. "I hate Oakland, and ache for the old misty, windy San Francisco hills."[3]

The library board continued to cut expenses and make changes. They closed the main library an hour earlier (which was better for Ina), cut newspaper subscriptions (though Trefethen added one from his small hometown in Maine), and reduced the budget for books. They also removed books from the shelves that they considered unseemly, such as the novels of Emile Zola. They appointed themselves to a committee to revise the rules and regulations of the library, including an item that gave present and future library boards free rein to fire an employee at will.[4]

In October, the board decided that the catalogue should be updated. They ordered Ina to visit the San Francisco library and report back on the feasibility of using that system. At that time, the system of classification and cataloguing was unique to individual librarians and no two libraries were alike in how they approached it. At the next board meeting Ina told the board that it would be impractical for their small library to attempt the same system being used in San Francisco, and instead suggested an approach that would take less time to implement and be simpler for staff to use.[5] The librarian in San Francisco also sent a letter warning the board that it would take a year to reclassify the books, and that the librarian would only be able to get it done in that time if she were relieved of other duties.

Trefethen and his cohorts ignored the advice and told Ina to start reclassification using the San Francisco system. They also directed her to rewrite the catalogue, and offered no assistance or relief from her regular tasks. Ina complied. She told Stoddard that she hurried through twelve-hour days and still left things unfinished. She was so tired at the end of each day that she often went to bed in her clothes. She told another friend that she was expected to know all the books in the library but was reported if caught reading. "I confine myself to the titles, in which I am becoming very learned, indeed!"[6]

The antics of the board had become public knowledge. One year into the board's two-year term, San Francisco's *Daily Evening Star* reported that the "ring" of Trefethen, Long, and Walker were trying to push Ina out of the library. Ambrose Bierce termed the board's reign the "Trefethenization" of the library. Even though Bierce had been critical of her poem in the new *Overland Monthly*, Ina appreciated his support in this case and told Stoddard, "If I were younger and he single I might be tempted to fall desperately in love with him."[7]

Six months after she started the reclassification process, Ina had prepared three thousand cards of the five thousand needed, and by the end of June had completed thirty-eight hundred cards. She told the board that she hoped to be finished by November. In August they told her to compile a list of reference books to purchase and gave her a month to do it. When she protested, they questioned her competency. She was so tired that she did not rhyme them, but sent a serious letter:

> While I have never presumed to any superior
> degree of excellence in my capacity as librarian,
> feeling myself, on the contrary, only a very begin-
> ner in a profession which finds me every day at fault
> and with something to learn, I can say with truth,
> that during my (nearly) ten years service in this
> library ... it is the first time, within my knowledge,
> that my competency to perform my work had been
> called in question.[8]

Enough was enough. In a strategic move, Ina requested a six-month leave of absence without pay. It was granted. For years she had said good-bye to her friends as they boarded eastbound trains, and now it was her turn. Her first destination was her mother's birth-place in Scarborough, Maine, an old coastal town seven miles south of Portland. Agnes had been one of eight children, and Ina met many of her aunts, uncles, and cousins for the first time during her month-long visit. From Maine she went to Boston, where her mother had lived as a young woman. The *Boston Evening Transcript* reported that although the California poet had been born in Illinois, she was vis-iting New England for the first time. In Boston she visited libraries and talked to librarians about procedures, wages, and working hours. She communicated with Henry, who acted as head librarian in her absence. He told her that the board had voted to raise the salaries of the first and second assistant to seventy-five dollars a month. Henry also reported that the board had hired a full-time cataloguer to com-plete the job, and instructed the cataloguer to adopt a different sys-tem. The cataloguer estimated that he would be finished by January if he worked full time. He didn't finish until April. In his final report he told the board that the task would have been more efficient had they directed him to use the system Ina had used so he didn't have to redo the thirty-eight hundred cards she had already completed.

Ina told Henry not to work too hard. For one, she worried about his health. Henry smoked, had a chronic cough, and stayed out late. She was also worried that he would take her job. "[Don't] work yourself to death proving to the trustees that only two are needed in the library ... If I can't get back into the library we will have to break up," she said, only partly in jest.[9]

In Boston, she sent her card to Oliver Wendell Holmes and John Greenleaf Whittier, the two surviving members of the Fireside Poets. Henry Wadsworth Longfellow had died the previous year. She met with Holmes briefly, and Whittier replied that he was eager to meet her.

Under a cold, gray October sky, Ina's carriage pulled up in front of Whittier's two-story home in Amesbury, Massachusetts, forty-four miles north of Boston. Whittier had moved to Oak Knolls in Danvers in 1875, but kept his place in Amesbury. Ina sent the driver away with instructions to return in an hour. She entered a gate and walked down a path covered with damp autumn leaves. The porch was covered with red and yellow leaves that had fallen from the vines that blanketed the sides of the house with green shutters. Whittier's friend, Mrs. Cates, answered the door and asked Ina to wait in the parlor. Ina later said she was so nervous that she considered bolting. She was looking out the window with her back to Whittier when he entered, and heard his deep and gentle voice before seeing him. She recreated the visit years later for an audience of presswomen.

"I give thee welcome friend," said Whittier, who used Old English pronouns in his speech and poetry. Ina remembered reading a description of him in his early years when he was graceful and handsome, but when she turned around, she saw "an *old* man, tall, a little bowed, thin grey hair, features regular almost to severity, except the almost pathetically tender mouth, and dark eyes ... The most wonderful eyes, with the exception of Edwin Booth's, I have ever beheld."[10]

She held out one of her hands in the conventional manner, but he reached for both and said, "So thee are Ina Coolbrith. Thee are welcome child," and without taking his eyes off her, he recited her poem "In Blossom Time" in its entirety. He took her to his private study and asked so many questions about California writers that she finally stopped him. Why ask about "our crude beginnings in the West" when she wanted to hear what he had to say?

"You call them crude beginnings?" he replied. "In my estimation, and that of all the unbiased critics, you are giving America the strongest, most original, most virile work it is producing today."[11]

He told her that he knew her "California" poem by heart, and challenged her to say the same about any of his work. She told him that she had memorized only one, his tribute to Starr King.

"Did thee know Starr King?" he asked.

"Yes, but only for a short time. I came to San Francisco not long before his death. But Starr King really made me acquainted with you, Mr. Whittier."

"Friend Whittier," he corrected.

Whittier told her how hard it had been for him when King left Boston for California. "I believe his loyal voice helped greatly in saving California to the Union. I take it for granted thee are a Union girl?" She said, yes, of course. He handed her a huge iron key that he took from the wall and said it was the key to the Libby Prison at Richmond, a confederate prison infamous for its deplorable treatment of Union soldiers. It was his most prized possession.

Mrs. Cates knocked on the door to say that Ina's carriage had arrived. Whittier left the room and upon returning said, "Is that what thee thinks of Quaker welcome and hospitality? I have sent that wretched driver away with strict instructions not to return before five."[12]

After lunch they talked of religion, the future of mankind, and the possibility of an afterlife. He told her he had received messages from the dead, and asked if she had had any similar experiences. She likely told him about her visit from John Rollin Ridge on the night of his death. He asked why she had come east, and she said she was considering a move. He warned her not to expect to make a living by her pen. "I published verse for twenty years before I received a penny of remuneration," he said. "Moreover, of those who could and would have helped thee, so many are gone. Longfellow would, I am sure, have liked thee and thy work, and he could have been of greater service to thee than I, for he dwelt more within the world and under-stood it better. And I'm sure Dr. Holmes would."[13]

Ina told Whittier that she had seen Holmes, and that he had greeted her kindly.

"If ever thee should come east, I want thee to remember that so long as he lives, Whittier's home is thine, whenever and for as long as thee should require or desire it," he said.[14]

When her carriage returned, he put on his coat and hat and said that he wanted to show her a bit of Amesbury. The two poets drove through the old town, with the horse clomping on the stone streets as Whittier pointed out buildings and houses of interest. When the carriage arrived back at his house, he kissed both of her hands. She later said that the last memory she had of him was as he "passed up the walk, with the rain-like mist covering him as with a thin gray veil and the autumn leaves drifting about his feet."[15]

12

Noble Mentor

When Ina returned to the Oakland Library, Trefethen and his ring had been voted out and replaced by a more reasonable board. Mrs. Plummer was also gone and a new library assistant was hired. Ina Lillian did not reclaim the position.

Within a month of Ina's return, her health deteriorated. After she left Boston she had spent a month in New York, where a doctor warned her that she would break down if she kept up at the pace she had been going. Stoddard, who had accepted a teaching job at Notre Dame University, asked Ina if she had any plans for her literary career. She said she needed a steady salary because she had borrowed against her house. Her brother, Don Carlos, had returned ill from a mining trip, and Ina was supporting him and Ina Lillian. "Someone has to provide the bread, and so I am back in my prison," she told Stoddard.[1] When Stoddard told Ina that Joaquin Miller had admonished him to write her always, Ina replied that she wished Miller would "right" her by giving her the money he owed for Calla Shasta. "Bah! Never mind. Keep it to yourself—or better—forget it, but don't repeat any more of his 'God Bless Inas' to me."[2] She instructed Stoddard to burn the letter. He did not.

In an undated photo taken in an Oakland studio, Calla Shasta sits on a garden bench. Her straight black hair cascades over her shoulders and frames a perfectly square face dominated by wide-set

Calla Shasta Miller, 1879. Courtesy Special Collections, Honnold/Mudd Library, Claremont University Consortium.

eyes that spark. The serenity of her folded hands and the soft lace and beads of her Victorian dress belie the energy that pushes through the photo. Though small in stature, Calla Shasta looks as though she might jump out of the picture. You can almost see the temper that Ina describes to Stoddard in a letter. "In one of her moods, at which times she is on the rampage, Pip!"[3]

Calla Shasta seldom saw her father. Miller lived first in Europe and then in New York after handing Ina the responsibility of his daughter. When Calla Shasta first came to Ina in 1872, she did not speak English or read and write. Ina changed that, and her influence as a poet and teacher is evident in three extant letters Calla Shasta wrote to her uncle, George Miller. The first, written on June 30, 1879, was in reply to one he had written her. In it she demonstrated near-perfect penmanship in a practiced cursive hand. She folded her pages correctly and spaced her lines evenly. On the left side she wrote "Dear Mr. Miller," with little o-rings to decorate her capital letters, and after a deep indent began, "We are unknown friends, but you give me your hand for your kindness in writing me a letter. Your welcome letter surprised me exceedingly and was received with great delight." She explained that she had been with Miss Coolbrith since her father brought her down from the mountains. "Father will never find a better friend than Miss Coolbrith has been to him. I know you will like her when you see her. She is the sweetest poetess in the Pacific coast," she said. Calla Shasta complained that her father had given Maud, his daughter with Minnie Myrtle, his first legal wife, everything, and her nothing. "And I a deserted wildflower by the wayside kept alive by the dew glistening on the morning air," she wrote with a poet's sensibility.

She told Miller that on her father's last visit he had promised to see her once more before leaving town, but he didn't keep his word. "Last I saw my father he lingered at the garden gate [and] by stars above he swears to live he took my hand in his. Father-like he placed his arm around me he called me all his own, but no power on Earth can make me believe him again." She didn't add line breaks to her letters, but you can hear where they might be inserted: "Alone I played with wild birds on the shore, singing a wild song to the sea; alone gathering wildflowers by the river, where the branches bend and quiver; could linger and watch it forever." She ended the letter with proper indentation, tabbing, and language: "I remain yours truly, Calla Shasta Miller."[4]

A month later she wrote Miller a second letter in which she said she had been considering a trip to the mountains in September but had decided to postpone it until spring. The prose in her letter is pedestrian until she spoke of Shasta: "Sometime, I in the stillness of some lonely hour, thinking of the dear old mountains, it seems pale sorrow hid away at twilight hour, while the peaceful moon looks down with tender light, pale and sad the young moon wanders, and gilds the withered rose with her smile."[5]

Calla Shasta's next and last known letter to Miller on November 3, 1879, reveals more of her personality. She says that she is as tired as "an old bat stuck with mud," hates the cold and damp weather in Oakland, and "misses the little snowflakes that I used to watch come fluttering down and the old oak trees grand and noble shivering with a weight of snow."[6] In response to his apology for being inquisitive, she told Miller he could ask any questions he wanted:

> I am always ready to answer you in anything. For I
> have my own judgment about me in everything. I
> am not afraid of anybody or anything ... I am sadly
> disappointed for not being a boy. I am not half as
> bright as I should like to be but I always feel intel-
> ligent and never feel too old to learn. If I had the
> money I would be an artist or a musician, that
> are my favorites. But it is only 8 years ago since
> I realized what kind of an animal I am. I did not
> even know how to speak English and did not know
> B from a bull's foot. Such was I when I first came
> down from Shasta where I was full of spunk killing
> skunks.[7]

Two years after Calla Shasta communicated with her uncle, her father invited her to come to New York and live with him and his third wife, Abigail Leland. Stoddard asked Ina what she thought of the idea. Ina responded that she didn't think it was wise, for "Carrie" would be lost if Miller failed to look out for her. Providing for Carrie meant "drives, and parties, and amusements of various kinds."[8] Calla Shasta saw things differently. She told her uncle that she used to go out in society for balls and parties, but hadn't for two years and was generally "discouraged and disgusted with everything."[9]

Ina told Stoddard that Calla Shasta had many fine qualities, but that she could be publicly embarrassing. One such incident occurred at Ina's house when a friend came to call. The two women had tea while the friend's son played in Ina's large backyard. When it came time to leave, the woman looked for her son and could not find him. Everyone joined the search, and eventually they found the boy hiding under the house. He refused to come out. Calla Shasta said she would get him out and went to the kitchen for a large knife. She crawled under the house with the knife clenched in her teeth. "You'd better come out or I'll cut your heart out," she threatened.[10] The boy came out, and the shaken mother and son left. Calla Shasta laughed loudly and Ina and Ina Lillian suppressed the urge to join her.

It is unknown exactly when Calla Shasta left Ina's house. She was still there, and ill, in July 1883 when Ina wrote Stoddard that she was dying of consumption.[11] Calla Shasta recovered, and soon after insisted that Ina pay her twenty-five dollars a month for housekeeping services. Ina said she could not pay, and Calla Shasta moved out. For years, Ina did not know of her whereabouts.

Calla Shasta, Ina Lillian, and Henry were not the only young people whom Ina took under her wing. Oakland was a small town, and Ina noticed when new patrons climbed the stairs to her desk. The first thing she noticed about the scrappy new kid who brought a stack of books to her was his age. According to library rules, patrons needed to be at least fourteen years old to borrow books, and even then they needed a sponsor. The new boy kept his head down when he placed the books and his mother's card on Ina's desk. She praised him on his selection, and when he looked up, wide-eyed at her comment, she saw a good-looking boy with warm eyes, a small nose, and full lips. He didn't look more than ten, and was clearly a voracious reader. He returned frequently. At first Ina couldn't get a name out of him. In time, he told her his name was John London, but people called him Jack.

London had moved to Oakland from his stepfather's farm in Pleasanton. His family was poor and he was looking for a way to escape his life through books. One day he asked for a book on

Jack London, age nine, with his dog Rollo. Courtesy
Oakland Public Library, Oakland History Room.

Pizarro, and after Ina retrieved it from the shelves, she told him it
was a fine choice. London remembered the moment for the rest of
his life. Years later, he told her what her words had meant to him.

> Do you know, you were the first one who ever
> complimented me on my choice of reading matter.
> Nobody at home bothered their heads over what I
> read. I was an eager, thirsty, hungry little kid—and
> one day, at the library, I drew out a volume on Piz-

zaro in Peru (I was ten years old). You got the book
& stamped it for me. And as you handed it to me
you praised me for reading books of that nature.
Proud! If you only knew how proud your words
made me.[12]

As a boy he named everything in adjectives, and he named her
"noble," even though at the time he didn't know who she was or
that she was a published poet. "No woman has so affected me to the
extent you did," he told her years later.[13]

Perhaps London's hunger for books reminded her of the first novel she had read, *The Red Revenge*, which she read "surreptitiously and
chiefly by moonlight."[14] When he asked Ina to recommend something to read, she handed him the complete collection of Tobias
George Smollet, a Scottish poet and author of picaresque adventure
novels. London asked for more books and she brought him Horatio
Alger and Washington Irving. "More," he said. To get his fill, he used
the library cards of his mother, his married sister, and her in-laws.

London frequented the library during elementary school, but after graduation his family could not afford to send him to high school
and he took a job at a local pickle-canning factory. He hung around
the waterfront and learned how to pirate oysters. When that career
proved too dangerous, he joined the oyster pirate patrollers. While
working the docks, he learned about a job on a sealing vessel bound
for Japan, which launched him into a life of adventure like those he
had read about in books. He sailed out of Ina's life and in time became one of the world's most famous writers.

It isn't a cliché to say that Isadora Duncan danced her way to the
Oakland Free Library at ten years old. She wrote as much in her autobiography forty years later. "There was a public library in Oakland,
where we then lived, but no matter how many miles we were from it,
I ran or danced or skipped there and back."[15]

Isadora was the daughter of Joseph Duncan, Ina's friend and
probable lover. In October 1877, after Ina had been in the library

for several years, Joseph Duncan's bank crashed. His was not the only bank that did. California's economy teetered in reaction to the close of the silver mines, and many banks took drastic measures to compete. Duncan's competitive edge had been a vault that held safe deposit boxes, the first of its kind in the West. When news hit that his bank was in trouble, thousands of working-class depositors showed up to claim their money and found the impenetrable steel vaults empty—and no Duncan. He was charged with forgery and other crimes, the news of which Ina read as she put the newspapers out in the reading room. Duncan eluded the police for months. They scoured the streets and kept watch on outgoing ships until getting a tip that Duncan was holed up in San Francisco at the house of a female friend. There police found him and the disguise that enabled him to go out on the streets undetected. His outfit had been a sewn-together ensemble of dress, bustle, underskirt and chemise; a chestnut-colored wig topped with a sewn-on black hat crowned with dainty violets; and a thick brown veil to pull over his face.

Duncan's trial began in May 1878. He was still in court when his youngest child, Isadora, celebrated her first birthday. She later referred to this period in her family's life in her autobiography. "Before I was born, my mother was in great agony of spirit and in a tragic situation. She could take no food except iced oysters and champagne."[16] Mary Dora, Isadora's mother, divorced Duncan during his trial. After he was acquitted, Duncan moved to Los Angeles and eventually remarried.

Mary Dora moved to Oakland with her four children and supported them by teaching music. She struggled financially and moved the family from house to house when she couldn't pay rent. Each evening, in the same spirit that Edna St. Vincent Millay's mother raised her children, Mary Dora kept music, art, and literature alive in the house. She told her children that these were the things that mattered in life, not security or material possessions. She filled their ears, minds, and hearts with the music of Beethoven, Mozart, and Chopin, and the words of Byron, Shelley, and Shakespeare. When she had a little money, Mary Dora took the children across the bay to dine in San Francisco, even if it meant being without food for a week.

Isadora was seven when Joseph Duncan knocked on the front door of the family's Oakland house. She saw an older, handsome man who introduced himself as her father. That confused her. She had heard such awful things about him that she envisioned him to be an ogre; but this man seemed kind. She asked him to wait. She went inside and told her mother who was at the door, and her mother started to cry. Then Isadora told her brother, and he hid under a bed. Isadora decided to join her father anyway. They went out for ice cream and cakes and she found him charming. Because his fortunes were on an upswing, Duncan bought Mary Dora and the children a house in Oakland, where they lived until his finances collapsed again.

Isadora was already a serious and precocious child when she quit school at ten and turned to the library for her education. "The librarian was a very wonderful and beautiful woman, a poetess of California, Ina Coolbrith. She encouraged my reading and I thought she always looked pleased when I asked for fine books. She had very beautiful eyes that glowed with burning fire and passion," Isadora wrote in her autobiography.[17] By candlelight Isadora read Dickens, Thackeray, and Shakespeare. She kept a journal, and wrote and edited her own newspaper filled with stories and news of the neighborhood. She found places to dance alone in the woods and on the beach near San Francisco's Cliff House. "My heavy shoes were like chains; my clothes were my prison," she wrote. "So I took everything off. And without any eyes watching me, entirely alone, I danced, naked by the sea. And it seemed to me as if the sea and all the trees were dancing with me."[18]

Her first public performance was a dance to a Longfellow poem. She recited "The Arrow and the Song" to neighborhood children and led them in movement. She began to teach dance classes, first in Oakland and then in San Francisco, and off she danced in search of an expanded life that matched those that she had read about in books. "Afterwards I learnt that at one time my father had been very much in love with [Ina]," Isadora wrote in her autobiography. "She was evidently the great passion of his life and it was probably by this invisible thread of circumstance that I was drawn to her."[19]

Years later, Joseph Duncan and his third wife were sailing on the S.S. *Mohegan* from London to New York with their daughter. The

Mohegan sank near Cornwall on October 14, 1898, and 106 people went down with the ship, including Joseph Duncan and his family. Ina hadn't written about love in decades, but eighteen months after Duncan died she published a poem in *Current Literature* titled "When Love is Dead." In it she wrote, "Oh, how can love be dead / And yet not I!"[20]

In addition to Isadora Duncan and Jack London, Ina had one other famous mentee who acknowledged her help. In 1892, a young woman came into the library and introduced herself as Mary Austin. Austin was living in San Francisco temporarily with her husband, who was trying to develop an irrigation project. The irrigation scheme didn't pan out, but the trip paid off for Austin. She was born in 1868, the year the *Overland Monthly* had launched, and at twenty-three she wanted to submit a short story to the relaunched version of the same. She needed advice on how to prepare a manuscript for publication, and someone suggested she seek Ina's guidance. In Austin's autobiography, *Earth Horizon*, she described Ina as a "tall, slow woman, well filled out ... She had a low pleasant voice, [and] now and then a faint smile swam to the surface of her look, and passed without the slightest riffle of a laugh."[21] Austin said she saw something in Ina's countenance that she would later recognize in her own image, that of someone "accustomed to uninhibited space and wide horizons."[22]

Ina was matter-of-fact and helpful, said Austin, and introduced her to *Overland*'s editor, Millicent Shinn. Shinn accepted Austin's story "The Mother of Felipe" for the October issue, and it was Austin's first published piece. Ten years later Austin published *The Land of Little Rain*, which established her as a serious regional writer on the national stage.

The examples of London, Duncan, and Austin represent young people who recognized Ina's influence after they had become famous, but there were hundreds of others who appreciated Ina's encouragement and guidance. For the rest of Ina's life, she received notes from strangers who thanked her for helping them at the Oakland Public Library.

13

Escape from the Inferno

Ina turned forty-nine on March 10, 1890. For sixteen years she had served as the administrative and departmental head of the library where she managed staff; wrote budgets and worked within them; ordered, repaired, and catalogued books; kept the library neat, clean, and welcoming; prepared monthly reports for the board and the press; served as a reference desk to student and adult learners; and encouraged aspiring writers. And yet, she did not have the right to vote. California did not grant women suffrage until 1911. National suffrage for women would come in 1920 when the Nineteenth Amendment was added to the United States Constitution.[1]

Since starting work at the library, Ina rarely published more than two poems a year, and these were either eulogies for friends or poems of occasion. Only a few stand out. One was a eulogy for Helen Hunt Jackson, the novelist and Native American activist who died in 1885. "Helen Hunt Jackson" was published in the *Overland Monthly* and later included by Edmund Clarence Stedman in *An American Anthology, 1787–1900*. In the same anthology, Stedman included "The Mariposa Lily," a poem Ina wrote in 1886 that captures the essence of one of California's native flowers: "Insect or blossom? Fragile, fairy thing / Poised upon slender tip, and quivering / To flight!"[2] T. W. Higginson cited the same poem in an *Atlantic Monthly* article, "Butterflies in Poetry." Ina wrote "California Rain" in 1888, a poem

Ina Coolbrith at age fifty, c. 1885. Courtesy Oakland Public
Library, Oakland History Room.

in the mood of her earlier nature poems. It appeared for one day in
the *Oakland Tribune*, as ephemeral as autumn rain. The first of the
five stanzas starts with a soft patter: "Float down upon the tawny hills
/ O misty banners of the rain! / With murmur as of forest rills / Sweep
softly down from hill to plain." The next stanzas describe the thirsty,
sun-baked earth, and the odors released by the woods after the rain.
Yet another reads:

> O pure, sweet spirit of the rain,
> No fairer thing the fair earth knows!

In you the gold of harvest grain,
In you the redness of the rose.[3]

Since entering the library sixteen years earlier, Ina did not have any love interests. In a letter to Stoddard she asked about a mutual friend, whom she described as handsome. "Had I been humanly susceptible I should have lost my heart and wits for him—but alas! I fear I am not."[4] When Stoddard encouraged her to marry another mutual friend (who remained unnamed in their letters), Ina reported back that she had considered it but was turned down. "I tried to fall in love with the Doctor, but he would [have] none of me. He snubbed me awfully. Don't know why."[5] She told Stoddard it felt odd to grow old with crow's feet and gray hairs.

She did not see much of her old friends. Stoddard had moved to Washington, DC, in 1889 to take a job as chair of the English department at the new Catholic University of America. And even though Miller lived in the Oakland hills above the library, she rarely saw her flamboyant friend. Ina wrote Stoddard, "[Miller] dashes out in broad sombrero and Spanish saddle & spurs upon his 'fiery untamed' and plays the vaquero; upon which occasions I steadfastly refuse to recognize him, much to his disgust ... Then he comes in, in rancher's garb, looking more like a tramp than anything else human, and tries to make friends again. He says, 'The worst thing in me, Ina, is my vanity;' and I answer: 'And you are so vain of your vanity you would not lose it for all else the world contains!'"[6]

One young library patron had a different perspective of Miller's visits to the library: "I well recall standing patiently at the loan desk when Miss C. and Joaquin Miller, whom we all knew by sight, stood apart and apparently read poetry to each other," said E. M. Wilder in a letter sent to the Oakland Library seventy years later.[7]

In 1889, Ina had a surprise visit from one of her Mormon cousins and she invited him to dinner. She had not seen Joseph Smith III, the eldest surviving son of the prophet and president of the Reorganized Church of Jesus Christ of Latter-day Saints (known today as the Community of Christ), since childhood in Nauvoo, though they had communicated by letter. In the early 1860s he sent her a ring that had belonged to her father. When *A Perfect Day and Other*

Poems came out, he sent for a copy. She sent the book along with a request that if he were to publicly acknowledge her or the book, he not connect her to the Smith family. He replied that he would honor her wish, but gave her a lecture about how as a poet she might "champion" his church and work.[8] As a general rule, Ina didn't trust those who bragged of piety. Years earlier she told Jeanne Carr that she was beginning to "distrust *everybody* who is over-church-ey … Someone should suggest to Edwin Booth the propriety of changing a certain line of Hamlet into, 'Angels, *from* Ministers of grace defend us.'"[9]

Ina still slogged through seventy-hour workweeks at the library, and Henry and Ina Lillian continued to live with her and her cats, which reportedly had reached fourteen in number. Ina was particularly fond of white angora cats, whose long hairs clung to Henry's wool coats, much to his frustration.

By spring of 1890 her nerves were shot. The board had ordered her to begin work on a new catalogue and to make haste. She pushed herself, but one Monday morning she couldn't get out of bed. She made it to work by noon but broke down within the hour. Her confident, rebellious nature had abandoned her, as evidenced by her weak complaints to John Vance Cheney, a librarian in San Francisco. She asked Cheney not to repeat her grumbling to the board. "They will say, 'Miss Coolbrith has been complaining' … [and yet] I cannot give satisfaction because I cannot do the work of a dozen persons. To continue the effort means serious result to my health."[10]

Ina did not want to cross the board because she knew that her nephew had gained the upper hand. Now thirty, he was an able administrator, and as assistant secretary at board meetings he provided cigars and performed magic tricks while waiting for the members to arrive. Henry's salary had been raised to one hundred dollars a month, equal to Ina's. He was free to come and go during working hours, while she was not. She told Cheney that she had no privileges, and could not go across the street to the post office without "putting it down in writin'."[11] Ina and Henry worked on the catalogue, and eventually two part-time assistants were hired to help. Henry, who had a thin but handsome face with a long moustache that accentuated his cleft chin, dated one of the assistants, Elizabeth "Bessie" Welton, who didn't care for Ina.

In September, Henry moved out of Ina's house. An article in the *Oakland Tribune* said it was due to Ina's cats. But the trouble between Ina and Henry had been brewing for some time. Two months before Henry moved out, Ina wrote Cheney that he should not breathe a word to the board about "Henry and the base of troubles."[12] She did not elaborate.

Henry moved to a boarding house and submitted his resignation. It is probable that he also issued an ultimatum that either he or Ina should go. When Ina learned of Henry's resignation, she convinced him to stay, and told Ina Lillian, "The only way for peace and quiet with Henry is to give up absolutely, everything at home, and in the library, into his hands."[13] Henry married Bessie in December 1890, and the following September they named their first child Ina Dorothy Peterson. The board increased Henry and Ina's salaries to one hundred and twenty dollars a month. They earned equal pay, though she was still head librarian and he the first assistant. Ina was trying to leave the library, but in August 1892 wrote Stoddard that the bars had clamped down again.

Calla Shasta was back at Ina's house. When she left years earlier she had "drifted from one place to another, and finally into a 'dive'" she told Stoddard. She married a Wells Fargo agent named Landon, but the marriage didn't last and she returned "homeless, helpless, and a victim to drink."[14] Ina called a doctor who would try hypnotism to cure Carrie's alcoholism, and if that didn't work they would try the Gold Cure, a popular abstinence program that called for four injections a day of a brew that supposedly contained gold. In actuality the snake oil was 30 percent alcohol mixed with ammonium, strychnine, and boric acid.

"All failing her father must take her to the hills. I am *willing*, but I am not strong enough, and she is dangerous," said Ina. "She tried to cut her husband's throat; so she told me in a moment of pleasant confidence." Joaquin was drinking heavily, too, said Ina. "Alas, poor humanity! How I thank the God who helped me," she said, perhaps in reference to her own previous problem with alcohol.[15] Ina closed by asking Stoddard to keep what she said in confidence and destroy the letter. He did not.

Writer and feminist Charlotte Perkins (later Gilman), who lived across the street from Ina for a short time, wrote in her autobiography that Calla Shasta worked for her room and board. Gilman ran a boardinghouse where as many as eight women lived, including Gilman's terminally ill mother. Journalist Adeline Knapp had her own room, though she and Gilman were lovers and likely shared a bed until their relationship soured.[16] Gilman wrote, "Ina Coolbrith, the beloved poet of California, lived opposite to me ... A daughter of [Joaquin's], part Indian, was in service with Miss Coolbrith at the time."[17]

Ina Lillian also continued to be financially dependent on Ina. Like other young people whose families could not afford to send them to school after the age of ten, Ina Lillian got her education from books. She also wrote poetry and short stories. Ina told Stoddard that her niece had talent but seemed incapable of striking out on her own. Ina also said her niece had a crush on Ambrose Bierce. On several occasions Bierce had come for her with his carriage in the morning and didn't return her until after midnight. "Alone," Ina emphasized. Ina Lillian was twenty-eight years old and single. Bierce was sixty-one, separated from his wife, and had children nearly as old as Ina Lillian. Ina tried to interfere, but Ina Lillian defied her.

If there had been an affair, Ina Lillian later denied it to Bierce's biographer. She said that she met Bierce in Ina's home, and became better acquainted with him while on vacation with Henry in Auburn and Sunol, locations that were warmer and drier than San Francisco where Bierce sought relief from his severe asthma. Ina Lillian helped administer Bierce's chloroform on occasion, and during a particularly difficult asthma attack Bierce asked her, "Do you think I should stand this?"[18] Bierce was known to mentor young writers and helped Ina Lillian place a few of her pieces in *The Wave*, a weekly journal. He also coauthored a short story with her called "An Occurrence at Brownsville," which was published in the *San Francisco Examiner* and later included in his book *Can Such Things Be?* The story is about a young woman who is spellbound by a man who convinces her to commit suicide. "Would he have written [the story] with any woman

Ambrose Bierce. Courtesy The Bancroft Library,
University of California, Berkeley.

he was not in love with?" Ina asked Stoddard.[19] Ina Lillian said of
Bierce, "I never felt I deserved the distinction he accorded me by
publishing this story in his book, but it was his way of giving me the
encouragement which he deemed I needed." In 1892 Bierce gave Ina
Lillian a photo with the inscription "To my dear friend, Ina Lillian
Peterson."

Ina's friends knew she was trying to leave the library. In an
attempt to help, Joaquin Miller published an article in the *San
Francisco Call* on August 12, 1892, in which he suggested that the

University of California pay her an annual stipend. They owe her, he argued in "California's Fair Poet," for the two epic commencement odes she wrote for the university. He said that one thousand dollars a year would relieve her from the "dusty, musty atmosphere of cheap novels ... [and] give a hard-worked woman a chance to do divine work, to do great good, to rest."

Miller wrote that he had wanted to include a biographical sketch in the article but admitted he knew little about her, even though he had known her for decades. All he wrote was that she was "cradled in the camp, amid the stormy splendor and savage glory of the Rocky Mountains." He knew that she believed her work should speak for itself, and had been present at her house years earlier when a reporter probed Ina about her past. In response, she turned to a bookshelf, took out her book of poems, handed it to the reporter, and said, "That is all; good-bye."

Miller tried to learn more from the Bohemian Club. "She is the patron saint of the Bohemian Club, and has been since its birth," one member said. "Her life has been as pure and pathetic as her poems. In fact, her poems are her life."

"Ah, her life," said Miller. "Now tell me a bit about that."

"There are about eight hundred Bohemian club [members] waiting for the head of the man who puts our patron saint in the newspapers," sneered the gatekeeper.

In time, Ina would learn to tell select stories about her life, but at this point all the public knew about her was what they gleaned from her poetry and took as truth from gossip. Ina's reticence to market her life was alien to Miller. He believed that vanity was a necessary tool to get heard above the din. "The empty wagon will clatter and clang along over the cobblestones; ten thousand of us all at once chattering and crying out to be heard, lying like Satan about ourselves—shooting rockets, red lights, blue lights, yellow lights—all in the vain hope to be heard and seen for a second above all others, till life is a Babel, a bore, an abomination unto the Lord." Miller admired Ina for not taking part in such clatter. He praised her beauty, her poetry, and above all, her silence.

Miller was not the first to champion Ina's cause. A few years earlier Stoddard had written a profile of her for "The Magazine of

Poetry," in which he positioned her as a poetic queen who had been knocked off her throne. "Her muse was speedily and cordially recognized in the best quarters," said Stoddard, and dubbed her the "pearl of all her tribe."[20] Although both articles helped put her back in the public eye, the university did not act on Miller's suggestion to provide her with a stipend, and Ina continued to climb the stairs to her desk six days a week.

On the first day of September in 1892, Henry Peterson left on a month-long vacation with his wife and one-year-old child. Two days after he left, an *Oakland Times* reporter came to the library to interview Ina about the reduced budget she had been given for 1893. She had requested $22,152.67; the city said she would get $13,000. Ina told the reporter that with the given budget the building would continue to be unsafe. She explained that her proposed budget had included $5,000 to be set aside for a new building, and had suggested that the city do the same for three years so a new building could be built without putting too much pressure on taxpayers. She also would not be able to keep up on needed reference books, purchase duplicates of popular literature, or take advantage of opportunities to add rare books, like those offered by a wealthy collector at a reduced rate. "We will have to forego these opportunities unless we can buy without money and without price, and we are hardly near enough to the millennium for that," she said.[21]

The article appeared the next day, and the board said nothing to her about it or her frank responses. When the members convened for their monthly meeting, they left the building early. Ina did not know that they reconvened at another location for what one board member called a "star chamber" session, a secret meeting in which the board voted to dismiss her. She would not learn about their decision for another twenty days.

With Henry gone, Ina scrambled to keep up with the workload. She also had a poem published in a special California issue of *Lippincott's Monthly Magazine*, a literary journal out of Philadelphia. Other contributors included Gertrude Atherton, Joaquin Miller,

M. H. DeYoung, Hubert Howe Bancroft, and Charles Warren Stoddard. They got her name wrong though, with credit going to Ina H. Coolbrith instead of Ina D. Coolbrith.

On a busy Monday morning at the end of September, a messenger handed Ina a letter. The return address indicated it was from the board. Two of the members, S. H. Melvin, a druggist, and John A. McKinnon, a tailor, had been on the board when Henry Peterson threatened to resign. The new board members were F. S. Osgood, also a druggist, B. A. Rabe, a surgeon, and Jeremiah Tyrrel, an insurance man. Not a literary man in the bunch.

She slid the letter opener across the seal to open it and read, "After a full and careful consideration of the subject, the undersigned have unanimously but with reluctance arrived at the conclusion that the efficiency and usefulness of the library will be promoted by a change in the office of librarian."[22] They asked her to file her resignation within three days, and gave no reason for their action.

Ina asked someone to cover her desk and strode to Osgood's drugstore to ask why she had been fired. Osgood told her that the board merely believed that her resignation would be for the good of the library. She said that if he or the board could not give her sufficient and specific reasons for their dismissal, she would demand a public hearing to clear her name. She also insisted that a three-day notice was untenable. He agreed that the notice was short, and suggested she could stay until the end of the year if the other members agreed to the extension.

Ina did not return to the library that day, and an *Oakland Tribune* reporter found her at home. She told the reporter that the letter was the first inclination she had had that the board was dissatisfied with her work. The reporter asked if the board's move had anything to do with Henry. Ina said that it had been two years since she and Henry had quarreled about the cats, and at that time had agreed to keep their personal differences out of the library. But she also told the reporter that when she tried to get the reasons for her dismissal, one member had said, "You know your relations with Mr. Peterson are strained ... We have agreed that we can do without you better than we can without him."[23]

When news of her dismissal hit the local papers, Ina learned more about the board's reasons for firing her. President Melvin told the *Oakland Morning Times*, "She allows books to lie about on the floor, and is not as prompt as she should be in getting new books ready for use."[24] Circulation at the time was seventy-nine thousand books a year. Tyrrel said that after she resigned they would move the first assistant up to head librarian, and not replace the first assistant slot, thus saving one hundred and twenty-five dollars each month. No hearing was necessary, he said. (Trefethen's ring had seen to that when they rewrote the rules of the library to allow the board to fire an employee at will.) Osgood said that the trouble between Ina and Henry had created friction, and it had been clear for some time that one of them had to go.[25]

When Henry returned to work on the first of October, the newspapers accused him of being behind the board's actions. He denied any wrongdoing, but admitted he hoped to be head librarian one day.

Three days later, on October 4, 1892, Ina tendered her resignation. A *San Francisco Examiner* reporter noted that Ina sat "smiling and dignified" at her desk outside the smoke-filled room as secretary Osgood read her letter aloud:

> Gentlemen—I hereby, agreeably to your request, tender my resignation as librarian of the Free Public Library, said resignation to take effect January 1, 1893.
>
> Inasmuch as no charges of incompetency upon my part have been made and I am ignorant of the causes which have led you to make this request, I therefore tender my resignation under protest.
>
> While I am aware that your actions as a board are not governed by the provisions of the Oakland charter, still I think the principles enunciated there should govern your board in this matter.
>
> The charter guarantees to all holding positions under the city government a fair and impartial hearing, and permits those accused the privilege of making their defense.
>
> Had this course been pursued, myself and the

general public, who are presumed to have some interest in this matter, would not have been left in ignorance of the causes which determined your action.

During the time that I have acted as librarian of the Free Library I have sought faithfully and diligently to discharge the duties of the trust reposed in me and it seems to me that I should have been heard before summary action was taken against me.

I am, gentlemen, very respectfully yours,
Ina D. Coolbrith[26]

After the letter was read, Melvin removed the cigar from his mouth and said, "What's your pleasure?"

"I move that the resignation be accepted," said Tyrell.

"I second the motion," said McKinnon. All of the board members gave their ayes and after the meeting lit fresh cigars and went outside, wrote a reporter, "where for a few moments, beneath the bright October moon, they discussed the evening's acts."[27]

The entire affair made news in local and regional newspapers. The *San Francisco Chronicle* described her letter as a "tart communication."[28] The *Herald of Berkeley* suggested that the board rethink its move lest Berkeley wrest the mantle "Athens of the Pacific" from Oakland. The *Oakland Times* claimed the board knew little about books and even less about libraries, and accused them of getting rid of Ina *because* she was literary. *Blue Lake Advocate* admonished those who defended her to rethink their position. "Ye gods and little fishes! Gentlemen, pray be calm. When a lady comes to regard the institution that gives her employment as her special property and the trustees thereof as her subordinates and entertains for the public the peculiar sentiments of the lamented W. H. Vanderbilt, she has outlived her usefulness and ought to be removed."[29] Ina pasted this last clipping in her scrapbook and inserted three red exclamation points next to "ought to be removed."

Ina had served as head librarian and reigned as Oakland's literary hostess for two decades. Library science and catalogue systems hadn't yet been developed when she took the job, yet she knew the location of every book and had the literary sense to recommend books to fit her readers. Jack London recognized the skill, as did Isadora Duncan. There were also thousands of less-famous patrons whose reading and pursuit of knowledge she had helped to direct. There was—and still is—a charm and a great advantage in approaching a live human being who is enthusiastic about reading and literature and who knows the ins and outs of the stacks. But in the end she didn't want a fight—she wanted out. On the day she received the letter from the board telling her to quit, she told a reporter, "If the place were offered me now I would not under any circumstances take it. I am sick and tired of the constant trouble and annoyance connected with it."[30]

She was done—or nearly so. For the next three months she continued to work in the library alongside Henry Peterson.

Her fans were not happy with how she had been treated. One week after her resignation, she attended a memorial service in Oakland for John Greenleaf Whittier, who had died at age eighty-four on September 7, 1892. As requested, she had written a poem of occasion that was read by poet David Lesser Lezinsky. At the end of the program, Charles W. Wendte, minister of the First Unitarian Church in Oakland, took the podium and told the crowd that he had recently visited Wordsworth's grave in England. While there he had cut a sprig of yew that shaded the poet's grave site and promised himself that he would give the sprig to the first "true poet" he met. At that, Wendte walked across the hall and presented the yew clipping to Ina. Many Californians had come to place Ina on Parnassus, including those in this room who applauded loudly when Wendte handed her the yew sprig.[31]

There was one who had come to disagree with Ina's preeminence. Ambrose Bierce's commentary on Ina had run hot and cold over the years, and in 1892 his comments were downright frigid. He wrote in his column "Prattle" that though her talent was unmatched by few women in America when she was at her best, she had two handicaps that kept her from good work of late. The first was too much local adulation coupled with a lack of literary critique that might improve her work. The second handicap—which he claimed to be the most debilitating of the two—was that she blamed her fall from literary grace on her niece and nephew. Bierce argued that most people do things they don't want to do in life, and that the "supreme proof of greatness is found in its superiority to circumstance." He asserted that her challenges should have fueled her art, and not festered internally: "That way madness lies—and badness."[32]

"He was my friend," Ina told Stoddard. "Now he never loses a chance to give a covert sling at me in his 'Prattle.' I wish to God he were dead!"[33] Ina blamed Henry and Ina Lillian for turning Bierce against her. "Have I not cause to love these dear children whom my sister bequeathed to me? And yet, Charlie, the hardest of it all is my inner struggle to keep from hating them. They have ruined my life. Pray for me, Charlie, pray for me, that they may not ruin my soul as well."[34]

On Christmas Day, Ina published "Millennium" in the *San Francisco Examiner*. In the poem, which the newspaper gave a full page, she wrote that "the cloud legions, gathering force and form / Shut, with closed ranks, all gleam of moon or star." She prayed for peace to come to the tempestuous waters and asked where was the peace and "love-pulse" that should be on Earth?[35]

At the library, Henry Peterson was named Ina's successor and his salary was raised to one hundred and forty-five dollars a month. Like Ina, Henry kept a scrapbook, only his was filled with articles about library management and its advances. They both pasted articles about Ina's removal in their respective scrapbooks, including one from the *Oakland Daily Evening Tribune* with the headline, "UNEASY, H. F. Peterson to the Front." Henry pasted the article in his scrapbook and crossed out the word "UNEASY."

Ina never publicly blamed Henry for taking her job, but to Stoddard said, "If God ever put a snake's heart and nature in a human body, that body is Henry Peterson's."[36]

Henry served as a competent librarian at the Oakland Free Public Library for seven years. His chronic cough turned into tuberculosis, and in 1899 he was forced to quit due to poor health. His marriage didn't last, and Ina Lillian nursed him until his death in 1902. By that time, Ina was working at another library in San Francisco, where her days were as long and her workload as heavy as they had been in Oakland. It seemed there was no escaping the Inferno.

Part IV:

San Francisco Redux

How may the poet sing
When Song is far away?
—*Ina Coolbrith, "The Flight of Song," 1894*

14

Out of the Fire

At fifty-two, much of Ina's dark hair had turned gray to match her eyes. One reporter described her as having "almost fault-less features," and another observed her as having an "elo-quent eye and tender half-sad mouth."[1] Ina wanted to write again, but wasn't sure how to entice her muse. In late April 1893, she went with David Lesser Lezinsky and Edmund Russell to Joaquin Miller's house in the Oakland hills. They took a streetcar to the Hermitage stop in Fruitvale, an area southeast of Oakland named for its apricot and cherry orchards. Lezinsky, a young Jewish poet, had sparks in his eyes and a passion for sociology and psychology. Russell painted por-traits of society women and preferred to wear silk robes and heeled shoes. Charles H. Scofield, a reporter for the *Stockton Evening Mail*, tagged along to record the outing.

At the streetcar stop, Lezinsky said he knew of a shortcut up the hill. Russell said that he couldn't possibly tramp through the coun-tryside in his shoes, and lifted his pant leg to show what Scofield described as "kid pumps."[2] Lezinsky went to a nearby stable and re-turned with a small horse and cart, and a boy to drive them. Ina and Russell climbed aboard. "Gee-up," the boy demanded of the horse, whose steady trot slowed to a crawl as it pulled its passengers up the hill.

Lezinsky and Scofield set out on foot through fields and brush.

Joaquin Miller at The Hights. Courtesy The Bancroft Library, University of California, Berkeley.

Along the way they stopped at a cottage where geese squawked at their arrival. Poet Edwin Markham appeared, his gray-streaked beard and moustache neatly trimmed. Markham had left his family's farm in Vacaville, California, to pursue a career in teaching and literature, and at forty-three years old was the principal at Oakland's Tompkins Observation School. He joined the other two on the well-worn path to "The Hights," the intentionally misspelled name that Miller had given his homestead.

Miller's complex at The Hights included four whitewashed structures, one for dining, one for work and sleep, and one for his mother.

The fourth structure, which was largest by far, was reserved for the gardener, whom Miller kept busy with his trees and terraces of roses.

Miller welcomed his invited guests but wasn't as friendly to the uninvited tourists who tramped up the hill to gawk at him and his homestead. Miller had become one of the most famous writers in the West, and he and his eccentricities drew the curious. The tourists brought picnics, left their trash behind, and lifted so many "souvenirs" that Miller had to nail things down. Journalist Adeline Knapp lived in a nearby canyon on a small ranch she called Adelheim. In an essay for the *San Francisco Call*, Knapp wrote that there was nothing romantic about living near a famous poet. One day two women showed up at her door asking about Miller. They had been to Miller's place, but he was on his way out and suggested they visit Knapp instead. They lingered for so long that Knapp shared her lunch of cornmeal and molasses with them as they drilled her about Miller's habits. When they asked about his views on woman's suffrage, Knapp replied, "I suppose probably if a woman wanted to suffer, Joaquin would be willing to let her."[3]

On the day Ina and company visited The Hights, Miller fed his friends roast geese and claret. After the meal, Lezinsky read an article by Miller about Westminster Abbey, Russell recited a Rudyard Kipling poem that they proceeded to analyze, and Miller told stories about his London escapades. Miller gave them a tour, which likely included the seven-foot-tall rock funeral pyre he had built with his own hands so that when he died and was cremated, he could have his ashes thrown to the four cardinal directions. Miller showed them his sleeping cabin where cards, letters, and photographs plastered the walls; saddles, bridles, and lariats hung from the rafters; bear rugs covered the floors; and the pelt of an extinct Rocky Mountain wooly horse was thrown across his bed. He kept no books in his rooms. When someone once commented on the lack, Miller bellowed, "To hell with books. When I want books I write them!"[4]

Miller offered to demonstrate his famous "hoodoo rain" for his friends. He pointed to three bear paws hanging from the rafters, which he claimed were from a three-legged bear. He closed the curtains and told Markham, Russell, and Scofield to take a paw, face east, and pull. As they did, Miller chanted a Native American song until rain fell on the roof, softly at first, and then in a steady shower.

"It is a big medicine. If you work it right, it never fails to make rain," said Miller, according to Scofield.[5] Miller failed to mention that he had trained Yone Noguchi, a young Japanese poet living with him, how to turn on the sprinkler system that made his hoodoo rain.[6]

With the shadows long in late afternoon, Ina and Russell climbed aboard the cart for the ride down the hill. It's likely that the hills were filled with wildflowers that April day. Ina loved California's wildflowers. When an East Coast visitor claimed that the West lacked flowers, Ina wrote an article in defense of the state's native flowers, which she pasted in her scrapbook with no date or publication noted. She wrote that no other state can boast of such diversity and beauty in its flowers, and proved it by listing them. First there were the buttercups, she wrote, with "cups called 'gold' and 'cream' and 'sun,' all filled to the brim with perfume." Other favorites included lupine, shooting star, yarrow, wood-balm, pansies, Indian paintbrush, columbine, and Canterbury bell. The lilies, she wrote, "what a group with white, black, brown, lemon, ruby, the leopard, the tiger, the fawn, the chamise and the coast lily, the little Alpine and the beautiful Mariposa lily, hovering like a butterfly, indeed, above the grasses." There are too many small flowers to name, she said, but had to mention just one, the "*trientalis*, a small, tender plant bearing its tiny pink stars on a stem so thread-like as to be almost invisible," a flower she learned to love on a "never-to-be-forgotten day in the redwoods with John Muir."[7]

The California poppy, which was certainly aglow in the Oakland hills in the afternoon as she and Russell rolled down the road, was still ten years away from being named California's official state flower. In 1816 the orange poppy had been given the Latin name of *Eschscholtzia californica*, but Ina preferred the older Spanish name, *la copa de oro*, a cup of gold. Ina chose the California poppy as the subject for the first poem she published after leaving the library. In the final stanza of "Copa de Oro," she credits California's soil and sun for the poppy's unique color.

> ... Nurtured from the treasure veins
> Of this fair land; thy golden rootlets sup

Her sands of gold—of gold thy petals spun.
Her golden glory, thou! On hills and plains
Lifting, exultant, every kingly cup,
Brimmed with the golden vintage of the sun.[8]

"La Copa de Oro" was published in the *San Francisco Bulletin* on May 24, 1893. Years later, when botanist Luther Burbank hybridized a poppy and named it *"crimson eschscholtzia Ina Coolbrith,"* Ina told him that when she wrote the poem she hadn't known she would become a member of the family. More than a century later, poet Robert Hass selected "Copa de Oro" to represent Ina on the Addison Street Poetry Walk in Berkeley, California.

"La Copa de Oro" was also printed on a broadside and distributed to everyone who visited the California Building at the World's Columbian Exposition, a spectacle more commonly known as the Chicago World's Fair. In late September 1893, Ina boarded an *Overland Limited* train to attend the final month of the fair. She had been commissioned to write a poem for the unveiling of a Harriet Hosmer sculpture of Queen Isabella of Spain. While the fair was commemorating the four hundredth anniversary of Columbus's discovery of America, a group of Chicago suffragists had commissioned Hosmer to make the sculpture to remind people that although it was Columbus who made the trip to America, it was Queen Isabella who financed him. Ina attended the unveiling of the statue in the California Building when her poem "Isabella of Spain" was read to a prestigious audience that included feminists May Wright Sewall and Susan B. Anthony.[9]

While in town, she received press attention, thanks in part to Charlotte Perkins Gilman, who sent a note to Sewall asking her to introduce Ina to the best writers in Chicago. Journalist Mary Hannah Krout responded to Gilman's request and profiled Ina in *Chicago Inter-Ocean* on November 11, 1893. She characterized Ina as being a delightful conversationalist with a voice that had "perfect modulation." A *Chicago Evening Post* reporter asked Ina which were her favorite poets. "If I were fashionable, I suppose I should answer you Browning, but I confess to a greater love for Tennyson," she said. "Omar, too, is one of our household words. Mark Twain once said that old Omar Khayyam was the only poet he kept on his shelves."[10] When the same reporter asked if she had ever studied the rules of poetry, Ina admitted that she had not and had better start. She wanted to use her pen again now that she was out of the library. "Use makes such a difference in facility," she said.

Ina was one of 27 million people who walked the exposition grounds that covered six hundred acres with buildings largely designed by Daniel Burnham and Frederick Law Olmsted. She saw Nikola Tesla's groundbreaking electricity, the original Ferris wheel, and the classic and elegant lines of the architectural heart of the fair, the White City. All that she saw, including the forty-six pavilions that represented countries from around the world, could have been fodder for her pen. But the subject that captured her attention was a Lakota Indian warrior on display in a cabin.

Chief Rain in the Face, a live Native American on exhibit, had fought in the 1876 Battle of Little Bighorn, a battle also known as Custer's Last Stand. In that armed battle, members of the Lakota, Northern Cheyenne, and Arapaho tribes who resisted resettlement fought the United States Seventh Cavalry. The cavalry lost the battle, and George Armstrong Custer, the golden boy of the Indian Wars, was killed. Rain in the Face was rumored to have cut out the heart of Tom Custer, the popular commander's brother, a rumor that became legend when Henry Wadsworth Longfellow wrote "The Revenge of Rain in the Face." The cabin on display at the World's Fair had once belonged to Sitting Bull, a Lakota warrior whose vision of a cavalry defeat led to the engagement at Little Big Horn. Fourteen years after the battle, police murdered Sitting Bull at his cabin on the Standing Rock Indian Reservation. The cabin was transported to the World's Fair and put on display with Little Bighorn battle artifacts, including Chief Rain in the Face. The chief did daily "war dances" at the fair, though as he told Native American writer Charles Eastman, the fight had long left him.

Ina's feelings about Native Americans had changed since she was a girl. She had been afraid during her journey on the Overland Trail when one of the wagons carrying food got stuck in a stream and a band of Indians yelled and screamed from nearby bushes in hopes of scaring the party into abandoning the goods. On another occasion her party was resting in camp when a group of Indians came out of nowhere, jumped on the traveler's best horses, and "disappeared in the mountain fastness."[11]

As she grew older, Ina was a witness to the Native Americans who had been forced to the fringes of Anglo American society. While she was living in Los Angeles, an old blind Gabrielino made an impression on her, and she wrote about him more than sixty years later.

> Poor old Polon,
> The old blind Indian,
> I saw in the street today,
> And it took away
> All beauty of earth and sky,
> And made the daylight wan ...
> The matted, grizzled hair
> Of the uncovered head,
> Rags and the naked feet;
> Staff in the hand to guide—
> And defend beside—
> And in the blanket-hem
> Stones to throw back at them,
> Muchachos, who baited him.[12]

In "The Captive of the White City," Ina describes how jarring it was to come upon Rain in the Face in the middle of the World's Fair:

> ... And the throngs go up and down
> In the streets of the wonderful town
> In brotherly love and grace,—
> Children of every zone
> The light of the sun has known:
> And there in the Midway Place,
> In the House of the Unhewn Trees,
> There in the surging crowd,
> Silent, and stern, and proud,
> Sits Rain-in-the-Face!

In her second stanza she contemplates the reason for his being there. Is he there to be judged? If so, she doesn't think there is just cause given that "the beautiful City stands / On the Red Man's wrested lands." She understands the hate in his veins.

> Then seek as well to tame
> The hate in the Red Man's veins,
> His tiger-thirst to cool,
> In the hour of the evil day
> When his foe before him stands!
> From the wrongs of the White Man's rule
> Blood only may wash the trace.
> Alas, for the death-heaped plain!
> Alas, for slayer and slain!
> Alas, for your blood-stained hands,
> O Rain-in-the-Face!

The contrast of the chief's presence to the merry fair is stark, as shown in the final stanza.

> And the throngs go up, go down
> In the streets of the wonderful town;
> And jest of the merry tongue,
> And the dance, and the glad songs sung,
> Ring through the sunlit space.
> And there, in the wild, free breeze,
> In the House of the Unhewn Trees,
> In the beautiful Midway Place,
> The captive sits apart,
> Silent, and makes no sign.
> But what is the word in your heart,
> O man of a dying race?
> What tale on your lips for mine,
> O Rain-in-the-Face?[13]

The poem was not published until two years later, when she included it in her second collection.

Ina spent Christmas in Maine with her mother's family, and New Year's Eve in Boston. In January she went to New York, where she was one of the guests of honor at "Ladies' Night," an annual event put on by the wives of members of the Authors' Club, an all-male literary organization. Children's author Mary Mapes Dodge was the most well-known woman of the group. The event was held in the state apartments of the Hotel Waldorf, where the opulence of the room and the pedigree of the crowd inspired a *New York Times* reporter to remark, "The great New Yorkers have nothing, desire nothing, and are personally as disinterested as monks in a convent in Asia. They desire to be New York, and they are New York."[14]

The *New York Times* reporter did not mention Ina's presence, but a reporter from the *Boston Herald* who profiled each guest of honor said Ina was a "guest from abroad" whose latest contributions "placed her in the front ranks of female poets."[15]

At the event, Ina introduced herself to Edith M. Thomas, an accomplished poet about ten years younger than Ina. By way of introduction, Ina told Miss Thomas that she knew her uncle, Colonel James Vaughn Thomas, who was known as Tiger Jim and one of Joaquin Miller's oldest and dearest friends.

"He was a superb man when I met him, Miss Thomas. I fell desperately in love with him," Ina told her.

"Oh, all women did that," said Thomas.

"But he fell in love with me," said Ina.

"Yes, he did with all women."

"I don't think you appreciate your uncle, Miss Thomas."

"It is that I fully appreciate him, Miss Coolbrith!"

"Well! I think you might be nice, real nice," said Ina, "and say you are sorry I am not your aunt."[16]

Ina stayed in New York for two months and spent nearly every day with Philip Verrill Mighels and Ella Sterling Cummins, a widow who had a daughter named Viva. Cummins was a California historian and writer from San Francisco, and Mighels was a struggling New York writer who looked older than his twenty-four years due to two bouts of typhoid fever. Cummins and Mighels would come to marry (and divorce), but on this trip it was Ina who was romantically involved with Mighels. Upon Ina's return to California, she wrote love letters to him, which Cummins claimed to have saved for years until she destroyed them. According to Cummins, when Ina learned that she and Mighels were to marry, Ina wrote her, "You have Viva, you might have left Philip for me."[17] It's hard to know if Ina truly said this given the rancor that developed between these two women twenty years later, a friction that led to the formation of the Ina Coolbrith Circle, a poetry group that still meets today.

15

A Wily Muse

B y the time Ina returned to Oakland, her celebrity status had grown. While she was away, the news of her being entertained and admired by literary circles in Chicago and New York hit San Francisco newspapers and added zing to a long-smoldering complaint that California didn't nurture its artists. "It is to be feared that California is not a congenial soil for the placing of her children of genius," Ella Sterling Cummins Mighels wrote in *The Story of the Files*.[1] When word came out that Ina wanted to move to New York, the topic of California losing its artists was bandied about in clubs and in newspapers. The Bohemian and Century clubs heeded the criticism and formed a book guild to publish and promote writers on the Pacific Coast. For their first project, the clubs agreed to finance a collection of Ina's poetry. It had been fourteen years since her first book, *A Perfect Day and Other Poems*, was published with a run of only 550 copies, and a new book would satisfy the demand for her work. By the 1890s, Ina Coolbrith was seen as a prominent writer in the West's "local color movement." Writer Hamlin Garland characterized Ina and others in the movement as those whose work had "such quality of texture and background that it could not have been written in any other place or by anyone else than a native."[2] As time passed, San Francisco was seen as the incubus of the local color movement in American literature, especially during the years in which Harte edited the *Overland Monthly*. "There is perhaps no other writer in the State so thoroughly imbued with the spirit of California as Miss Coolbrith,"[3] wrote the *San Francisco Call* in its applause of the book guild's decision to promote her work. Houghton, Mifflin, & Company published it, poet and critic Edmund Clarence Stedman served as advisor, and William Keith provided four illustrations.

Though others had confidence in her work, Ina had little. She told Charles Keeler, a young writer she had recently met, that as she edited and made corrections to the manuscript, her stepfather's words reared up from the dead: "Awful stuff, Sis! Awful stuff!"[4]

By May, Ina was living alone, which was a first. Ina Lillian had married attorney Finlay Cook and moved to San Francisco, and Calla Shasta lived at the Hights with her father. Since leaving the library Ina had written six poems, and wanted to keep it up. To entice her muse she read poetry, drummed her fingers on the table, and stroked her cats. She also tried to lure her by making a dress, mending socks, running errands, and writing letters. Ina thought of her muse as the engine of her work—and as a free spirit. She believed that her poems came of their own accord, such as the time in 1875 when she was in the redwoods on the Mendocino Coast and her poem "Meadowlarks" "wrote itself because it couldn't help it."[5] She told a reporter years later that poems were like children waiting to be born, explaining:

> I have dreamed entire poems, and stranger still, I
> have lost them to other writers. This is one exam-
> ple. I had the idea for a poem one day, and did not
> have time to write it ... Six weeks later I opened a
> new magazine and there was my poem! Just as I had
> thought of it, almost word for word. I could hardly
> believe it ... That is why I say poem are things.
> They will find birth.[6]

A few years later, Ina wrote and read a poem for the annual Pacific Coast Women's Press Association convention about her muse's attitude toward poems of occasion. In the poem she explained that she had put off writing it until the night before the event. She sat at her desk late into the night playing with words and their rhymes to try and entice her muse, who hardly ever came when commanded. She did on this occasion, and was disgruntled for having been summoned so late. She had "upon her brow / A look which questioned, 'Well, what is it now?'"[7] With a yawn of boredom, Ina's muse asked if Ina was after a poem about Columbus, or an epic as large as the world, or,

> ... maybe 'twas this Golden West of ours,
> To rhyme with vine and wine, and fruits and flowers;
> Or were you, from a flight upon my wings,
> To ring the Mission bells again—poor things!
> And wake the Padres from their peaceful pall
> To hear the least you know about them all?
> "Westward the Star of Empire takes its way,
> And settles over San Francisco Bay!"
> She laughed. "That really sounds quite like your stuff
> When I'm not near. It's almost bad enough."[8]

At the sound of rain her wily muse flew off and Ina locked the door. She sank into her rocking chair and fell asleep. She dreamt that she stood before the conventioneers with blank pages in front of her, and the crowd broke out in thunderous applause with words like "relief," and "thanks."[9]

Ina treated the subject lightly in her poem, but in truth her dependence on her muse stifled her work. Her colleagues who made livings from their pens could not afford to wait for inspiration. Twain, Harte, Stoddard, London, and Gertrude Atherton had routines, word-count goals, and a commitment to write each day whether inspiration hit or not. Ina gave the power to write a poem to an ethereal entity, which made her think she was powerless to wrestle a poem to the ground on her own. She counted on her muse and as a result had little belief in her own ability.

On a mild July day in 1895, Ina attended an outdoor gathering of writers at Adeline Knapp's ranch in the Oakland hills. A reporter from the *San Francisco Call* took notes and an artist sketched those in attendance. At the center of the ink-line drawing was guest of honor Charles Warren Stoddard in a three-piece suit, wide tie, and fedora. Stoddard was visiting San Francisco from Washington, DC. He was fifty-one and had not had a chum in a while. When he returned to Washington in the fall he would meet a fifteen-year-old boy, Kenneth O'Connor, with whom he would live for three years.

At the far left of the picture were Charles and Louise Keeler, the youngest of the bunch. Charles Keeler was a poet, author, and self-taught ornithologist with the California Academy of Sciences. His frail and talented wife, Louise Mapes Bunnell Keeler, was an artist who illustrated his books. The Keelers told the group that they were building a house in the Berkeley hills based on a design by a new architect, Bernard Maybeck. Theirs was Maybeck's first house. Ina had met the Keelers a year earlier and liked them immediately. Charles Keeler wrote about their first meeting in his unpublished autobiography, *Friends Bearing Torches*. "[Ina] had lost the slender lines of girlhood, but there was playing about the sadness of her face a mischievous smile that made her seem youthful."[10] Ina gave them a copy of *A Perfect Day*, of which Keeler wrote, "It may not have been great poetry, but we were sure that it was genuine. It rang true."

Next to the Keelers sat Knapp with her sharp chin, pursed lips, and wire-rimmed glasses. Markham was there, too, his beard trimmed tightly and his three-piece suit impeccable. William Greer Harrison, an insurance man and one of the founders of the Bohemian Club, was also in attendance. Ina sat at the far right, her face round and chubby. She wore a heavy coat that she clutched at the collar as if she were chilled. No one else was wearing a coat.

Missing from the group was David Lesser Lezinsky, the young poet who had shot himself in the head earlier that month. The newspapers blamed Ambrose Bierce for attacking Lezinsky because he was a Jew. When a friend asked Ina about the suicide, she said that she had always known that Lezinsky was "mentally unbalanced," and his father insane.[11] "My heart aches with it," she told a friend. "He was such a pure, good, kind boy, and with the cloud lifted from his brain would have been one of the noblest and most brilliant leaders of the day. I cannot bear to think of such an ending."[12]

Knapp served fruit and cream and strong coffee to the guests, who sat near a small stream shaded by willows. The pleasant air, dappled sunlight, and stupendous view of the bay put the group into a philosophical mood. Harrison suggested that each in the group define poetry, and asked Ina to go first. Ever ready to put poetry on a pedestal, she said it was the "language of the gods, translated for man."[13] Louise Keeler defined it as rhythmic language. Markham said it was the interpretation of life. Stoddard said it was that which touched the heart most deeply.

Knapp had a different (and heretical for this group) take on poetry. "We have passed the stage of racial development when anything can be said in verse that cannot be better said in prose," said Knapp, who was known for her strong opinions. "Our poets strive after the weird, the grotesque, the uncouth in their agonies at what they are wont to call their self-revelations, but which are rarely more than painful exposures of their cranial caverns. I believe that the great poems have all been written; that the poetic form of expression belonged to a less highly specialized period of the world's history."

Everyone began talking at once. Knapp spoke above them, the sleeves of her dress puffed out like a blowfish. "Look over the field of modern poetry and say what sane man can tell what our poets are driving at. They talk about 'lewd stars' and 'mounting waves.' They tear the language from limb to limb in their efforts to express what is inexpressible, unexistent. They give us words, words, words, wrenched from their natural meanings, and arranged in all sorts of unnatural forms … At this period of our intellectual development the natural vehicle of our intellectual expression is prose."

"Poetry will exist so long as the world exists," defended Markham. "Science itself cannot destroy poetry. Science only removes one veil of mystery to reveal another. Prose cannot express all that there is to be expressed. We need poetry to express that fleeting, elusive song of life that is as real as anything in life."

"We shall never be able to live without poetry," said Ina. "Poetry we take into our hearts and lives, and it sings itself to us always."

"[Poetry] is a lower form of art than prose," insisted Knapp, "and one which will not continue to prove adequate to express the intellectual life of so highly civilized a creature as nineteenth-century man."

"Aristotle tells us that poetry possesses a higher truth and a higher seriousness than history," said Markham. "Like some airy and invisible architect, it shapes character." His words lingered in the quiet canyon.

"Many of the opinions of the world have been formed by the poets," he continued. "The editor strengthens his argument from Shakespeare; the lawyer, the orator, all turn to [poets] for confirmation. The poet in his highest aspect may be considered a seer." His comment would prove prophetic for him. A few years later Markham became one of the most famous poets in the world due to his poem "The Man with the Hoe," inspired by Jean-François Millet's painting *L'homme à la houe*. The painting and the poem protested the abuse of the working classes and symbolized the need for workers' rights and unions. The life of a laborer was not romantic to Markham, nor was it unfamiliar. As a youth he had worked on his family's farm in Vacaville, north of San Francisco. Markham's poem touched the zeitgeist of the times and was translated into thirty languages. Ironically, it was this poem about labor that would forever remove Markham from the working class.

The discussion of poetry came to an end when Knapp's guests had streetcars and ferries to catch. Everyone but Ina gathered their coats. She had never taken hers off.

Early symptoms of peritonitis, an inflammation of the tissue that lines the abdomen, include fever, chills, and nausea. The infection can lead to organ failure and death. The day after Ina's visit to Adelheim, she fell ill, and by the time the doctor arrived she was in critical condition. He administered opiates and diagnosed her with peritonitis. She drifted in and out of consciousness, and her doctor called Ina's brothers to her bedside, thinking she was near the end. Josephine Zeller, a friend, nursed her day and night. Newspapers reported on her grave illness and several said she was dying. Just as Ina began to gain ground, pneumonia struck. Zeller nursed her some more, and Ina finally recovered.

Songs from the Golden Gate came out in October 1895, two

months after she was stricken. For the most part, her book received positive reviews. The *Oakland Times* said that in reading her poems "one breathes the air coming in through the golden portal so strong and fresh and sweet."[14] The *San Francisco Chronicle* said that her poems were born "distinctively of the soil of the Golden Gate."[15] The *Portland Maine Transcript* said one could feel "the balmy air of the Pacific coast" in its pages.[16] The *Boston Beacon* said that while she sang of California, her poems transcended provinciality. The *Los Angeles Herald* reported that her work was good enough that "not even the professional lampooners who have so banefully affected literary workers on this coast have dared to profane or belittle her offerings."[17]

Apparently they hadn't yet read the review in the *New York Times*. "Given an ordinary, common-school acquaintance with the English language, a good ear for rhythm, a genuine love of nature, and a large desire to write, anyone can produce this kind of verse … One may be a pleasing rhymster without earning the right to wear the name of poet."[18]

The *New York Times* review did not hurt sales. The first edition sold out in two weeks.

At the suggestion of her doctor, Ina went to Los Angeles for a rest, where she stayed with her childhood friend Mrs. Perry. While in Los Angeles she met journalist and Indian rights activist, Charles Fletcher Lummis, who earlier that year had taken over as editor for *Land of Sunshine*, a magazine that became *Out West* in 1902. In 1904 he would become head librarian at the Los Angeles Public Library, a job he kept for about six years.

In March, Cora Older, a reporter for the *San Francisco Bulletin* (and the young wife of Fremont Older, its editor), interviewed Ina at her house. Ina answered the door in a cream-colored morning gown with a piece of pink crepe draped across her shoulders and head. Older wrote in her article published on March 21, 1896, that Ina lived in the sort of house appropriate for a poet, and that her parlor was just as Older would have ordered it, with comfortable chairs and sofa, and treasures in every corner of the room. To describe Ina, Older said, "Her eyes are gray-blue that look at and through the meaning of things. The entire cast of her countenance is strong, and her features would make those of a virile man."

Ina told Older that she was trying to sell her house and move to Boston or New York. "I want to try to achieve something during the few remaining years of my life, and here I am as helpless as an art-ist would be without paint." There were no magazines in the West that paid for poetry, she said, and poets had to rely on the journals of the East. The problem was money, she said. "Anyone could be good with an income of five thousand a year or more." Thirty years later Virginia Woolf said a woman didn't have a "dog's chance of writing poetry" without money and a room of her own.[19]

Ina had not worked in three years and needed money. The re-ceipts from her book and the few poems she had published since leaving the library were not enough to pay her bills. Several of her friends had made a good dime at lecturing so she decided to give it a try. For two years she lectured in homes and for clubs, but her lectures did not earn enough money for her to live on, and she grew depressed. "If this coming year brings me nothing more than did the one now going out—in which I tried so hard in so many directions—I am going to leave the world," she told Charles and Louise Keeler.[20]

Instead, Ina entered another Inferno. In January 1898 she ac-cepted a full-time position as librarian at the Mercantile Library in San Francisco.[21] The Women's Auxiliary, a club that helped to keep the financially strapped private library afloat, had chosen her for the position. Before Ina set foot in the door, she nearly lost the job when a contingent of male members protested her appointment as "petticoat rule." One member said that it was nothing against Miss Coolbrith but "a mere question of sex and the weaker is in disfavor."[22] When the San Francisco Examiner heard that Ina might be barred from the position because of her gender, they suggested that the library burn everything written by women. "No intellectual petticoatism! Down with the Mrs. Brownings, the Jane Austens, the George Eliots and the Charlotte Brontës!"[23]

The issue was resolved and Ina took the job. When she com-plained to Stoddard, he told her that she should be grateful. "Don't!"

she snapped. "If you were to enter upon a position where you had to remain each weekday from 9 a.m. to 10 p.m. with only *just* time off for lunch and dinner; and on Sunday from 10 to 4, *with no moment off*; if that meant *steady work*, without reading or resting, or writing, or *anything* but drudgery … would you feel like smiling *or striking* when you were congratulated upon your position?"[24]

Ina was librarian, cataloguer, and bookkeeper. Her only assistance came from the son of a board member. The library was open until ten o'clock six nights a week, and the assistant split the night shifts evenly with Ina. One night, the young man sauntered in and informed her that he had better plans. She said it was up to her to decide which nights he worked. He laughed and left. She wrote a letter to the board requesting that they either clarify duties and positions or she would resign out of self-respect.

They backed her. When she was charged with hiring another assistant, the board suggested that she hire a young girl. Ina replied,

> I have had in my library work a score of [young girls]. Dress, chit-chat, parties, beaus, marrying and giving in marriage! It is the almost invariable result, that just as you have them broken to harness and going at an even gait, some miserable masculine appears on the scene, and they come to you with a blush and tremble, and "please ma'am, I'm going to be married." They are off, and you have your work all over again with another. Now a [mature] *woman* has responsibility and intelligence, and patience if she be anything at all. They really do better work in a library than the generality of men.[25]

As for Ina the poet, she had learned earlier that year that her work had been discovered in England, thanks to Albert Kinross, *London Outlook*'s associate editor. In a three-page profile about Ina, Kinross concluded that America didn't appreciate her or her poetry. He blamed California for shelving her in a library for twenty years, and the East Coast literary establishment for not recognizing her talent. He said that whenever he asked cultured Americans about

Ina Coolbrith, their disdainful reply was, "Oh, she's a Californian then."[26]

A few days after Kinross published his glowing review and profile, he printed a letter from Gertrude Atherton who said she was glad to see that Ina was getting her due, but added, "I am afraid it is too late now."[27]

Charles Keeler asked Ina if she was writing. "Do you not suppose if I could command one moment that I would grasp it to write *now*, while the tide is on for a moment from that London notice?" she said. "I can do nothing. I go to my room more dead than alive."[28]

At fifty-eight years old, Ina was headed for a complete physical breakdown. Thankfully, the Bohemian Club offered her a part time job to run its library. The pay was half of what she made at the Mercantile, but the job was secure and the hours allowed her time to write. "This is the first time the doors of freedom have been opened to me since I was fifteen years of age," she told the *San Francisco Examiner* on April 23, 1899.

It's fortunate that she never learned the full story behind the Bohemian Club offer. Dr. Chismore, a club member and old friend, told her that her duties would be light and that the board had voted unanimously to hire her. What she did not know was that Chismore had convinced the board to offer her the job because he felt sure she was dying. In a letter to Charles Keeler several years later, the club's secretary said, "It was only upon the earnest solicitation of Dr. Chismore and his positive assurance that Miss Coolbrith could not live for six months longer that the Club as a matter of charity offered her the position which they never expected her to fill."[29]

Ina did fulfill her duties. She entered the club from the side door at 9 a.m. and worked until noon before any members arrived. She found a buyer for her Oakland home, one who agreed to her stipulation that the old oak in the backyard not be cut down. Ina moved back to San Francisco one month before the start of the twentieth century. First she took a room on Bush Street, and then one on Leavenworth. "I have been a bird upon the wing so long that I die with envy at the felicity of my neighbors, Mr. And Mrs. Sparrow, in the cozy nest in the next door porch," she told Lummis.[30]

Eventually, she found a place with a view on Russian Hill and started work on a book about early California literature. "Brain and soul and heart are as dry as a flame-swept prairie," she admitted to Lummis.[31]

16

Into the Flames

On April 17, 1906, the audience gasped as Don José, played by Enrico Caruso, stabbed the beguiling Carmen on the stage of the Grand Opera House. When the opera was over, *San Francisco Call* reporter James Marie Hopper walked back to the office to write a review and turn it over to the night crew. While walking down Post Street at 2 a.m., he heard a stabled horse let out a weird scream and stopped to ask the stableman what was the matter. "Restless tonight don't know why," replied the man.[1]

Ina lived nearby at 1604 Taylor Street in a flat large enough to accommodate two boarders, Robert Norman, a law student, and Josephine Zeller, who had become Ina's live-in housekeeper and health attendant. Josie was like a member of the family and took care of Ina when she was ill. Since the turn of the century, Ina's health had deteriorated. She suffered from severe rheumatoid arthritis that kept her housebound for months at a time. When her health allowed it, she worked at the Bohemian Club, where her salary of fifty dollars a month included editorial services for club members.

She wrote only a few poems of her own. When Bret Harte died in England on May 5, 1902, she wrote a memorial poem that was published in the *Overland Monthly*. Five days later her nephew died, but she did not write a poem for Henry Peterson. Lummis published her poem "The Cactus Hedge" in October 1902, and "William

Keith, Artist," in April 1903. Ina wrote a sonnet for Edmund Clarence Stedman's seventieth birthday, and sent it to him with a sprig of redwood and leaves of bay laurel. He replied that the poem was "strong, compact, high-phrased, showing your gift and art at their ripest."[2] When he died in 1909, the *Atlantic Monthly* published it and paid her twenty dollars.

Ina had spent most of her time working on her book A *History of California Literature*. The manuscript traced the growth of literature in California from the printing of the first book at Monterey in 1854 to the rise of notable newspapers and journals in San Francisco and throughout the state. Six years after she had started the book, it was nearly finished, she told a visitor on Easter Sunday, April 15, 1906. On that day a young man knocked on Ina's front door and introduced himself as Jessie Winter Smith. He was a student at Stanford University, and asked if she would critique a poem he had written. Ina invited him in, his last name hovering like a question mark. They talked of poetry. Zeller served coffee, and perhaps a slice of her famous pie. Smith looked around Ina's parlor at a lifetime of treasures. A conch shell as large as a football sat on a small table rubbed bright with beeswax. Native American baskets were displayed bowl side out on the floor of the unused fireplace. Along one wall, a four-tiered, double-wide bookshelf held so many books—mostly signed first editions—that even one more slim volume of poetry would not fit. Leaning against the wall on the top of the bookcase were unframed William Keith paintings. Restless beads hung from a doorway near a framed portrait of Lord Byron swathed in an orange Albanian robe and turban.

Ina told Smith what she thought he could do to improve his poem. She told him about her book, and showed him the manuscript. The young man didn't stay long. Ina hadn't been well, and her poor health was exacerbated by the fact that the Bohemian Club had recently dismissed her, leaving her without an income. On his way out, Jessie Winter Smith turned and asked Ina if she was a Smith.[3] She said yes, and asked how he fit into the family. He said he was the grandson of Samuel H. Smith and Mary Bailey Smith, Ina's mother's best friend. She may have shown him a ring that once belonged to her father, and a watercolor of her father and Joseph Smith.

Three days later, on April 18, 1906, a waning crescent moon hung in the sky and the sun had not yet risen over the East Bay Hills when an earthquake ripped through San Francisco at 5:12 a.m. For forty-five seconds waves of energy rolled through the ground, cracked streets in two, and felled buildings. During a ten-second lull the ship masts in the harbor swung like giant metronomes, and then a second one shook the ground for thirty seconds more. James Hopper said it was as if a hungry dog had grabbed the world in its teeth, and "the earth was a rat, shaken in the grinding teeth, shaken, shaken, shaken with periods of slight weariness followed by new bursts of vicious rage."[4] Writer Gertrude Atherton felt it across the bay at the Berkeley Inn where she was working on a novel. She sprang out of bed and made it to the door of her room during the first shake, which she said felt like "a regiment of cavalry charging across the world."[5] She was heading back to bed when "the earth danced, and leaped, and plunged, and roared."[6] Miller felt both quakes at The Hights, and forty-five minutes after the second one he counted sixteen fires in San Francisco. He took a ferry to San Francisco to try to rescue his manuscripts stored at the Bohemian Club and to bring Ina back to The Hights, but soldiers would not let him with his horse and carriage into the city. Mary Austin had been staying at the Palace Hotel while in town, until she had a premonition about the quake the day before it struck and moved to a friend's house at the edge of the city. Jack London left his ranch in Glen Ellen as soon as he heard the news, and by nightfall was on the streets of San Francisco. "In all those terrible hours, I saw not one woman who wept, not one man who was excited, not one person who was in the slightest degree panic stricken ... Never, in all San Francisco's history, were her people so kind and courteous as on this night of terror."[7]

The following day, General Frederick Funston ordered the evacuation of select neighborhoods in preparation for the dynamite he used to try to stop the fires. When the militia cleared Russian Hill, Ina and Zeller left with nothing but Ina's two cats. She did not bring her signed first editions, Keith paintings, or the letters from Muir and Whittier; and she did not bring the only copy of her manuscript that had taken six years to write. Ina picked her way down Taylor Street where people carried what they could in makeshift carts, baby carriages, and trunks on roller skates. At the Fort Mason refugee camp Ina slept on the ground for two days and three nights while monstrous clouds of smoke filled the air from the fires that consumed the city. From Fort Mason, she may have seen the fire roar up Russian Hill and take her house with everything in it.

On the day the fires finally subsided, a friend found Ina at Fort Mason and took her to Judge and Mrs. Boalt, whose home on Spruce Street had escaped the conflagration. Ina thought she had nothing left in the world save the clothes on her back until her renter Robert Norman delivered a surprise. He had been able to go inside the flat at the last minute, and on his way out grabbed what he could from Ina's desk. He handed her several precious stacks of letters and her twelve-by-eighteen-inch leather-bound scrapbook. Ina had been keeping a scrapbook for years. Beginning with the first poems she published in Los Angeles and including all her published poems and articles that mentioned her, she covered every inch of every page in the red and black book. She decorated the corners and bits of empty space with ink drawings of California flora and fauna. An oak, a few birds, or a garland of flowers added a personal touch to the pages. Only occasionally did she make edits or comments, such as the one she wrote below a post-earthquake article in the *New York Evening Post* that she added to her scrapbook. The article claimed that she had been delirious when taken off the streets.

"Where's Bret? Why doesn't Bret come with the proofs?" she allegedly said.

"Bret who?" said a friend.

"Bret Harte, of course," replied Ina.[8]

"False. False. False," Ina wrote in red pen next to the article.

The *Los Angeles Herald* reported that her health had been "shattered" by the earthquake. "While the fire raged near her home on Gaylord Street [sic], Russian Hill, she sat on the pavement with a pet Persian cat in her arms and a grip by her side. Friends had her removed to the hospital."[9]

"A lie!" Ina wrote next to the article.

Ina appreciated Norman's gallantry, but tragically, he didn't rescue her finished book, the one thing that might have provided an income as she tried to piece her life back together.

Letters of concern and cash found their way to her. Joaquin Miller sent fifty dollars. Eleanor Davenport sent a check from the Red Cross for five hundred. Mary Austin invited Ina to Carmel. "You and I have never had an opportunity to become properly acquainted," said Austin. "Come and sit in my Wickiup and write a poem and we will walk by the sea and talk and talk."[10] The Carmel Arts and Crafts Club had formed in 1905 to lure artists to Carmel. After the earthquake they sweetened the deal by offering cheap lots. Austin, George Sterling, and James Marie Hopper were among those who took advantage of the offer and formed the nucleus of the Carmel artist colony. Jack London also visited a few times, but he was pouring his energy into the Valley of the Moon at Glen Ellen.

Ina accepted Austin's offer the following year, and Austin gave a tea in her honor. Otis Notman of the *New York Times* attended the tea and described Ina as an "elderly woman, heart-broken by the fact that all her possessions were lost in the earthquake."[11] After the tea, Sterling and Notman took a brisk walk over the hills to the Carmel Mission, where they climbed the tower and rang the mission bell. Sterling told Notman that he was sorry that the day was overcast. "To see it today is like—why, it is like looking at a ruby in the dark."[12]

Ina wasn't spry enough to scamper over the hills, but she did appreciate the dazzle of Carmel on a sunny day, and wrote a simple poem called "Carmel-by-the-Sea."

> A cloudless sun in heaven's blue sweep;
> Great stars, how near that seem!
> The night an hour of sea-lulled sleep,
> The day a rosy dream.[13]

Two months after the earthquake, Ina walked to Russian Hill, where only a few trees and buildings had survived. She looked down on the city, which Atherton described as being "scattered with brown teeth, [and] old rotting tusks."[14] When Ina returned home she found a note from Charles Keeler that encouraged her to write something about the earthquake. She didn't respond right away because the walk to Russian Hill had depressed and tired her. Two days later she wrote Keeler, "I will try to write something but I fear the result will be proof of approaching senility—or rather of its advent."[15] The following day she sent him the result of her attempt with a note: "I know it is sad stuff but I told you I could not write, only I wanted you to know me willing to try. I don't imagine anyone will want to print it much less pay for it, so I shall not be disappointed if you send it back. I would rather you would do so than give to the world my failure."[16]

San Francisco: April 18, 1906

In olden days, a child, I trod thy Sands,
Thy sands unbuilded, rank with brush and briar
And blossom—chased the sea-foam on thy strands,
Young City of my love and my desire.

I saw thy barren hills against the skies,
I saw them topped with minaret and spire;
Wall upon wall thy myriad mansions rise,
Fair City of my love and desire.

With thee the Orient touched heart and hands,
The worldwide argosies lay at thy feet;
Queen of the queenliest land of all the lands—
Our sunset glory, regal, glad and sweet!

I saw thee in thine anguish tortured! prone!
Rent with the earth-throes, garmented in fire!
Each wound upon thy breast upon my own,
Sad City of my grief and my desire.

Gray wind-blown ashes, broken, toppling wall
And ruined hearth—are these thy funeral pyre?
Black desolation covering as a pall—
Is this the end—my love and my desire?

Nay! Strong, undaunted, thoughtless of despair,
The will that builded thee shall build again,
And all thy broken promise spring more fair,
Thou mighty mother of as mighty men.

Thou wilt arise, invincible! supreme!
The world to voice thy glory never tire;
And song, unborn, shall chant no nobler theme—
Great City of my faith and my desire.

But I will see thee ever as of old!
Thy wraith of pearl, wall, minaret and spire,
Framed in the mists that veil thy Gate of Gold—
Lost City of my love and my desire.[17]

Keeler found a home for her poem in *Putnam's Magazine*, which later merged with the *Atlantic Monthly*. He sent her money and asked for more poems. She wrote two more and he sent more money. She learned later that Keeler had gathered private funds to encourage her to write. Author Mary Halleck Foote sent fifty dollars; artist Anne Bremer, cousin to art patron Albert Bender, sent thirty-five; and others sent ten and fifteen dollars. Keeler kept a careful record of the money received and sent it all to Ina.

In May 1907 she paid Houghton Mifflin in advance to print a thousand copies of *Songs from the Golden Gate*. Within six months she ordered 468 more. The proceeds from her book sales were not enough to live on. She needed a steady income and told a friend that as soon as she could walk a few blocks without being prostrated she would try to work, "tho' what it will be, God knows, for no one seems to want an 'old woman' around."[18] Keeler asked the Bohemian Club to rehire her, but they declined.

Ina needed a home. A cousin in Maine offered her a place to live, but Ina decided against it. Another young friend invited her to live with him and his family in Mill Valley. She was grateful for the offer but declined. "I am homeless, desperate, [but] I will not be dependent upon anyone, *that* I am determined," she said.[19] After searching for a place for months she put an ad in the *Oakland Enquirer*: "Wanted immediately: Some kind of shelter; rent less than $2,000; can search no longer."[20] From that ad, Giuseppe Cadenasso, an artist and Mills College educator, offered her a flat on Russian Hill. He lived in the upper flat with windows that opened out to views of the bay; she lived in the lower flat, which had nice views too. The house on Lincoln Street (now Macondray Lane) is perched on a steep hill more easily reached by goats than by aging women with arthritis. She moved in with Zeller and Robert Norman.

People were aware of Ina's precarious situation and wanted to help. The Spinners Club, a woman's book group, offered to publish a book with stories from their members and give Ina the proceeds. She agreed to their plan, but unbeknownst to her they moved in another direction. First, they collected money by placing articles in newspapers about her need. In response they received a thousand dollars in cash, but instead of giving the money directly to Ina, they purchased a bond with the intent of giving her the monthly interest. The investment yielded a little over four dollars a month, and to Ina those few dollars were not worth the humiliation of having her name dragged through the press as a charity case.

The Spinners then deviated from the original plan for the book. Instead of having their own members contribute stories, they solicited stories from Ina's famous friends. Without consulting Ina first, they wrote letters to Jack London, Gertrude Atherton, Mary Austin, George Sterling, Frank Norris, and Charles Warren Stoddard, all of whom donated their work to the *Spinners Book of Fiction*. Ina soon learned about their generosity and wrote to thank each of them. To George Sterling she wrote, "I do not know why you should be so good to me—but I wish I could tell you how much I appreciate it."[21]

"I don't think I've been particularly 'good' to you," he replied, "not half so much so as I'd like to be … On the contrary, I feel indebted to you for the chance to link, however briefly, our names—a thing I was only too proud and happy to do. So please accept *my* thanks."[22] Their initial exchange marked the start of a lasting friendship.

The Spinners planned to buy another bond with the proceeds of

The Spinners Book of Fiction, but Atherton told them to stop messing around and give Ina the money. Ina found the experience so humiliating that after several years she withdrew her name from the group and sent them a check for $90.80, the entire amount that they had given her.

Another effort to help Ina obtain a house was spearheaded by writer George Wharton James under the auspices of the Washington Heights Literary Circle in Pasadena, California. James, whom Atherton called "Geewhillicins," collected autographed books and photographs to sell. When Mark Twain sent two signed photographs from New York, James decided the contribution wasn't good enough and went to New York to ask Twain to sit for a new set of photographs. His idea was a bold one. It was well known that Twain had vowed never to sit for a photographer again. He said the last time he did, the man had "photographed the immortal soul" out of him.[23]

James went to Twain's Fifth Avenue home and presented his card to Twain's secretary, who said that Twain had left strict instructions not to be disturbed. James said that he would do the disturbing, and pushed his way into the house. He yelled up the stairs to Twain, who he knew liked to work in bed. A waterfall of swear words came tumbling down the stairs, and Twain refused to come down.

"You profess the greatest friendship for Miss Coolbrith and say you would do anything on earth for her. Now let us see how much this means," James yelled up the stairs.[24]

Eventually Twain came down and agreed to sit for New York photographer A. F. Bradley, who devised a special rotating platform for Twain. The cantankerous writer later admitted to James that several of the photos constituted the best that had ever been taken of him.

With the sale of Twain's signed photographs and other items, James raised more than thirteen hundred dollars for the Ina D. Coolbrith Home Fund. The Washington Heights Literary Circle decided that the money was for them to give to a needy writer as they saw fit, and voted to offer the money to Ina as a loan.

Gertrude Atherton bristled at the botched attempts by Geewhillicins and the Spinners, and planned an event of her own. Atherton had already helped by donating a short story to the

Spinners Book of Fiction. She also sent Ina the fee for an article she had written about the earthquake for *Harper's*. In seeking support from Senator James Phelan and the Bohemian Club for an author's reading, Atherton said she'd go forward only if all the funds went directly to Ina.

On Thanksgiving Eve 1907, a smartly dressed crowd occupied every seat in the white and gold ballroom at San Francisco's Fairmont Hotel. Stoddard came up from Monterey, though earlier that year he told Ina he was depressed and had purchased a gravesite by the sea. "The fire in my heart is low," he wrote in February. "I have not been so blue, 'deeply, darkly, beautifully blue,' in years."[25] William Keith donated a painting as a raffle door prize. John Muir bought five tickets, but at the last was unable to attend and asked Atherton to give his tickets to someone who could not afford to go.

The *Evening Bulletin* reported that poet Edward Robeson Taylor, the mayor of San Francisco, presided, and the Bohemian Club quartet sang. Thirteen writers read for the program including Charles Keeler, Cora Older, Herman Whitaker, Herman Scheffauer, Luther Burbank, James Hopper, Joaquin Miller, and George Sterling. Sterling had recently gained notoriety after publishing "Wine of Wizardry" in *Cosmopolitan*. But he was in no mood to celebrate. Just a few weeks earlier, the young poet Nora May French had committed suicide in his Carmel home. Sterling was in San Francisco when his wife, Carrie, found French dead. Carrie tucked the bottle of cyanide away for use at a later time. At Ina's benefit Sterling read several of his own poems and Nora May French's "The Outer Gate."

When the grizzled Joaquin Miller took the stage, the audience was ready for him to lighten the mood. He read his most popular poem, "Columbus," in which Columbus's crew asks for reassurance from their captain at each challenging turn of events. Columbus responds, "Sail on! Sail on!" As Miller recited the poem, his arm gestures sent his long coat flying like a sail, and the audience responded to his call and joined him for each "Sail on! Sail on!"[26]

The event at the Fairmont Hotel would have cheered Ina had she been there, but she was home in bed with a high fever. It had been years since Ina experienced creative satisfaction, and more years would pass before she did again. But like Columbus, she would sail on, and like San Francisco she would rebuild. Atherton was true to her intentions and delivered a one-thousand-dollar check to Ina. With Atherton's gift, the five-hundred-dollar donation from the Red Cross, and a loan from the Washington Heights Literary Circle, Ina purchased a lot on Russian Hill and made plans to build a house on what she called "Atherton ground."[27]

17

A Laurel Crown

Ina moved into one of the two flats in her new Russian Hill house at the top of Broadway in December 1910 and began to rebuild her parlor. With gifts and loans she bought a bed, a pine table, and three chairs. She covered the windows with lace curtains, and the shiny wood floors with Oriental rugs. The Boalts loaned her books, pictures, a table, two chairs, and a writing desk. Ina acquired a few new knickknacks, including a cupid angel that sat on the wooden mantle with his foot dangling off the edge, ready to jump. To help rebuild her library of books, poems, and memorabilia by California authors, Jack London sent a signed copy of *Sea Wolf*, Muir sent three of his books, and George Sterling sent a poem and an autographed photo. "If you only knew what a pleasure it is to me to look upon it!" she wrote in thanks to Sterling. He replied, "I *love* to write poems and inscriptions to you! Wish you were 35 and I 36!"[1] The greatest contribution to her library came from the hundreds of books given to her three months later when the California Writers Club threw her a seventieth birthday party. The three hundred guests invited to the garden party in Temescal Canyon were asked to bring books for Ina. In return, she brought each guest a signed broadside of "In Blossom Time."

Visitors once again climbed the hill to Ina's parlor, and just as in the early days, she and her parlor elicited comment. One writer described it as being a "cheerful one with a fine view of the bay."[2] Another said, "Surely something of the charm of the old home is in this quiet, restful room."[3] As for Ina, one writer described her as wearing her slightly gray hair pulled into a Grecian coil and accenting her eyebrows with pencil to give a dramatic air. Another described her as being as "conscientious as a Baptist minister, but also as independent as an unbroken mustang."[4] *Notre Dame Quarterly* said, "Her wit has a fashion of darting from her lips like a keen-pointed lance of steel; only to break in the air into a cascade of crystal drops, pure and harmless as dew."[5]

Zeller moved in too. Zeller kept a meticulous house, planted the garden in the backyard, and administered to Ina when she was sick. But she also chattered incessantly, and when Ina asked her to stop, Zeller lost her temper. "I have not even a closet to get away and be alone in," Ina told Keeler. "I can't make Josie understand that she must not talk to me when I am busy with my pen."[6]

Ina was back on her beloved Russian Hill, but things were not the same. All of her "trues" were dying. Stoddard, her favorite, died at sixty-five years old of a heart attack on April 23, 1909. He had returned to California in 1905, lived in Monterey, and wrote articles about the missions and the old San Francisco days. Stoddard also suffered from rheumatoid arthritis. During one visit to San Francisco, he and Ina walked five blocks to a friend's studio, and even with his cane Stoddard found the going difficult. Ina suggested he use her shoulder for support. When they reached the studio Ina said, "You are walking more easily. Are you feeling better?"

"Very much. Almost well," he said as he patted her shoulder. "Application of girl, Ina, application of girl."[7]

Ina attended Stoddard's funeral at the Carmel Mission, where he was laid to rest in a simple casket with a tile from the mission under his head. After a requiem mass was given, the mission bells rang. Sterling told Ambrose Bierce that Ina looked like a "sibyl of stone."[8]

Writer and editor Charles Phillips was also at the funeral. Phillips had been a student of "dad Stoddard's" at Notre Dame University and was on his way to see him when Stoddard died. Phillips and Ina agreed that Stoddard's poems should be collected for publication. Stoddard had written and published poetry all his life, but had not published another collection since his first in 1867. Ina asked Stoddard's sister, Sarah Makee, to send his possessions to San Francisco so Ina could begin the selection process. When Ina opened the boxes, she found no poems. Ina asked Sterling if he knew anything about the missing poems. He suggested that Stoddard had burned them. Ina took a trip to Monterey, where she learned it was true. Stoddard's housekeeper told her that before he died, Stoddard had sat by the fire with a stack of his manuscripts, letters, and poems and read each line before feeding them all to the fire. But Ina was not deterred from her goal and began the more arduous task of collecting Stoddard's poems from friends, scrapbooks, and newspaper clippings. It took years, but Stoddard's poetry collection was published in 1917. The editor chosen for the book decided to reduce the number of poems that Ina had chosen and to eliminate the biographical sketch Charles Phillips had written. Ina was deeply disappointed in the finished product.

William Keith died on April 13, 1911. Keith had been a good friend to Ina, even if she didn't get to see him as often as she would have liked. Keith lost most of his life's work in the 1906 fire too; he lived in Berkeley when the earthquake hit and was denied access to his San Francisco studio. Friends went to his studio and rolled, flattened, and stacked two thousand canvases and took them to an area they thought would be safe, but the fire caught up to the relocated canvases the next day. Keith immediately set to work again. "I am unable to get up to see you as I have a tremendous fit of work—and it is going to be good," he wrote Ina.[9] He painted *With a Wreath of Laurel* sometime between 1900 and 1911. There is no proof that the tall, brunette woman carrying a wreath in the painting is Ina, but it is probable it is. The title he gave his painting was the same she gave her poem in 1870 after gathering laurel leaves for Byron's grave. Keith also sent Ina money after the earthquake, and she wrote to thank him: "I have only words wherewith to express myself and words are only words, not heartbeats. Sometime when souls stand clear before each other you will know me fully and all the love and gratitude I have for you."[10]

Joaquin Miller died on February 17, 1913. Ina was too ill to attend his funeral at The Hights, but asked a friend to read "Vale Joaquin," an original poem for the occasion. She asked another friend to

Joaquin Miller, George Sterling, Charles Warren Stoddard. Courtesy The Bancroft Library, University of California, Berkeley.

look for Calla Shasta's grave. She had died in 1903 and was buried in an unmarked grave. Ina vowed to mark "poor Indian Callie's grave" if she ever could afford to.[11]

Muir was next, dying of pneumonia on December 24, 1914. Although she didn't see much of Muir during his active life, they had remained friends and she always championed his writing. For example, when *Mountains of California* came out in 1894, she sent a note: "Your book is a song, a grand song!"[12]

Ina would outlive her friends by many years, though she was in poor health. She continued to suffer from rheumatoid arthritis, and medicine did not help. She told Keeler she was desperate, and that as a last resort she would try Christian Science. She was also apparently willing to try opium. She wrote Sterling, "Maybe a draught of 'the wine of wizardry' might make me well. You said you would, else I had not dare hint it."[13] At first, Ina's rheumatism was concentrated in her feet, but in the summer of 1910 one of her eyes became inflamed with it. A doctor came daily to treat her eye, but the painful malady persisted for more than two years. As the condition dragged on, she wrote Lummis to ask how he had coped with his blindness. Lummis had gone blind from a condition he self-diagnosed as "jungle fever," which he believed he contracted in Guatamala. At fifty-one, he refused to let blindness stymie his social life or his work, and continued to supervise the construction of the Southwest Museum with a bandanna tied around his eyes and the guidance of his son, Quimu. But Lummis already had a history of overcoming physical ailments. At age twenty-eight, after several years of working punishing hours as a reporter for the Los Angeles Times, he had a stroke that resulted in the paralysis of his left arm. Instead of going to the doctor, he went to New Mexico, where he trained himself to hunt and roll cigarettes with one arm. During his blindness, Lummis learned to shave with a straight razor, a practice that he continued for years after his sight returned. On November 3, 1928, he noted in his journal that he had completed his 5,534th blind shave.[14]

To Ina's question about how he coped, Lummis replied, "There was a glory of finding out that I could beat any old thing that God could put on my neck … I would not sell that 15 months blindness for all the money there is in the state of California. That money would not buy me that much education."[15]

In spite of the rheumatism in her joints and eyes, Ina was active with the Pacific Coast Women's Press Association, serving as vice president one year and as president the next. The PCWPA was founded in 1890 to provide camaraderie among women writers and to support women in journalism. The club's better-known members had included Jessie Benton Frémont, Jeanne C. Carr, Gertrude Atherton, and Charlotte Perkins Gilman. At the end of Ina's term as president, the members voted to host a "Congress of Authors and Journalists" during the 1915 Panama-Pacific International Exposition, a yearlong world's fair held to show that San Francisco had recovered from the destruction caused by the earthquake. The Press Association asked Ina to lend her name to the Congress by serving as chair, and promised her commitment would be minimal, given her health. That wasn't the case, however. In January 1914, Ina sent out four thousand invitations to authors, journalists, and poets for the Congress of Authors and Journalists, one of the 822 congresses, conferences, and conventions held during the Exposition.

One year after she sent the first invitation, Ina sent a reminder and schedule to the same four thousand people. Popcorn, her new pedigreed Persian Angora cat with orange eyes purred nearby. In the letter, Ina invited writers to "be with us in our great year of rejoicing over the coming together of the nations by the completion of the Panama Canal, 1915."[16] Some writers in Europe found the invitation offensive, given what was happening on their soil—Europe was at war while the United States remained neutral. That neutral stance was reflected at a peace rally in the Golden Gate Park in September 1914 when Ina's poem, "War and Peace," was read to a crowd esti-mated at a hundred thousand people. After the last line was read, white doves were released into the air as a finale.

One Englishman replied to Ina's invitation: "Possibly news of our domestic squabble here does not travel so far as California, but I may mention that there is a good deal of unrest in this part of the world at present."[17]

English author Gertrude M. Reynolds was more blunt:

> Your letter of invitation to the International Exhi-
> bition strikes so strange a note upon English ears
> as to sound almost ironical. You may or may not be
> aware that England is at this moment engaged in
> a war so vast that all the world is shuddering with
> shock: except, apparently, the United States …
> From this Titanic struggle your nation has elected
> to stand aloof. Meanwhile, you must forgive the
> English if the moment of the destruction of Inter-
> national law seems to us a bad time for Interna-
> tional celebrations.[18]

As the war raged in Europe and expanded into Asia, the Panama-Pacific International Exposition opened in February 1915. It featured a forty-three-story Tower of Jewels, a five-acre moving replica of the Panama Canal people could boat in, and more than six hundred acres of gardens, palaces, and exhibits. The Congress of Authors and Journalists, which took place from June 29 to July 3 in the new Exposition Memorial Auditorium at the Civic Center, opened with a "Spanish Fiesta" at the Cuban Pavilion on the exposition grounds. Ina received guests alongside Enrique Loynaz del Castillo, the commissioner general of Cuba. He was twenty years younger than Ina, yet they formed a bond. From Havana later that year, Castillo sent her a Cuban flag, his photo, a plant for her rooftop garden, and a note that said, "I would possess a fortune, if at every time that I have your remembrance past, like a caress, over my mind, the treasure of your letters would be mine."[19]

As acting president of the PCWPA, Ina opened the four-day congress. The presentations the first day included a paper given by Sin Lun, ex-speaker of the Chinese senate, about Chinese literature; one by music critic Redfern Mason about the song lore of Ireland; and another by Stanford University professor Aurelio M. Espinosa on Spanish drama. Other sessions throughout the Congress included those given by Charles Phillips on the poetry of California; Herbert Bashford on the American sonnet; T. Cochran, who read Gertrude Atherton's diatribe on the shoddy grammar of writing in magazines; Takuma Kuroda on Japanese literature; and Jeff C. Riddle, a Modoc Indian, on the Modoc War from the Indian standpoint. Zoeth Skinner Eldredge read Charles Lummis's paper "What is the Matter with California Literature?" When Lummis sent the paper to Ina, he apologized for not being there in person. He would have been, he said, if it hadn't been for the lower-back pain he had from carrying a piano at arm's length uphill.

On the second day of the congress, a standing-room-only crowd came to see Ina crowned poet laureate, a gesture that also gave her the title of America's first state laureate. Ina's popularity had soared due to a series of profiles written about her after the earthquake. George Wharton James was the first to unearth the colorful stories from Ina's past in the June 1907 issue of the *National Magazine*. For the first time, the public learned that she had come to California on the Overland Trail and that miners taught her to rock the cradle of a gold pan. They learned details about her experiences in San Francisco with Webb, Harte, and Stoddard, and that she had taken the Oakland librarian job to support her niece and nephew just as she was planning a trip to Europe to advance her career. They learned about her suggestion that Miller change his name, and that she had raised Calla Shasta. But James did more than tell her story; he embellished her life, crowned her with jeweled adjectives, and put her on a throne:

> Who was this young girl with the ... unconscious
> grace and dignity of a forest princess, the spontane-
> ous good humor and laugh of a happy child, the
> ready wit, the tender femininity and yet fearless
> camaraderie with governors, statesmen, bohemi-
> ans, authors, artists, miners, preachers, women and
> children, mountains, trees, and flowers.[20]

Ina did not like being on that throne, and did not like the liberties James took with his pen. A few years later, a profile of Ina by Laurie Haynes Martin contained so many errors and inflated truths that Ina wrote to Martin to set the record straight. Martin replied that she had gotten all her information from James. Ina wrote to James: "You are, as you know, addicted to word painting. I wish you would not. I wish you would be content with the simple truth, however slim."[21]

James was the first, and by no means the last, to sentimentalize Ina. Writer Kate Kennedy called her a queen, and about her poetry said, "Breathlessly we follow through vistas of light, color, motion, joy, and sorrow in her superb sonnets."[22] In a profile of Ina for the *Overland Monthly*, Marian Taylor wrote, "Let us pledge ourselves to be faithful gentlemen and ladies-in-waiting to our Queen of Song, giving her loving service and the flowers of life now."[23]

The dye was cast. Reverence and appreciation turned to sentiment, and that sentiment has persisted for a century. Reporters turned a strong, sensitive, and witty woman into a one-dimensional character caught in the fixed paint of her own story. When they talked about the "sacrifices" she made for others, it was with the typical reverence held for martyred women who sacrificed themselves willingly. But let's be clear: Ina did not assume her inherited responsibilities without complaint of what it did to her art.

In early 1915, Ella Sterling Cummins Mighels told Ina that she and the Native Daughters of the Golden West had hatched a plan to name Ina the state's poet laureate. Ina responded, "Poet laureate! I? May the Lord forfend. Why the dear good friends do not realize that the opposition would not leave me a fig leaf, much less a laurel!"[24] Indeed, it was George Sterling, and not Ina, who wrote the exposition ode, though Ina agreed with the choice. She knew that some of her friends had suggested that she write it, but she thought it should be Sterling or Markham. "I am perfectly aware that I do not approach their plane; indeed, no one can have a more humble opinion of the quality of my verse than myself," she told poet Lorenzo Sosso.[25] The idea to endow her with the crown was advanced by poet Richard E. White, historian Zoeth Skinner Eldredge, and *San Francisco Chronicle* editor George Hamlin Fitch. Senator James T. Phelan suggested that the ceremony be held during the Congress of Authors and Journalists.

Edwin Markham opened the session in which Ina was crowned. His beard had grown gray, and he wore his hair swept back from his bony forehead. In his paper "The Saving Power of Poetry," he touted the lofty and idealistic role of verse makers. "The poet points away from the selfish, ephemeral concerns to the higher issues of life and death. He thunders his averments that to be something is more than to get something; that to make a life is more than to make a living; that we must put back into the world more than we take out of it."[26] In response to his talk, an unidentified poet told a *Los Angeles Graphic* reporter that Markham's speech best represented the new generation of poets. "In this backward looking congress, it was with great joy that I welcomed the more down-to-date ideas of the promising young Edwin Markham, one of the most modern persons there and by far the nearest to the younger generation in thought and purpose. His insistence on the use of the plain human words, of common speech, his rebellion against poetic license and affectation and his insistence that 'every theme is a theme for the poet' were as grateful to me as fire on a frosty night."[27]

Senator Phelan approached the podium to introduce Ina. "[She] has not flooded the press with her compositions. She has written little, but that little is great. It is of the purest quality, finished and perfect, as well as full of feeling and thought."[28] He called for Ina to approach the stage. University of California president Benjamin Ide Wheeler stood ready to endow her with the laurel crown. Before leaving her seat, Ina removed her large feathered hat. Normally, she wore a white lace mantilla in public to cover her thinning hair, but on this occasion she left her head bare to receive the crown. Dressed in black satin adorned with a sash embroidered with California poppies, she labored up the steps to the stage. A reporter from the *New York Times Book Review* said the crowd "stood in hushed silence."[29] With crown in hand, Wheeler spoke with a hint of Old English: "Upon thee, Ina Coolbrith, by common consent of all the guild of those who write—upon thee, sole living representative of the golden age of California letters, coadjutor and colleague of the great spirit of that age, thyself worthy by natural and inherent rights to hold place in their forward rank, upon thee I lay this poet's crown and name thee our California poet laureate."[30]

Ina bowed her head slightly to allow Wheeler to place the crown on her head, but instead he handed it to her. She recovered quickly and put it on her own head. The audience cheered, waved white handkerchiefs in the Chautauqua salute, and threw flowers at her feet.

The applause and whistles drowned out her first few words. Then the room hushed to hear her say that she was grateful for the honor, but unworthy. "Senator Phelan has spoken justly of the little I have published. By me poetry has been regarded not only as the supremest of the arts, but as a divine gift, for the best use of which its recipient should be fitted education, time, and opportunity. None of these have been mine … and in a life of unremitting labor, time and opportunity have been denied. So my meager output of verse is the result of odd moments, and only done at all because so wholly a labor of love."[31] She said the honor was more a recognition of the group of talented writers with whom she had the pleasure of being associated than of her own contributions. "For that reason—for those who are passed away and for my sister women—I accept this laurel, with deep gratitude and deeper humility."[32]

During the applause Ina called for Josephine Clifford McCracken to come up to the stage. Ina knew McCracken from the *Overland*

Monthly days and they had remained friends. McCracken worked as a reporter for the *Santa Cruz Sentinel* and had come up for the day for the ceremony. McCracken later wrote that it felt like a dream to be led to the stage and share the glow of applause with Ina.

"There was no lack of enthusiasm in the crowning of the laureate," reported the *New York Times Book Review*. "To the cold and 'effete East' it may seem a little overwrought at times. That, however, is probably due to envy. New York has no poet laureate—and California has."[33]

When it was all over, Ina was exhausted. Lummis invited her to El Alisol for a rest. It wasn't the first time he had invited her to his house of stones northeast of Los Angeles. She replied that it would be impossible because she could barely get from room to room. "Our Big Fair I have seen for three hours in a wheeling chair," she said.[34]

When another friend congratulated her on the Congress, she replied, "I would not undertake such another, for anything short of the *peace of Europe*."[35] That would take years and the involvement of the United States.

There was no peace abroad and no peace at home. Zeller's tantrums had gotten worse. "She's a perfect Virago," Ina told Keeler. "I wish I could have her under hypnosis. It is the only thing that would help her in the least."[36] The next five years would prove to be a challenge for Ina, but challenge and desperation often bring about change.

18

"Lady Moon"

Two months after the Congress, *Sunset* magazine published "From Russian Hill," a poem Ina had submitted three years earlier. Clearly her new title influenced the magazine's decision to print the poem, which captured the magical mood of a quiet San Francisco night in these last two stanzas.

> How stately and serene
> The moon moves up the sky!
> How silvery between
> The shores her footprints lie!
>
> Peace, that no shadow mars!
> Night and the hill to me!
> Below, a sea of stars!
> Above, of stars a sea![1]

In the year following the Exposition, Ina wrote no poetry, and over the next two years she wrote only four poems. She told one friend that she was "on the rack" of rheumatism, and told another that her bones were knitting together. One friend suggested cream of tartar in lemonade; another said she should try buttermilk or Mexican mustang liniment. Lummis suggested she take Salitha, a concoction he took every morning that contained magnesium sulfate, lithium, and colchicine. But his love of and appreciation for her probably did more than any pills. "Your fist ain't no different from many other fists—but I always know it. And I felt a little warmer under my left nipple when I picked up the envelope this morning, which I recognized," he said.[2]

Ina turned seventy-six on March 10, 1917, one month before America declared war on Germany and entered the Great War. For her birthday a hundred schoolchildren climbed Russian Hill and serenaded her from the street as she sat at her second floor window with a swath of lace covering her eyes. The seventh- and eighth-graders stood in neat rows, their feet together, and sang Leoncavallo's "La Mattinata" in Italian. In English they sang "Boat Song" and "Come Where the Lilies Bloom." For a finale they recited Ina's "In Blossom Time."

Ina gained comfort from children. Years earlier, she told Keeler she would rather live on the streets than be so alone. "O, what a blessing and wealth in your lovely, lovely children. If I only had *one*, I should have something to live for."[3] Ina never told him about her child, said Keeler, but the "exceptionally tender interest she took in our eldest daughter, Merodine, who was our only child during the first few years we knew her, made us feel that there was a loss and yearning in her own heart."[4] Ina was also fond of Lummis's daughter, Turbesé. "Bless little Turbese! I wish she were my young' in," she told Lummis.[5] Her love for children reached back decades. In an undated letter to her sister's first daughter, Mary Peterson, Ina wrote in clear block letters, "Aunt Ina will put a kiss down in the corner. Mary, put your lips there and the kiss will jump into your mouth." Ina wrote "KISS" at the bottom of the page and put a circle around it. "Give Henry, Ina, and Willie a taste of it." Mary Charlotte, Ina's favorite niece, died at seven years old.

Ina was confined to her house, she complained by letter to Josephine McCracken. Her friend replied that there were many times she would love to stay home when she *had* to go out. McCracken was two years older than Ina and still worked as a beat reporter for the *Santa Cruz Sentinel*. Like Ina, McCracken had escaped a husband who tried to kill her. After the Civil War, she was living in a tent in

New Mexico during the Indian Wars when her husband confessed to being an outlaw from Texas who had changed his name after murdering a man. After he threatened to chop off his wife's head with a hatchet in the middle of the night if she revealed his secret, she managed to escape. She moved to San Francisco, where she wrote short stories and worked as Harte's secretary at the *Overland Monthly*. Unlike Ina, Josephine Clifford married again. She and her husband, Jackson McCracken, lived at Monte Paraiso, a twenty-six-acre ranch in the Santa Cruz Mountains she had bought in 1880. In 1899, a forest fire burned the house and much of the surrounding countryside. The house could be rebuilt and was, but the redwoods were not so easily replaced. McCracken wrote an article for the *Santa Cruz Sentinel* that lamented the loss of *Sequoia sempervirens* by fire and ax, and her letter led to a public discussion about the possible loss of all redwoods unless something was done. That led to the founding of the Sempervirens Club and to California's first state park, California Redwood Park. Today, that park is part of Big Basin Redwoods State Park, the largest stand of old growth redwoods south of San Francisco.

McCracken lived at Monte Paraiso with her husband until he died in 1904. After his death she took a job at the *Santa Cruz Sentinel*, where she earned five dollars a month. In 1909 she received a raise to ten dollars a month, one-tenth of what Ina had made as a librarian. "For this I furnish everything, articles on the growth and expansion of Santa Cruz; criticisms on music and the drama; business write-ups, climate, scenery, health, flowers, views, sea and land, and protection of children, animals, birds, game; and write-ups of clubs and societies," she told Ina.[6] Her salary was not enough to live on and she sold the house she and her husband had rebuilt for fifty thousand dollars. She was forced to sell it for one thousand and blamed the giveaway on the meanness of men. She threatened to become a socialist, but instead continued to work as a beat reporter to earn a living.

Unlike McCracken, Ina rarely went out, so the California Literature Society came to her. Ella Sterling Cummins Mighels had divorced Phillip in 1910 and returned to San Francisco. In 1914 she formed the California Literature Society, and moved the meetings to Ina's house so Ina could attend. More chairs were borrowed and once a month local writers, poets, artists, and historians climbed Russian Hill to Ina's parlor. Joan London, Jack's eldest daughter from his first marriage, was fifteen years old when she first attended the meetings. London said that Ina rarely spoke, laughted, or smiled. "When she did speak out it was electrifying. I confess that she awed, and even mystified me," said London, adding that dead writers such as Joaquin Miller, John Rollin Ridge, Charles Warren Stoddard, and Bret Harte seemed always in the room.[7]

It is certain that the spirit of Joan's father was evoked when he died at age forty in 1916. The newspapers reported that the cause of Jack London's death was kidney failure, but George Sterling said London killed himself because he was in love with two women. Sterling didn't know who the other woman was, but Charmian did. "[She] will have to tell me some day, when I force her to drop the pretense that he died of uremic poisoning. He died of twelve grains of morphine," Sterling told Ina.[8] Elsie Whitaker Martinez, wife of painter Xavier Martinez, corroborated Sterling's assertion that London had a lover, saying that London was ready to leave Charmian because he had fallen in love with a Hawaiian woman.[9]

According to Elsie Martinez, Jack London was among a group of writers and artists who carried cyanide in their pockets. The group included her husband, George and Carrie Sterling, Ambrose Bierce, and Nora May French. Carleton Bierce, Ambrose's nephew, worked in the chemical division of the US Mint and supplied it to the group. Nora May French used hers in 1907. When Ambrose Bierce went to Mexico and vanished, his friends suspected cyanide. Sterling labeled the cyanide he carried in his pocket "peace."

Ina did not belong to this club, but her ongoing bouts with rheumatism were a certain kind of death. Prolonged rheumatoid arthritis can lead to the destruction of joints, the deterioration of bone, and deformed feet. She didn't get out of the house for months during an inflammation, and she was lonely and nervous. She had acquaintances and admirers, but it had been a very long time since she had someone to love.

Carl Gunderson Seyfforth showed up at a California Literature Society meeting in 1914 with Bram Nossen, a wayward young man whom Mighels looked after. Before Ina and Seyfforth met, Mighels

Carl Seyfforth. Courtesy Oakland Public Library, Oakland History Room.

wrote Ina that a young man was coming to play piano for her. Ina loved the piano, and had one in her parlor; Charles Phillips had asked to store his in her house while he was in Europe with the Red Cross. Alice Bashford, who played for Ina once a week, said that Ina's gray eyes glowed during her private concerts of Chopin and Beethoven.

Seyfforth was in his late teens when he and Ina met. He had a square jaw and buoyant blonde hair. He was training to be a concert pianist and had an ego to match his dreams. He later wrote in *Ulven*, his autobiography, that his given Norwegian name was Ulv Youff. "I am an ulv, which means wolf in Norwegian ... My teeth are white and sharp with ambition, and I am hungry for fame. My eye is greedy, and my thoughts are cruel, but my lungs are panting and my soul is ravaged, and this book is my howl."[10] Seyfforth had been a self-avowed troublemaker as a youth. He stole fruit, threw cats in water, and spent idle time in the cemetery waiting for the dead to come back to life. He was a circus of one, in search of something to help him stoke the fire that roared in his belly. "I lived every moment. I could not breathe fast enough," he wrote of himself as a youth. He hated work and regular hours, and about religion said, "I loved sin with ardor. I was too alert, too active, too intelligent, too vital to be religious."[11]

As a teen, he decided to become a concert pianist. Nearly all the teachers he consulted said it was too late to start, but eventually he found one willing to give him a chance. His father was unhappy with his son's career choice and forbade him to practice at home where a piano sat idle. Instead, Seyfforth practiced to exhaustion at a nearby church. He acquired a solid technique, showed talent, and at a student reception was the star attraction. An emboldened Seyfforth asked his father for five hundred dollars to study in New York. His father gave it to him and Seyfforth got on a train. In New York he couldn't find a teacher to believe in him, so rented a grand piano in a deaf and mute asylum to practice on his own. The streets of New York matched the electricity coursing through his veins, and he was up at five each morning to walk them. He spent his money on galleries, museums, and opera. One night he met Kenneth Sultzer, a young man his own age who became his best friend. Six months later, Seyfforth returned to San Francisco broke. His father did not let him back in the house. Seyfforth stayed at a friend's house in Sausalito, worked part time as a clerk, and found his way to the home of California's poet laureate. "The first time I saw her she sat receiving in a lavender robe with a lace fichu over her head, and holding a small bunch of primroses ... Her tragic personality inspired great reverence, and I was prostrate before her," he wrote.[12] After Seyfforth played at the meeting, Ina told him he was a musical genius. He began to visit often. Ina was not the first elderly woman that Seyfforth befriended. In *Ulven* he wrote about another woman with "handsome eyes" with whom he was "very near the clutches of romance" when he ended it.

To return to New York, Seyfforth lied to his father, telling him that a woman in New York had offered to pay him to teach her daughters piano if he could get there on his own dime. His father gave him the money. "I lost a night's sleep over the matter but kept the funds," he said. Seyfforth arrived in New York with twenty-six dollars in his pocket, and the only place he could afford to live was a windowless, unheated attic. He mooched off Sultzer, and ate and slept little. He wrote to Ina about his dire circumstances, and she asked Gertrude Atherton, who was then living in New York, to help. Atherton agreed to meet him, but wasn't impressed. "Young Seyfforth is certainly engaging and interesting, but I should imagine [he] would be a handful if I gave him an inch ... I shall not see much of him for the present, which is rather a relief, for I have not that form of vanity that welcomes adoration."[13] Atherton went to the Paris Peace Congress for the *New York Times* when the war ended on November 11, 1918, and when she returned saw Seyfforth again. "I like your infant more the more I see of him," said Atherton.[14] She introduced him to the right circles and he was invited to luncheons, dinner parties, and the opera.

"I kept many an engagement at the Ritz and the Plaza, with ten cents in my purse," said Seyfforth. "New York is full of these young men."[15]

Seyfforth had other benefactors that winter. One man took him to dinner three times a week and bought him new shirts. Seyfforth lived at another man's house in Westchester for three weeks and practiced on a ten-foot Steinway in the music room. But these alliances were temporary. Broke and cold, he sat in churches during the day and one night broke into a restaurant to eat. Sultzer, who was going to school and working, earned six dollars a week and gave his friend five.

Seyfforth wrote Ina that he wanted to go to Norway or kill himself. Ina knew that Seyfforth's window would close if he didn't advance his career soon, and took matters into her own hands. She borrowed seventeen hundred dollars (nearly twenty-three thousand today) against her life insurance policy and gave it to Seyfforth. When her insurance provider, Albert Bender, questioned her decision, Ina said, "I am not taking this poor boy on my old shoulders, 'tho I wish I could, in order to save. If this poor lad cannot get the help in the next few months to carry him thro' his trial, he will go, or die by his own hand."[16]

When Seyfforth received the money, he wrote to Ina, "I look you full in the eyes, Ina Coolbrith, and ask you to read my soul … You give me back my Art! Do you know the despair of not being able to do what you know you have the ability for? Is there keener torture? I had begun to feel that I should never attain my goal, knowing the fatality of it."[17] Of course, Ina knew that despair. She had felt the edge of that sword for decades. She believed that her art had been torn from her in her prime, and when she tried to get back to her literary life twenty years later, illness, poverty, and tragedy knocked her down again. She was unable to get back on her feet, literally or figuratively.

Ina asked Seyfforth to come to San Francisco and see her before going to Norway. He brought Sultzer with him, and they stayed at Ina's house. Zeller didn't like Seyfforth, and the boys got a taste of her temper. While in San Francisco, he gave a concert for the San Francisco Musical Society and was a critical success. Seyfforth left San Francisco for a health holiday in Norway, and upon his return to New York leased and furnished an apartment complete with a piano. For the first time in his life he had one at his fingertips, thanks to Ina.

For years Ina had wanted to move to New York, and in the summer of 1919 she asked her friends what they thought about the idea. Her doctor said the change in climate might improve her health, and encouraged her to go. All her friends thought it was a good idea—all but Lummis. "How [will you] adjust yourself to that horizon of those who scratch it with their elbows every time they turn around?" he asked. "Your only salvation will be, of course, that you will carry California in your heart, and they cannot narrow you to themselves."[18]

Ina knew that her own window was closing. She was lonely without her trues and there was one death in particular that closed a

chapter in her life. In early 1912, Ina had renewed her correspondence with Joseph F. Smith, her cousin who in 1901 had become the
sixth president of the Church of Jesus Christ of Latter-day Saints.
The Mormons had denounced polygamy in 1890, but Joseph F.
Smith had practiced it for most of his adult life and fathered forty-
three children with five wives. Ina's correspondence with Joseph was
friendly. He sent sympathy and money. She signed her letters "Josephine" as she had in the old days. At times he lectured her, but she
decided to "answer only with aloha."[19] He sent faith-based magazines
and other Mormon publications that she agreed to read, but made it
clear that she didn't believe in the religion. "I know that if I thought
and believed as you do, I would be happier, but I cannot," she wrote.
"I am as I am, and I pray that God will help me if I am right and not
wholly desert me if wrong."[20] When he asked her to visit Utah, she
said no. When he offered to take care of her if she did, she still said
no. "God is in all His World, and I trust Him not to forget me utterly," she said.[21]

Ina explained her reasons for not wanting to visit or live in Utah
to Adele (Bio) Terrill Jones, a friend and distant cousin. Bio was not
a Mormon, but was related to the Smith family. Her grandfather was
Stephen Mack, brother of Lucy Mack Smith, the prophet's mother.
Bio was living in San Francisco when she began a correspondence
with Joseph F. Smith, who told Bio that Ina Coolbrith was a Smith.
Bio introduced herself to Ina and the two women became friends.
After Bio visited Joseph in Salt Lake City several years later, she
suggested that Ina do the same. Ina replied, "Joseph and his sister are
good, I do not doubt that, but absolutely fanatic in their religion, and
would not, I fear, know anything different from their belief for all the
Universe. To me, in this age of reason, it seems almost impossible."[22]

In January 1917, Ina sent Joseph a copy of *Songs from the Golden
Gate*. He had asked for it months earlier, but she had been laid up for
two months with rheumatism and sciatica and had to learn to walk
again with the aid of canes and chairs. "What a helpless old hulk,"
she wrote in the note she sent with the book.[23]

One month later, on February 18, 1917, she learned that he had
revealed her background publicly. She sent him a note:

It was not kind of you, Joseph dear; in fact, without my knowledge and permission, I do not think you had the right ... I have wanted to tell you what my mother told me (but you give me no chance) that you might understand why I cannot think as you do, tho' I wholly respect and consider your side.[24]

For years, Ina had wanted to have a frank, in-person discussion with her cousin, but the few times he visited her he never came alone. In 1914 Ina wrote, "You know, Joseph, there is but one portion of the Church creed upon which we diverge. You are honest in your belief, and I in mine. Your own father condemned it in the presence of Joseph and my father and mother, and in the most emphatic terms ... I suppose you would be angry with me and with my dead mother if I should tell you what I ought to tell."[25]

The last letter Ina wrote to Joseph F. Smith is missing, but the contents of it can be inferred by his angry reply.[26] In her letter she apparently claimed that her father had promised her mother to take the family back to Kirtland, Ohio, and not take any more missions. She also told Joseph that her father was opposed to polygamy and that at his deathbed Joseph had asked him if he had any final wishes, to which Don Carlos replied, "Yes, I have, Joseph Smith. I want you for the rest of your life to be an honest man."[27] Ebenezer Robinson, coeditor with Don Carlos for *Times and Seasons*, corroborates Ina's assertion, saying Don Carlos said, "Any man who will preach and practice spiritual wifery will go to hell, no matter if it is my brother Joseph."[28]

Joseph F. Smith responded to Ina's claim. "To say that your father was quietly or secretly laying plans to go back to Kirtland in 1842, with intentions of abandoning the Church, or in consequence of disagreement with his brothers Joseph and Hyrum, is nothing less than infamous libel on your father's character ... Nothing but the spirit of dissatisfied and lying apostates could possibly put any other meaning on it."[29] There was no other way to spin it. He was calling her mother a liar.

Joseph quoted passages from *Times and Seasons* to prove Don Carlos's devotion to the church. "Who should we believe?" said Joseph. "The record which your father has left behind which cannot be destroyed, or the malicious charges of those who, having lost the spirit of the Gospel and having departed from the truth, would have us believe that he was also one of them and as miserable?"

Again, he called her mother's character into question.

Joseph wrote this letter from a sick bed in April 1918. Ina likely read it in her sick bed. She did not reply. He wrote her again on October 21, 1918, and sent some religious materials for her to read. He reiterated that salvation would be given to those who believed in the church and its dogmas, and condemnation for those who didn't. She chose not to reply again and Joseph F. Smith died on November 19, 1918. She had made her position clear when a year earlier she told him, "To be crucified for a faith in which you believe is to be blessed. To be crucified for one in which you do not believe is to be crucified indeed."[30]

In the summer of 1919 Ina decided to move to New York. Before she did, she had to tell Zeller she was going without her. Life with Zeller had become unnerving, and Ina feared Zeller's reaction. The trouble had started years earlier when Ina began to misplace her papers and letters. At first she blamed her own absentmindedness. "I don't know how my letters disappear so but they do. If I only had one little closet to get into alone," she told a friend.[31] As time went on, Zeller's thefts became blatant. Once, after Bender sent Ina some tea in a beautiful jar, she told him that Zeller had "appropriated it," and that she'd rather die of thirst than spark an outburst.[32] Zeller's tantrums had grown worse, and she screamed at Ina loudly enough for the neighbors to hear; Ina's friends became concerned for her safety. One friend told Ina that Zeller was dangerous and should be locked up in an insane asylum. Ina admitted that Zeller had said she hated her, and one time twisted her arm until Ina screamed for her to stop.

When Ina told Zeller she was moving to New York, and that to do so she would have to rent out both flats, Zeller reacted as expected. Ina knew that Zeller had assumed she would live with Ina to the end, either her own or Ina's. Zeller told Ina she was a "miserable fool of an old woman" who had no right to move.[33] She accused her of putting her out on the streets, even though Ina promised to help her financially. The tension in the house heightened as the time neared for Ina to leave. One night with the house dark, Zeller opened Ina's bedroom door and hissed her hatred. Zeller threatened to "slap her face, mash her head, and throw her out the window."[34] Ina prayed as she finished packing the next day while Zeller hurled verbal abuses. Ina knew Zeller was also capable of physical violence because she had once attacked Ina's brothers.[35] "If I had not got out, I would not be alive today," she later wrote.[36]

Ina boarded a train in September. Six months earlier, her title as poet laureate had been made official by the California legislature after another poet tried to wrest the crown from her head. A *Sacramento Bee* reporter claimed that no one deserved the laurel crown more than Ina. "The old rhythms and rhymes are best," said the reporter, who didn't like free verse or the poets who wrote it. "They are the Bolshiviki of literature. They would throw off all trammels, all restraints, all reason, all custom, all sanity."[37] With her title confirmed (though with no stipend attached), Ina headed for New York, the incubus of free verse.

Part V:

New York

I must have solitude for my writing ... I never was able to fully command that except during the four winters I passed in New York, when I was for the first and only time—*Free.*

—*Ina Coolbrith to Albert Bender, 1925*

19

Welcome to Manhattan!

On October 26, 1919, Ina's train rolled into a maze of tunnels at Grand Central Terminal, the largest train station in the world. On her first trip to New York twenty-seven years earlier, her train had pulled into an aboveground glass and steel shed on Forty-second Street. This time the seventy-eight-year-old poet emerged from underground tracks to find a great hall with high arched windows, grand staircases, and columns as tall as redwoods. Seyfforth met her at the station and took her by motorized taxi to her hotel on Forty-fifth Street. The Hotel St. James was near Times Square, where Fanny Brice, W. C. Fields, and Ethel Barrymore headlined in shows, and one street over from the Algonquin Hotel, where Dorothy Parker, Robert Benchley, and Alexander Woollcott sharpened ideas over cocktails at the Algonquin Round Table. A young writer named F. Scott Fitzgerald joined them on occasion. In the spring of 1920, he would become one of New York's hottest authors when his first book, *This Side of Paradise*, sold twenty thousand copies in two weeks.

Once Ina settled in, she wrote dozens of letters to friends. She wrote Bender that she didn't feel as tired as she did at home, and concluded that her lack of fatigue proved how much her mental state dominated her physical one. "In fact, I feel like a first-class fraud when I tell people I have been an invalid."[1] To historian Charles Beebe Turrill, a loyal attendee of the literature group that met at her house, she admitted that she felt like a stranger in "this Babel of the 20th century." Although she enjoyed the bustle of New York, she lamented that her window looked out on twenty-story buildings instead of views of the bay. Turrill replied that he didn't like New York. "I recall Muir's objection to the cañons of Wall and other streets and his preference for those in the Sierras."[2]

In November Ina sent a note to her old friend Edwin Markham, who had moved to Staten Island with his third wife, Anne Catherine. In 1910 Markham had helped found the Poetry Society of America, a club whose recognition Ina craved.

"Welcome to Manhattan!" wrote Markham after receiving word from Ina. "Your letter fills the house with surprise. As soon as I can pull my foot out of the deep rut, I shall drop in on you. When I am not fast in the rut, the wild-haired Fates are on my track. Life is hard. But I shall try to elude these enemies of man, and soon be knocking at your door."[3]

When Ina answered Markham's knock, she was surprised to see how large he had grown. He was so round that she couldn't have hugged him had she tried. Still, the old friends were glad to see each other, and Markham gave Ina a fitting welcome by asking her to be the featured guest at the next Poetry Society meeting in December.

Ina also sent her calling card to Adele "Bio" Terrill Jones, now De Casseres, her distant cousin who had left her husband earlier that year and moved to New York to marry author, poet, and journalist Benjamin De Casseres. Bio, a dark-haired woman decades younger than Benjamin, arranged for a visit right away, and Benjamin requested an interview for *The Sun*. They arrived and Ina greeted Bio and her new husband, a bespectacled man with deep furrows between his brows and a receding hairline. Benjamin noted that Ina wore a loose linen dress and a white lace mantilla. Flowers from friends filled her room. By now, Ina had grown accustomed to giving interviews and knew the good stories to tell. She told De Casseres about the time that Harte had been livid when the proofreader objected to "The Luck of Roaring Camp," and how Ina had gotten him to relax by rhyming him. Ina repeated the rhymes for De Casseres, and then added, "I could never understand why such squibs adhere to one's memory so much more readily than many things of real worth—unless perhaps just as in passing through a flowering field it is not the blossoms which stick to one's garments but the burrs."[4] Ina told him it was she who had suggested that Cincinnatus Hiner change his name to Joaquin, and showed him a letter Jack London had sent her after the earthquake, a letter that closed with:

> I was only a little lad. I knew absolutely nothing
> about you. Yet in all the years that have passed I
> have met no woman so noble as you. I have never
> seen you since those library days, yet the memory
> picture I retain of you is as vivid as any I possess ...
> Do forgive me what you may deem my foolishness.
> I am all iron these days, but I remember my child-
> hood, I remember you; and I have room in me yet,
> and softness too, for memories.[5]

The full-page profile of Ina that Benjamin De Casseres wrote appeared in *The Sun's* "Books and the Book World" on December 7, 1919, and the stories of Harte, Twain, Miller, and London added to the interest about her. Ina sent copies to California friends, who offered their congratulations. "I am glad that old New York is paying you proper tribute," said Robert Norman. "It should have done so long ago. New York will yet claim you as one of her own and then California will dispute her title."[6]

Soon after, Ina had an opportunity to shine in front of New York poets. On the day after Christmas, she took a taxi to the National Arts Club for the December meeting of the Poetry Society of America. Seyfforth and writer Jeanne Francoeur joined her. It was cold. The day before, New Yorkers awoke to snow so deep that the city sent three thousand street cleaners in a hundred horse-drawn carriages and five hundred Ford trucks with open beds and canvas-covered cabs to plow through it.

Ina arrived at the club building across the street from Gramercy Park. Facing it in the park was a larger-than-life statue of actor Edwin Booth immortalized as Hamlet. Ina had known Booth in San

Francisco when he was at the height of his acting career, and she remembered his having the most beautiful eyes she had ever seen. Seeing the statue may have triggered a story about Booth that she once told a reporter. While visiting art collector Lawrence Sutton in San Francisco, she admired his collection of plaster hands cast from famous men. She picked up the largest hand in the collection and learned it was a cast of President Abraham Lincoln's hand. Sutton told Ina that Edwin Booth had also recently visited and picked up the same. When Sutton told him whose hand it was, Booth pressed the hand to his lips and kissed it. Then he laid it down and left the house without another word. Booth had never gotten over the fact that his brother, John Wilkes Booth, had assassinated the president.[7]

Ina entered the club through heavy, steel-framed glass doors and climbed the stairs to the second floor using Seyfforth's help and the brass handrail. On the second-floor landing was a set of tall doors that opened to a roaring fire that faced the door. Above the fireplace was a mirror that stretched to the ceiling. If Ina looked at her image, her gaze did not linger. She disliked her aging image so much that she had rubbed out her face in several photographs, and when Joseph F. Smith had asked her for a portrait in 1916, she replied, "The only vanity I have left (I never did have much) is in the determination not to perpetuate my ugly old face."[8]

Instead, Ina focused on the beauty of the rooms, where Persian rugs carpeted the floors, art covered the dark walls, and stained glass decorated the windows. Although there is no known record of who attended the meeting that day, the membership roster of the club included Witter Bynner, Amy Lowell, and Edna St. Vincent Millay, the *poet du jour* due to her recent hit play, *Aria da Capo*. Millay was born a year before Ina was fired from the Oakland Public Library, and at twenty-seven was busy living the words from her poem "First Fig," published in *Poetry* the previous year:

> My candle burns at both ends;
> It will not last the night;
> But ah, my foes, and oh, my friends—
> It gives a lovely light.[9]

In an article published on January 6, 1920, a reporter from the *San Francisco Bulletin* wrote that Edwin Markham presided at the meeting. Markham introduced Ina as the Sappho of the West, and said that Ina practiced her art not for the sake of those listening, but "only for the honor of the muses."[10] The notion that a woman wrote only for the joy of writing while a man could expect to feed his family was a platitude that irked Ina. Joaquin Miller had made a living and bought land by using his pen. Charles Warren Stoddard sold his work and taught at a university, even though he had never attended one. Bret Harte had earned ten thousand dollars in one year at the *Atlantic Monthly*, a remarkable sum even if the contract did not last. When a fan once told Ina that his family lived on her poems, she replied, "That's nice. It's more than I've been able to do."[11]

California-born Anna Catherine Markham took the floor and scolded the audience for not knowing Western writers as well as Western writers knew those in the East. "No woman poet of the East has a place in the hearts of the people as Miss Coolbrith has in the hearts of the West," she said. The *Bulletin* reporter said, "Miss Coolbrith, stately and handsome in her black silk gown and quaint lace headdress, took the floor and for nearly an hour held the audience charmed, first by her reminiscences and then by her poems. She spoke without notes with ease and grace in an intimate friendly way. Her words were touched with pathos and humor and a fine common sense." Ina told stories about Harte, Stoddard, and the *Overland* days, and promised that her audience would be able to read more stories in her memoir that would be published before long. She told a story about Joaquin Miller that may have been triggered by Booth's statue across the street. Ina said that when she first met Miller he wore fairly typical clothing, but after he moved to England she began to hear rumors that he was dressing in costume and telling exaggerated Western tales. She discovered that the rumors were true when he returned to San Francisco several years later and showed up at her house wearing corduroy pants tucked into his boots, a shirt with an open collar, and a floppy sombrero that he wore over hair that flowed past his shoulders.

"Joaquin, how could you!" she said.

"That is the welcome to a man who has been for two years the lion of London?"

"Lion!" she answered. "Is that why you have grown a mane?"[12]

He ignored her criticism and invited her to see Edwin Booth in *Julius Caesar* that evening. She refused to go unless he paid a visit to the barber. Miller returned later that evening with a more conservative outfit and hair that no longer flowed.

"Oh, how much better. How very, very nice you look, Joaquin," she said. All was well until she glanced at him at intermission between the first and second acts. "In all its pristine glory there was his hair flowing over his shoulders, and he quietly and solemnly reached me a handful of hairpins. Every glass in the house was upon us," she said.[13]

Ina closed her talk to the Poetry Society by reading several of her own poems. When she finished, the group gave her a "long continued applause" and her acceptance into the Poetry Society was a success.[14]

Ina stayed indoors for most of the winter. The *New York Globe* reported on January 16, 1920, that "one of the most remarkable women that the West—or America, in fact—has produced has been living here in New York and nobody has noticed." Ina, who the *New York Globe* said represented "all that is great and liberal and strong in the old American pioneer stock," stayed inside because the final wave of the Spanish Flu pandemic, which had begun in January 1918, crested in the city as it did across the world. By the time the pandemic played out in 1920, it had claimed the lives of at least 50 million people worldwide. Ina wrote Bender that although officials were leaving black crepe on nearly every door, there still wasn't enough housing for those living, and she continued to live in her hotel. In February a great blizzard hit. After it passed, she peeked through her window to watch workers building fires to melt the snow and using war tanks to clear the streets. Icicles a yard long hung from roof and window ledges. "I suppose when summer comes, melted human beings will run in streams along the same streets," she wrote Bender.[15]

Ina was not completely alone. Seyfforth visited when he could, but he was ill for most of the winter. Kenneth Sultzer and Ned Blossom, Seyfforth's friends, visited Ina when the weather allowed. The Markhams brought her books. Edward L. Burlingame, an editor at Charles Scribner's Sons, visited her in February. She also communicated by letter with friends in California and by February she had written 250 letters. The biggest news she shared was that since coming to New York she'd had no rheumatism. She credited the change in climate. "I keep well and a little ambitious," she wrote Bender. "New York is surely *alive.*"[16] Ina was writing more than letters, and sent a few new poems to Charles Phillips. He wrote that he was not surprised she was writing.[17] "If you had never written 'New York' in that first letter, I would still have known that it came from a new, free person, it was so full of life."[18]

She submitted "Listening Back," a poem that compared the silent snows in New York to the singing rains in San Francisco, to *Sunset* magazine. They replied that they would publish it the following autumn. "As if I had years to wait," she wrote Turrill.[19] When the issue came out the following November, she discovered that they had changed the last line of the poem without her knowledge. Her last lines read, "In snow the window wreath'd instead of roses / And snow is very still / I wonder is it singing in the grasses / The rain on Russian Hill?"[20] They had changed the last line to read, "the rain upon my hill." Ina wrote Bender that the change made the poem "common, cheap," but let it go with an "Ah, de mi Alhama," a Spanish phrase of regret.[21]

Ina also wrote two love poems that winter, one of which was titled "Love's Age":

> "Love is so old," I said, "no more
> Of him be said or sung" ...
> But since love entered at my door—
> Love how forever young!"[22]

Ina never explained the nature of the love she felt for Seyfforth. Sometimes she talked about him as a lover; other times like a son. No matter what form her love took, it made her feel alive.

Come spring, Ina was socially active. She was a guest of honor at the "New Club of Women Poets," where she read by request. She told Turrill, "[I] heard some of the women poets of the East—*real ones*—read and recite. I like them all."[23] Ina went to the theatre, attended Poetry Society meetings, visited the Players Club, and went to several club teas. Markham invited her to read at an "Authors' Matinee" benefit at the Waldorf-Astoria with Witter Bynner and Yone Noguchi, two poets with California connections. Bynner had spent a year teaching poetry at the University of California. Noguchi had lived in San Francisco between 1893 and 1899, where he was a fixture with the literary bohemians and published several books of poetry. He had moved back to Japan but was on a lecture tour in America that spring.

In late March, Turrill sent news as welcome as spring. "'Shout the glad tidings, exultingly sing' the Ina Coolbrith Circle is a thing of life and activity."[24] Prior to Ina's move to New York, the California Literature Society had split in two and half of it morphed into the Ina Coolbrith Circle. The split was due to the soured relationship that had developed between Ina and Mighels. Ina felt Mighels's iciness as early as 1916 and asked in a note what was the matter: "Think, girl. Don't hurt me again. If you only knew one-millionth part of my burden you would not add the weight of a fledgling's feather, as God knows I would not to yours."[25] Mighels wrote a note of complaint on the back of Ina's letter. "[She] has no more troubles and sorrows than the rest of us, but has no philosophy to help her bear them."[26]

Mighels explained to Ina that she was still mad at her for pulling a photo from *The Story for the Files*, a photo that Mighels had paid to have formatted. Mighels also accused Ina of hurting her feelings during meetings. At one Ina had derided Mighels for opening the meeting with prayer when Mighels was merely struggling to write down the names of attendees. At another meeting, Mighels told Carl and Bran they needed a guardian angel, and was mortified when Ina chimed in, "They don't need one! They are young and innocent. If anyone needs them it is us, because we are old sinners!"[27]

Mighels wrote barbs on the backs of notes frequently. On one she wrote, "I have wasted tons of sympathy and concern over [Ina], only to be dealt with treacherously by her at the last. I am glad I can say,

'Love is dead. She cannot hurt me anymore.'"[28]

Ina contributed barbs of her own. To Turrill Ina complained that Mighels had changed the subject of a meeting, and another time wrote that she had received the "most Mighelish card."[29]

In May 1919, Mighels announced that she was dividing the group. It would be the same members and the same format, but members could choose to meet on the third Sunday at her house or the fourth Sunday at Ina's house.[30] In July of 1919, Mighels published a poem in the *San Francisco Bulletin* called "Broken Friendship," in which she compared her friendship with Ina to shattered glass.

After Ina moved to New York, those who had met at her house changed the name of the group to the Ina Coolbrith Circle. The group floundered until they moved the meetings to the elegant Blue Room of the Fairmont Hotel in March 1920, when more than thirty people attended. Ina sent a letter from New York to be read aloud at the next meeting:

> This is like saying "how d' y' do" to oneself, almost, isn't it? ... You represent Ina Coolbrith's Circle; she being the last of that group comprised of Bret Harte, Charles Warren Stoddard, Joaquin Miller, Mark Twain, Prentice Mulford ... If you could hear the questions asked, the praises spoken of these, my old comrades, *here,* you would appreciate more fully what manner of minds they were, never to be again on those sunset shores! Even I wake to a fuller realization and wonder "did I walk with giants in those days?"[31]

The popularity of the meetings grew, and the members wrote a constitution and elected board members. Despite Ina's difficult relationship with Mighels, she reminded Turrill that the Circle should always acknowledge Mighels's California Literature Society as the founding organization.

As summer neared, Ina wanted to stay in New York but knew she could not tolerate the heat and humidity. Going to California cost less than a summer retreat, so she got on a train. "I wish the summer were possible," she told Turrill. "I never felt so full of 'write' in my life. Maybe it's the last spun-out filaments of my poetical web."[32] Instead of returning directly to San Francisco, Ina took a train to Los Angeles, where she stayed with her childhood friend Mrs. Perry. It was Perry who made Ina's time in New York possible with a monthly fifty-dollar check. When Lummis found out that Ina was in town, he planned a "noise," a party the likes of which he had not hosted in years. Prior to Ina's leaving for New York Lummis had written, "Why not be a good neighbor, and come this way and stop a bit among Real People. Will give you such an Old California Time as will warm the ways of your heart."[33]

On June 12, 1920, Lummis opened his "housebook" to a new page. At the top of the page he wrote, "This night is dedicated, with reverent love, to the Last of the Old Guard of the Golden Age of California Letters, Ina Coolbrith—Ina, of Ours—Poet by the Grace of God, Laureate of California by the sense of Governor and Legislature obeying our will."[34] Fifty-eight people signed the book. It is unknown whether Lummis named Ina as a defendant in the Court of *Alcalde Mayor*, a party game in which he forced the guest of honor to stand trial for "not knowing an Old California time" while everybody drank. Lummis placed a double-barreled shotgun and a bowie knife on the table in front of him and forced the defendant to prove that she knew what constituted a good time. If Ina was put on trial during the party, she was in good company. Her friends John Muir and Joaquin Miller had also been tried in Lummis's court. After dinner, Lummis read several of Ina's New York poems to the guests.

For Ina, it wasn't the time at the party she most cherished. It was spending time during the day with Lummis "the true" in El Alisal's central courtyard. In the peaceful shade of the sycamore trees, she listened to the birds and the fountain, and wondered what Methuselah, his century-old turtle, thought about immortality.

20

Courting Moonlight

Ina returned to San Francisco for the summer. One of her flats
was empty and she lived in her own house. Bender sent her Kona
coffee, her favorite. It warmed her heart but couldn't remedy her
rheumatism, which returned almost immediately. "Why could not
California be *good* to me, and not tear my joints into fragments and
not stab my soul?" she asked Bender.[1] In early September she was
the guest of honor at a California Writers Club dinner, where she
read her New York work. In mid-September she told Bender she
was in a hurry to get away because she was in danger. She didn't
elaborate, but it was likely Zeller she feared. Ina had tried to give
Zeller a monthly allowance but Zeller refused to take it. To Ina's face
Zeller said she didn't want her money because she knew how hard
she had worked to earn it. To Ina's friends, Zeller complained that
Ina had put her out on the streets to starve and swore she'd "have her
rights."[2] Ina's brother said that he would feel justified to kill a man
who said the things that Zeller said to Ina. And yet, Popcorn, Ina's
beloved Angora cat, lived with Zeller while Ina was in New York.
One Thanksgiving, Ina's niece delivered some turkey to Popcorn
at Zeller's sister's house in Oakland. She dropped it off with a note
while it was still dark to avoid seeing Zeller, who she said was "like
a person standing in an elevated position with a large supply of mud
nearby with which she bespatters everyone who approaches her be

he friend or foe."[3] Ina Lillian had hoped to see Popcorn in the window as she ran from the porch, but did not.

Ina sold some furniture and books to accrue cash for the winter, and left for New York in late October. She told Turrill that on the train she enjoyed the "thrill of whirling thro the snow-mantled Sierras! There is nothing like our mountains and our forests, no where, no how!"[4] It was odd, she added, to travel as an unknown after a summer in San Francisco, where she was seen as a celebrity. "Not a soul on that train from conductor to fireman knew of the precious load it was carrying in the person of the poet laureate of California. Alas! For the bubble of fame! Outside the limits of one's own ego it doesn't even bubble."[5]

Back at the Hotel St. James, which offered her reduced rates for her former good behavior, Ina unpacked her bags and pulled out a gift from painter Maynard Dixon. The painting came with a note from him and his wife, Dorothea Lange. Dixon said he and Dottie had been talking about how hard it must be to leave California, and wanted Ina to have a painting to "renew to your eyes a vision of this bright land of sun and space we so love … May the thickness of the paint not hide our good intention."[6]

In November, *Sunset* magazine sent a check for seven dollars and fifty cents for "Listening Back." The publisher said that was all he paid for "that kind of poem."[7] He was likely referring to the fact that the poem was not in the modernist style popular at the time, such as those penned by E. E. Cummings, Djuna Barnes, and Carl Sandburg. The spark of the free verse movement had originated from Filippo Tommaso Marinetti, the leader of the Futurists, who cried, "Let's murder the moonlight!" Yet Ina still courted it. She told a Los Angeles reporter that the free verse "bolshevists" couldn't touch the depth and strength of Tennyson and Browning. While she appreciated the freedom of expression that Amy Lowell brought to the art form, she believed the trend had gone too far. "Pegasus has gone cavorting like a wild mustang during the last few years in this country. It is now time to rein him in and make him return to his beautiful paces."[8]

"Isn't what you mean to express more important than the form?" asked another reporter.

"You might as well say that a snowman is a fine piece of sculpture if it represents a man. Form is as essential to poetry as to sculpture."[9]

Ina stood for the old guard, yet the pull of a vibrant city fueled a desire to make new work. She wrote more poems during the four winters she spent in New York than she had in the previous twenty-five years. Perhaps what inspired her were the similarities between post–World War I New York and post–Gold Rush San Francisco. Both cities during postwar times underwent great change and teemed with immigrants. Although she was unable to explore the streets of New York the way she had as a young woman in San Francisco, she would have seen enough to know that the city was alive with renewal. While flapper dresses and bobbed haircuts ruled Times Square, the poorer parts of the city looked similar to San Francisco in earlier days, with balconies filled with bedding; children shooting craps on street corners; hungry Irish newsboys in suits daring the world to give it to them on the chin; and colorful laundry hanging from lines between buildings that represented the Italian, Romanian, and Hungarian people who lived there. She would have seen children sleeping on grates to stay warm; Chinese girls in long, silk dresses; English women in layers of brocade; children in snow-white coats with fur hoods; Jews with long beards and dark eyes; and women balancing towers of rags on their heads. Every neighborhood teemed with people who had been displaced by the Great War or were changed because of it.

"The World War [had] just ended, and a mad era in art and poetry had set in," Keeler wrote in his memoir. "If a California poetess nearing her eightieth year, who still wrote poetry after the manner of Lowell and Whittier and Tennyson, did not electrify jazzy Manhattan of 1920, it was no great wonder … [She was] of the era of the great James Russell Lowell. New York in 1920 was in the era of Amy Lowell."[10]

Still, Ina kept busy socially. She had a visit from Mildred Leo Clemens Schenck, Mark Twain's second cousin. Schenck was on her way to Europe with her traveling show, "Happy Hawaii," which promised stories, song, dance, and an exploding volcano. Ina also asked Lummis to introduce her to some of his New York friends, and he said he would. "God bless you, dear Ina, and loan you (as my Indians say) strength and physical comfort, that your indomitable soul and pure poetic fire may be untrammeled."[11] Thanks to Lummis she had visits from Fanny Bandelier, the widow of anthropologist and historian Adolph Bandelier; poet Edna Dean Proctor; and author and historian J. Salwyn Schapiro. Ina told Lummis that it wasn't until Schapiro came to her door that they realized they had already met at Maynard Dixon's studio, where they had shared a meal of "frijoles and tortillas."[12] In December she went to a dinner party hosted by poet Miles Menander Dawson, the treasurer of the Poetry Society of America. Other guests included poets Edwin Markham, May Riley Smith, and Edith M. Thomas.

For Christmas, friends and family sent greetings. Editor Edward Francis O'Day sent a festive holiday telegram: "THE RAIN IS SINGING IN THE GRASSES ON RUSSIAN HILL AND IN THE HEARTS OF MANY HERE A CHRISTMAS SONG OF LOVE IS SINGING TO INA COOLBRITH."[13] Popcorn (with the help of Ina's niece) sent Ina a Christmas telegram, and Bender sent a gift, as he did every Christmas. During a visit in December with John Farrar, the *Bookman* editor, Ina said, "It's nice not to have rheumatism, but I miss the *Sequoias*."[14] From her single window she looked over rooftops and swirling steam. Her window faced north, which meant she couldn't see the sun, the moon, or the stars. She read of new stars being discovered in the *New York Times*, and told Turrill, "I'd like to see the old!"[15]

In the New Year, Ina read at several events, and Seyfforth accompanied her. She read alongside Edna Ferber, Zona Gale, Edwin Markham, and Amy Lowell for an Authors' Matinee at the Waldorf Astoria; she read Bret Harte's "Dickens in Camp" at the Dickens Fellowship dinner at the Astor Hotel; and at the Poetry Society's eleventh annual dinner at the Hotel Astor, she sat at the speaker's table with Rabindranath Tagore, Edwin and Anne Catherine Markham, May Riley Smith, Sara Teasdale, Jessie B. Rittenhouse, and Elinor Wylie.[16] The younger poets in New York accepted and welcomed Ina with hospitality and kinship, she said. "It is a mistaken idea that the people of the East are less cordial than those of the West."[17]

As the New Year ushered in stimulating social events, it also brought sad news. In January Ina learned that Josephine Clifford McCracken had died on December 21, 1920. McCracken's companion, Etta Aydelotte, wrote that McCracken had been going blind for years and that Aydelotte had served as McCracken's eyes so she could work as a beat reporter to the end.

"The world has not used us well, Ina," McCracken once wrote.

> California has been ungrateful to us. Of all the
> hundred thousands the State pays out in pen-
> sions of one kind and another, don't you think you
> should be at the head of the list of pensioners, and
> I somewhere down below? Ina Coolbrith has always
> been called "the sweetest note in California litera-
> ture" ... No later writer has ever approached you,
> and still you are not an independent woman. As for
> me, I claim to have done more for the preservation
> of the redwoods of California, for the conservation
> of birds and game, than any Native Daughter of
> California, but who thanks me for it?[18]

Ina felt blue when she turned eighty years old in March 1921. That month the *Overland Monthly* published her four-stanza poem "Alien." Here are the first and final stanzas:

> The great world has not known me,
> Nor I the world have known;
> The great world will not own me
> Altho' I am her own ...

> My Mother-World, I wonder
> When no more of life a part—
> A clod your bosom under—
> Will you take me to your heart?[19]

She wasn't well. "Not rheumatism, but heartsick with the world," she told Bender.[20] In April she said good-bye to Seyfforth, who was going to Norway to audition for an impresario, a concert manager. It should have been a joyous occasion, but Ina was worried about him. His health had been poor for a year or more, and even short practices at the piano exhausted him. Friends took him to Florida to rest but it didn't help. "I wriggled like a centipede, with as many quivering nerves as it has legs—and was quite as dangerous to handle," said Seyfforth.[21] Ina missed him after he left, but was soon happy to learn that Seyfforth's audition had resulted in a twenty-three-performance tour with a debut that included a full orchestra. With only four months to prepare for the big debut, Seyfforth hired a coach to help him gain the strength he needed for the physically demanding tour.

Once again, Ina returned to San Francisco for the summer because it would be cheaper than paying for a summer retreat in the mountains or on the coast in the East. Both of her flats were rented and Ina checked into a hotel. Bender sent Kona coffee and the summer fog settled into her joints. She wrote Lummis that she was lonely and missed being made love to in Spanish. He replied, "*Alma de mi Alma* (soul of my soul), *aborada and idoltrada* (adored and idolized) Ina, *tus ojos divinos* encienden de alma (thy eyes divine inflame, kindle, my soul). Likewise, *labios de rubí* (lips of ruby), *cuello de marbil* (neck of ivory), *mi bien, mi tesoro, mi cielo* (my beloved, my treasure, my heaven) *tus brazos* (thine arms) ..."[22] He ended there.

That summer, Ina learned that Mrs. Perry had died in Los Angeles. Ina would miss her old friend, and would sorely miss Perry's monthly fifty-dollar checks that enabled her to live in New York. To save expenses, Ina moved into her niece's house in Berkeley. In late August, Seyfforth wrote and pleaded with her to return to New York as soon as possible. He said that in preparation for his tour, he had pushed his health and stamina, and three days before his debut woke up coughing blood and didn't stop for three hours. Doctors told him he had tuberculosis and had suffered a hemorrhage. His tour was canceled and for twenty-three days he lay in bed taking morphine, racked with the fear of having another hemorrhage. He would return to New York for another opinion as soon as he was able.

"As his need is great, a sick boy alone, I shall go as soon as I can," Ina wrote a friend. "I suppose it will be hard to go in the heat, but I seem called upon to stand all things."[23] Ina spent her first month in New York nursing Seyfforth. She told a friend that he was very sick and as "temperamental and difficult as a prize prima donna or a bear with a very sore head."[24] When he was well enough to travel, Seyfforth boarded a ship bound for Europe, where he would go to a sanitarium in the mountains. Ina was depressed. "The Lord's good not to hold us here forever," she wrote Clemens. "Though I wish He'd make the trip a little easier and let us know the name of our getting off station."[25]

Ina had always wanted to see England and Egypt. Instead, she financed Seyfforth's trips abroad and never once complained about it. His care, comfort, and creative fulfillment were all she desired. With the loss of her steady income from Perry, Ina was broke and did what she could to cut corners. Her hotel room was the cheapest she could find that was safe and warm. She made her own morning coffee and ate just one meal a day. She bought no clothes or comforts, and still didn't think she could afford to stay in New York. She asked Markham if he knew where she could sell her autographs. He didn't. She asked editor Albert Kinross in England if there were opportunities to publish there. He advised her to concentrate her efforts in America. She asked George Sterling to introduce her to some New York editors. "*Les jeuners* don't know me," she said. "I don't belong to the Democracy of the Muse, *alias*, Free Verse, which seems to be the one and only *Real* today."[26]

But Sterling was having problems of his own. His life had tumbled into a freefall after his wife Carrie divorced him and then ended her life in 1918 with cyanide. Sterling lived in a room at the Bohemian Club and relied on the charity of its members. He told Ina he'd help her if he could, but that most of the Eastern magazines had rejected his verse for years. "I infer that I'm either too old-fashioned for them, or not respectable enough!" He was short on funds too, he said, as was almost everyone he knew, especially writers.[27] Several months later Sterling reported that he had written to critic H. L. Mencken about her and that Mencken had said he would be glad to hear from her. Sterling asked if she had tried the *Christian Science Monitor*. "I hear they publish much poetry, and pay well. Of course it has to be ultra-cheerful; but the glad note comes easy to you. I have to force it, as a rule."[28] His statement must have seemed odd to her; she hadn't written a "glad note" in years.

Ina could find nothing cheerful about her financial situation, and in December sent depressed letters to friends and family. "I'm up against it. All at once, as my knockdowns always come," she told Clemens. "I may have to go back to the Coast, almost at once and bury myself with give-up-a-tiveness."[29] She told Turrill that she might have to return to California, which for her meant the return of rheumatoid arthritis and the end of physical and mental health. Turrill replied that time in purgatory with friends was better than being in Hell alone. He wisely told her that while New Yorkers had greeted her cheerfully, they had their own lives to look after. "People must always keep their armor burnished, their weapons in readiness, in the battle of life," he said.[30] While that was also true in San Francisco, at least she was among friends. Come home, he beckoned. In his estimation, she had done what she had needed to do, which was "to be recognized as an American, and not only a California, poet."[31]

While it was true that she missed her friends, it was work that she craved. "The older I get the more ambitious I become and the more I see to do." she told Turrill. "I don't believe this Mother Planet will be able to shake me off even when I have shuffled off this mortal coil."[32] To Bender she wrote, "Here I am physically so well, and the freedom from the pain of 14 years on the rack of inflammatory rheumatism gave me back the vigor and ambition and ability to write again, which I thought lost forever. To go back means to give all this up, absolute death in life—the end!"[33]

She wrote a despondent letter to her niece, Ina Lillian Cook, which triggered a response from Ina Lillian's twenty-one-year-old daughter, Ina Agnes. She told "Grandie" to "brace up":

> For the love of Michael Moses, and Jehosaphat, what's eating you??? The next time I read a letter from you that sounds like the Dead March from Saul, I'll go to the St James Hotel for the sole and express purpose of paddywhacking you! There! Really, that letter was the limit! If you could see mama going around here with a face as long as a horse and her eyes like the bottomless pits of sorrow, you'd be surprised ... I guess the female line of this family is cursed with fits of morbid despondency—Mama is, I am, and I guess you are, too. We get the blues and

get 'em bad. It's part of our natures and I'm afraid
we can't help it to any great extent, but we don't
need to give in to it for very long at a time.[34]

Ina Agnes mentioned that her father had a cold, bought twelve
boxes of cough drops, and ate them all in one sitting. All he could
do was sleep the next day. "Honestly," she added, "I think men are
such oilcans."

In spring, Ina received a reprieve when Bender sent her a check
for fifty-eight dollars from the Bohemian Club. In May, he sent another.

"I can never repay you Mr. Bender, *here*," wrote Ina, who at
eighty-one still knew how to flirt.[35]

21

Last Dance

Ina left New York in late May to spend the summer in California. She landed at her niece's house in Berkeley, where a bout of rheumatism put her in the hospital. Her health improved enough for her to leave the hospital, but she was sick all summer and crossed the bay to San Francisco only once. She wrote no poems and told a friend that her mind was a blank in California. New York made her feel alive, and she planned to return in the fall.

A letter from Seyfforth postmarked Paris arrived in Berkeley. "Forgive me," he said. "I could not face a sanitarium."[1] Instead of going to the mountains as promised, he had settled in Paris and took excursions to Monte Carlo, Spain, and Switzerland. He had stayed up late, abused his health, and had another hemorrhage. He returned to New York, and so did Ina. For the fourth time in four years, Ina headed east on the *Overland Limited* train. The Hotel St. James did not have a room available when she arrived in late September, and she took a fifth-floor room at the Hotel Latham on Twenty-eighth Street between Madison and Fifth. She felt strong upon arrival.

"I salute you from the great Babylon of the Era," she wrote Bender. "I am not as tired as when I went out. The trip was really comfortable. What do you suppose I am made of? I give it up. I ought by every precedent to be sitting, wrapped up, in a chimney corner, and

237

preparing in thought for the closing scene, but I am *not*. I am only sweet sixteen!"[2]

Thanks to the Bohemian Club she no longer had to worry about money. During the club's semicentennial anniversary, and in recognition of her being made an honorary member when the club was founded, they sent her a check in August and let her know that monthly checks would continue indefinitely. The freedom from financial worry and physical pain gave Ina the strength to work. "As soon as I got back to the Inglorious, the indignant Muse took me literally by the heels (with a view to the feet, probably) and I've been in the throes of an extended rush of meter ever since," she wrote a friend. "I suppose you're aware that once subject to the muse, in however small a degree, you are henceforth its helpless victim."[3]

In her New York work Ina explored nature, love, and God, three themes that braided the wide-open floodplain of her memory. Alone in her hotel room, she wrote about a hill in California where meadowlarks sang and poppies set the slope aflame with orange. She recalled nature's "quiet welcoming," and recognized the "woodland orchestra" as comforter and teacher.[4] She believed that the answers to life's questions were found in the simplicity of a rose and a bird's song, a belief concisely rendered in "Honey-Throats":

> Honey-throats, upon the boughs,
> Piping all day long—
> Sun-flecks in the leaves that house
> Quickened into song—
>
> In your notes a gospel lies—
> Teach it ye to me!
> What the maker in the skies
> Meant His world to be.[5]

Nature could also be dark and reflective. In "Haunted," she likened her painful memories to water lapping against reeds on a dark shore. Fog hangs over the moonlit scene like tears, and the waves come in a steady rhythm like memories that don't die.[6]

Love was a complex subject. On the one hand, she professed

to believe in love above all else. In "The Birth of Love" she proposes that God created love to give the world its soul. In another she writes, "If I have never loved before / Yet love I now, indeed! / My lover's will is as the wind / Wherein I am the reed."[7] On the other hand, several of her New York love poems are about unrequited love, with titles like "Lost Love," "The Shadowed Room," and "Alone." Perhaps the poem that best describes her relationship to love is "Lady Moon," a poem in which the moon sails across the sky chasing the sun. The moon knows that satisfaction will never be hers, yet she vows to follow the sun through the ages.

She treated religion and God in unexpected ways. In "Atom," God is omnipresent; Earth is a "small sparkle of the Universe;" and man an atom.[8] Throughout her life, most of the religious poems she wrote, usually commissioned at Christmas, were based on the Christian faith. In New York she wrote two poems that touched on Islam and took place in Egypt, a country she had always wanted to visit. The narrator in "With the Caravan" dreams that she is in the Sahara desert at night with "great moons that blurred the stars / silver above / silver beneath."[9] Hassan, a camel driver, is trying to reach the city, but the gates are closed against him. He calls upon "A-l-l-a-h— i-l—A-l-l-a-h" to open the gates. In "Sahara," a man, a horse, and a camel are lost in a blinding sandstorm. The traveler is about to be consumed by a simoom, a strong dusty wind, just as he comes upon an oasis where "moon and stars and love are listening." Ina recognizes Allah in the poem's last lines: "'Allah be praised!' and bows him to the sod / 'Lo, God is God! There is no God but God.'"[10]

Ina had wanted to write about early Los Angeles for years. She fulfilled that desire with a forty-eight-stanza poem called "Concha," her most ambitious project undertaken and completed while in New York. In this epic poem, Ina depicted the cultural landscape of the old Californio pueblo and gave the poem a Mexican feel through the narrator's diction. The poem is told by Concha, a girl who lives at the San Gabriel Mission. Concha thirsts for knowledge, and wants to study alongside her boyfriend, Ramon, but is denied because she is female. Although Concha sees the value of learning from books, she also believes that true knowledge is found in a honeycomb, a bird on the wing, or a flower in the wind. She knows that if she can't unlock the truth in nature, the truth remains for "the thing itself, it knows."[11]

Through Concha, Ina communicates her preference for an ecumenical view of religion, one that defies the rigid dogma she had been taught as a child. For example, Ramon is studying to become a priest but decides against it. He says he will not worship in only one house when "God's vast spaces call," and declares, "My Church is the whole world / Man's heart my altar."[12]

As she finished up "Concha," she told Lummis she was obsessed with her "verse narrative" and wished she could submit it to him but was afraid he would "collapse" under the weight of the 740 lines.[13]

Autumn clicked from picturesque to harsh, and with the change of season came the unraveling. In the November issue of *Bookman*, a prominent literary journal, critic Witter Bynner gave a dismissive opinion of California poets. The genesis of the critique came when a woman in London wrote Bynner in New Mexico to ask his opinion of Western bards. Bynner replied and sent a copy to John Farrar at the *Bookman*, who published it. About the dead poets, Bynner had little good to say: Miller would be remembered for his eccentricities, not his work; Bierce's work he remembered not at all; and Charles Warren Stoddard was more of a scholar than a memorable verse crafter. Of the living California poets, he said that Edwin Markham and Erskine Scott Wood were the best of the lot; George Sterling had on occasion "written a poem crisply and vigorously human"; and Ina Coolbrith's work was "commonplace but gentle."[14] He also suggested that Sterling, not Ina, should be wearing California's laurel crown.

"I admit the truth of Witter Bynner that far," Ina wrote Sterling. "For the rest he's pretty much a blithering idiot."[15]

Sterling replied, "Bynner, besides being more kinds of an ass than I have ink to particularize with, is a sex-invert and a generally vain and envious character. I doubt if anyone takes him seriously, except such women as he perennially surprises and disappoints!" As for the crown, said Sterling, the next time it is awarded it will be placed on a brow far less a champion than hers.[16]

Ina's other friends were up in arms. Robert Shaw of the *Oakland Post Enquirer* called on all "literary warriors" to defend her. He reminded readers that the author of the letter was often called "Bitter Wynner."

"I suppose you know about Mr. Wittier Binner's [sic] rating of Cal. Literati," she wrote Bender. "I don't care a continental *D* … for *his* opinion, only the ass has a following in the modern razz-dazz-jazz clan, to which the day generally belongs—that will hurt me when I publish—and greatly, as I have the added brand of the *West* … Bah! Against Mr. Binner. I have the endorsement (unsolicited) of Tennyson, Geo. Meredith, Longfellow, Holmes, Whittier, Stedman. R. H. Stoddard, + a few others before this Modern Jupiter lorded Olympus."[17]

She was worried that his caustic assessment would hurt her chance of publishing. She had asked H. O. Houghton and Company to publish a collection of her poetry, one that mixed the old with the new. In December they replied that they first wanted to see her book of reminiscences about Harte, Miller, and Twain. They explained that from a publishing point of view it would be better for all the titles to publish the memoir first, which they believed would show good sales. "Will you let us see the manuscript of your Reminiscences as soon as it is ready, and we shall be glad to give very prompt and hospital (sic) consideration to the whole publishing situation in respect to your books."[18] Later that spring, Bender asked how the memoir was coming. She replied, "I hoped to have book out but the pubs are 'hold-ups,' and I am (except with verse) not quite ready. I am severe with myself in my work."[19] The Bynner incident spun her into depression. She was lonely and missed Russian Hill, even with the punishing fog. "It's hard to transplant an old tree," she wrote Sterling.[20] Her room at the Hotel Latham ran hot and cold, and she was feeling the New York cold for the first time. In February she had a bad fall when the elevator started up suddenly. Then she got the flu and had no one to look after her. By March she recovered but wasn't feeling well. Not rheumatism, she told a friend, just going. "Dear me! Is it not time? I am only one of the human grains of sand, blown here for a moment—and away! I think of Tutankhamun! The great king with all his riches, here for 18 years, and dead [for] 3300, and forever. What shadows we are!"[21]

Ina was anxious about Seyfforth. In January he had gone to a clinic in Switzerland to try Sanocrysin, an experimental treatment that had been tested on only a few humans. In the years to come it would be used on patients in Europe and the United States—until they started dying from it. The gold salts injected intravenously and intramuscularly proved toxic, especially to the kidneys. Seyfforth would receive the treatment three times. Before leaving New York, Seyfforth sold everything and presented Ina with an address book as a gift. On the flyleaf he wrote, "A record of your friends, but I come first—for I love you more than any—and that love could only be first."[22] His inscription is the only known extant written communication between them, though they corresponded frequently. Ina kept a notebook in which she logged letters written and received between 1922 and 1926. In May of 1922, she wrote thirty-eight letters, including seven to "Carl." In June, nine of sixty-five were to Seyfforth. On average she wrote about eight letters a month to him, none of which are known to have survived.

After his first treatment, Ina received word from a nurse at the clinic that he was extremely ill. Ina wrote Clemens, "I have passed a bad winter. Sick at heart and in body ... Carl is very bad. I have little hope ... and there is the financial burden added to the poor boy and he is as dear to me as if he were a son from the flesh."[23] Seyfforth did recover, and as his health improved he worked on his memoir, *Ulven*. "The Furies are upon me, the furies of musical unrest and work undone," he wrote. "Art is my Achilles heel. My urge is fierce and grows fiercer ... Only Death can stop me. And Death will be peace. For I cannot stop believing in myself, in my talent, my intelligence and my temperament—I cannot stop believing in my EMOTION."[24]

Ina believed in him too. Apparently, the money she had given him was gone, and she worked to raise more. She asked David Belasco, the "Bishop of Broadway," if he knew of any financial assistance for artists. He did not. While Ina scrambled to find him money, Seyfforth wrote in his journal, "Most people are made of sawdust. Sometimes fools past sixty think they have longings when it is only acid in the system."[25] He blamed his own shortcomings on others: "If I knew the really interesting people of the world, and had them for my friends, there would be some purpose to life then. But I have had fools to deal with, and fools have undone me."[26]

At the end of May, Ina boarded a train bound for San Francisco. The *Overland* trips by train took only three days but had taken months when she walked it as a girl. "Such men and women had juice in their veins," said Lummis, who had also walked to California.[27] She told a reporter that rather than traveling in comfort she would prefer "roughing it along the way."[28] Before leaving New York, Ina went to see *Covered Wagon*, a silent film about an overland wagon journey from Kansas to Oregon. Paramount Pictures called the film "the greatest achievement in motion picture history" and boasted that during filming several hundred men risked their lives in a buffalo hunt, and the crew set nine square miles of "waste territory" on fire.[29] She went with Bio De Casseres, who wrote about the outing for the *New York Times*. While watching the movie in the Criterion Theatre on Broadway, Ina relived her own crossing seven decades earlier. She told De Casseres about crossing the rivers, and how her mother had propped feather beds on the inside of the canvas wagons to shield her children from arrows that never came. One of the characters in the film reminded Ina of a man in their party. "He swore terribly. My mother was afraid he would bring down the cholera on us, as he could out swear any other man she had ever heard. But he was the only one the mules would obey, and he said it was because of the language."[30] Ina said it was the best picture she had ever seen. It is unknown whether Ina knew that James Cruze, the director, had been raised a Mormon near Odgen. He left the church as a young man for a life in the movies, first as a silent-screen actor and then as a director.

Ina enjoyed her overland journeys. After one trip she told Turrill, "Never did 'Uncle Sam's Farm' seem so stupendously beautiful. I don't know what the other Worlds look like—I believe we are shortly to have a map of Mars—but this dear old, naughty, stubborn, unfortunate, suffering, ravishingly beautiful Earth could satisfy me for several more incarnations … Long may it spin!"[31]

She arrived in California with fifty-five poems ready for

publication, and she was eager to write more. One of the poems was "Unheeded":

> As bright the dew upon the rose,
> Though no eye sees it glisten;
> As sweet the song the singer sings,
> Though none may look nor listen.
>
> What matter if the world go by
> Nor praise nor incense bringing!
> Sing as the birds, God's poets, sing
> For the full joy of singing![32]

Ina moved in with her niece in Berkeley, where unfortunately her old archenemy rheumatism found her. She didn't know it yet, but she would not return to New York again.

Part VI:

Poetry as Home

What's the use of settling down and saying, "I'm old."
With work, life goes on by itself, and you forget about
anything miserable, such as a birthday.

—*Ina Coolbrith, March 8, 1924*

22

Heart-to-Heart

Several days before Ina's eighty-third birthday in 1924, she granted an interview to *San Francisco Call* reporter Evelyn Wells. Ina wore a velvet robe festooned with a long string of beads worn around her neck and a homemade white lace mantilla on her head. She began by saying, "I refuse to have another birthday. I'd even pass the day in mourning, but I don't like black."[1]

Several reporters described Ina in her eighties as Victorian. Her grandniece, Ina Cook Graham, debunked that cliché. "[Ina] was never the gentle, doddering, senile Whistler's mother type that is implied. She had a strong personality, a ready wit, and dominated every gathering at which she appeared. She did not like large crowds, she was bored with small talk, but when there was good conversation, sensible, serious or witty, with intellectual equals, she shone."[2]

As Wells interviewed Ina, Popcorn jumped into Ina's lap and sought her large hands. "All I ask of life is work. I could have given all my time, or nearly all of it, just to poetry," said Ina. "The rest of my life I intend to put in doing all the work I wanted to do and couldn't. That's just as beautiful as retiring is to other people. I'm just settling down to business now."[3] Ina had been back in California for nine months, living with her niece in Berkeley, where the summer fog's icy fingers challenged her will to work. "I do not like Berkeley," she told a friend. "It is shrubs and shingles, and cold. Ugh! It is cold!"[4]

In May, Ina moved back to San Francisco, but to an area that was even colder than Berkeley. "I tho't I was coming back to San Francisco, but my niece lost her mind and engaged an ice-chest west of Twin Peaks," she told Sterling. "Locally, the street is known as Terrible Street, more descriptive than Taraval."[5]

Seyfforth survived his Sanocrysin treatment and visited Ina in San Francisco. Turrill stopped by and asked to see Seyfforth, but Seyfforth declined to see him. Ina explained why:

> Please don't misunderstand and be vexed with poor
> dying Carl. His worst illness is from the nerves ... I
> fear to cross him because of the damage of a break-
> down. That is why he could not see you yesterday
> and he felt badly about it. I don't know if you have
> nerves, but I have been almost in his condition and
> understand ... With young girl graduates in the
> house I am nearly as crazy-nervous as Carl.[6]

To another friend she wrote, "Pray for him and for me. I built so much upon the beautiful, gifted being that he is! How can God let him die and the world lose such a genius!"[7] Bio De Casseres did not agree with Ina's opinion of Seyfforth. She told Ina's niece that she did not like to see Ina "surround herself with these feminine men and to be pulled around by the nose by them ... Carl was not a genius and never had a chance."[8] De Casseres told Ina directly that she thought Seyfforth was taking advantage of her. In response, Ina asked De Casseres how she would have felt had Ina criticized her for leaving her first husband for the man she loved. De Casseres also accused Ina of living too much for Seyfforth instead of herself while in New York. Ina replied, "I was far less unhappy and alone in my N.Y. hotel than I was in my Cal. Home. I lived my own life (not Carl's) far more than I ever had before. I read and wrote as I have not done since the death of my sister in 1874."[9] Ina loved to read. She kept a small notebook with reviews of books that served as her reading list. Ninety percent of the books on her wish list were nonfiction, and included such titles as *Egypt and Its Monuments*, *Easy Spanish for Beginners*, *Why We May Believe in Life After Death*, *Insomnia and Nerve Strain*, *The*

Babylonian Talmud in 10 Volumes, *Are the Dead Alive?*, and *Expedition of the Donner Party*.

Ina's passion for learning was recognized by Mills College on October 6, 1923, when she was awarded an honorary master of arts degree by President Aurelia Henry Reinhardt:

> You answered the call of the meadowlark in California's sunrise; you followed the song of the mockingbird under her fragrant moon; flower and melody, love of man and worship of God, you have wrought them into imperishable loveliness in the fabric of your song.[10]

Bender was a trustee of Mills College and likely attended the ceremony. His beloved cousin Anne Bremer did not. She died a few weeks later. Bremer was a celebrated California painter who had turned to poetry after developing leukemia in 1921. Ina did not hear about Bremer's death until a month later and was worried that Bender might think her delayed response ungracious. "I did not know! Surely you must know I did not know! You who help so many. If I could help you, or at least let you know how I grieve for you ... Sometime, when you can bear to speak of these things—the only really vital ones—may we have a heart-to-heart talk together."[11]

In December 1924, Seyfforth returned to Norway for more Sanocrysin. The journey across the ocean on a steamship took up to eight days and must have been miserable for a tuberculosis sufferer with bad nerves. The immediate physical reaction to Sanocrysin could mean life or death, and Ina was distraught when she didn't hear anything for a month. Finally in late January she received a letter from nurse Hanna Dahl. Dahl said that the worst of Seyfforth's reactions were over, and that he needed a year or two in the countryside for long-term care. Ina got busy, and her target was precise. Within a few months, Jennie Crocker Whitman, heir to Charles Crocker, sent Ina a check for five hundred dollars (equivalent to about six thousand today). Ina sent Seyfforth the money. But instead of going to a climate suitable for convalescing, he returned to New York.

Ina did not. She moved with her niece to a sunnier part of the city at 112 Lyon Street near Haight and Ashbury—the same house where Janis Joplin lived forty years later with Country Joe McDonald. She attended the Ina Coolbrith Circle, corresponded with colleagues and friends, and tightened up her New York poems. She asked Sterling to suggest a title for her new collection. He offered *Wings of Sunset,* a title she liked and used. "Wish the poems were worth it," she said.[12]

KPO radio thought they were. From a one-room station on the sixth floor of Hale Brothers department store on Sutter Street, a broadcaster read Ina's "Call of the Forests" during Fire Prevention Week in June 1924. They read more of her poems on March 10, 1925, her eighty-fourth birthday. A few days later, Clark Ashton Smith sent a letter with belated birthday wishes. He had read about the broadcasting of her poems in the newspaper and wrote, "It is good to know that one true poet, at least, is not without honor. Surely you deserve it, and more."[13]

Ina was asked by printer John Henry Nash to write an introduction to a folio printing of Bret Harte's "Plain Language from Truthful James," a special broadside designed and printed by Nash for his friends. The resulting eight-page essay gave her the opportunity to talk about those days in her own words. It also allowed her to express her gratitude for being associated with Harte during the "golden era of California literature."[14] She depicted the early San Francisco days as full of laughter and genius, and told stories about Harte as if he were family. She talked about his rise to fame with pride and said it was a sad day for California when he left for the East, a day she believed was sad for him too. She had heard that when he saw the Alps for the first time, he was not impressed. "I have known the Sierras!" he explained.[15]

Ina found out that it was Bender who had suggested that she write the introduction, and she thanked him for it:

> When I die some few will shortly say: "O, she? Yes,
> she was that aborigine who used to scribble dog-
> gerel in those primitive days. Quite forgotten now,
> of course." But you will carry your record beyond,
> imperishably. And sometimes I'll pipe up in some
> corner to add my quota: "I knew him. He was aw-

fully good to me back there on that queer little
Planet—what did they call it? O yes, the Earth,
I believe. Sort of odd and even place; not much
good, but he was tip-top."[16]

Bender had prodded Ina in his gentle and persistent way to finish
her memoirs, and she told him and others that she was working on
them. At one point he even offered to pay for an amanuensis to help
her finish, but she declined. "I must have solitude for my writing,
which I can depend. I never was able to fully command that except
during the four winters I passed in New York, when I was for the first
and only time—*Free*."[17] In spite of her promises, there is no evidence
today of a manuscript—either partial or complete. In New York she
had told a reporter, "Were I to write what I know, the book would be
too sensational to print; but were I to write what I think proper, the
book would be too dull to sell."[18]

On October 30, 1925, Charles Fletcher Lummis accompanied Ina to
an event held in her honor. Several women's clubs and the Parent-
Teacher Association sponsored a program at the Civic Auditorium
where children sang and danced for her. At the end of the program, a
curly-haired boy stepped up in his white sailor shirt to give Ina flowers and a wreath of laurel while five hundred schoolchildren gave
her a standing ovation. In those days, every child in school memorized poetry as part of their education. These children had grown up
reading and knowing the poetry written by Ina Coolbrith, the most
beloved poet in California. Lummis told Ina that the tribute should
make her feel as if she had lived a worthwhile life. "They could drill
school children to whoop it up for some great patriotic event; but to
pay homage to a Mere Poet [sic] means a foundation under the children, under the teachers, under the community which no fakir nor
politician nor hurry-up cause can command."[19]

During his month-long stay in San Francisco, Lummis visited
Ina several times. On one occasion he brought his guitar and played
Spanish songs for her and author J. Torrey Connor. How beautiful

Portrait of Ina Coolbrith with Popcorn, undated.
Photograph by Ansel Adams. Courtesy California
Historical Society and The Ansel Adams Publishing
Rights Trust.

it was, said Connor, to spend the day with "friends who speak my
language ... who are content to sit for a quiet hour with music."[20]
Before he returned to Los Angeles, Lummis visited one last time
and found Ina sitting in an armchair by the window with the sun
streaming onto her white robe. Ina Lillian said that he knelt in front
of her, took her hands, and put his face to them. "Ina!" was all he
said. It would be the last time he saw her, though they continued to

communicate. At the end of that year he send a card that said, "Precious Ina, Of Ours, Wishing you the best ever New Year and the desire of your heart. God love you—*I do!*"[21]

Seyfforth needed more money to pay for his medical treatments and convalescing, and Ina responded. On Christmas Eve she wrote a long, heartfelt letter to James Phelan saying that she feared Seyfforth would take his own life, as he had tried once before, and that she wanted to provide him hope by getting a pledge from her friends to commit twenty dollars a month for his care. "I know him for the most absolute genius who ever came into my life," she said sincerely. She told Phelan she had read Seyfforth's memoir, *Ulven*. "[It] gave me his inmost soul and I honor it," she said.[22] Phelan replied one month later that he knew of Seyfforth and had read his book, which left him with a bad impression. Since her appeal was so earnest, however, he said he would send twenty dollars a month in hopes it would help.

With the money Ina raised from Phelan and others, Seyfforth returned to New York. He visited Ina's New York doctor, who recommended a desert climate, but Seyfforth remained in the city. The doctor wrote Ina, "He will probably burn out his life pretty quickly, but in any event he will do it in his own way."[23]

In the January 1926 issue of the *Literary Digest International Book Review*, writer Maurice Andrews published a profile of Ina. He sent a copy of it to her along with a note: "You are the greatest American woman living, and it is the moral obligation of America, or at least of literary America, to pay homage to your high and noble purposes … The Fate is unjust in denying you recognition, a natural recognition which is yours according to all laws of heaven and earth."[24] He claimed that Ina had quit writing because she was discouraged with life. Lummis agreed and scolded her for it:

> You have nothing to be disappointed about, precious Ina! You surely can't be disappointed in what you have written—unless that you would like to have written more. You have struck the true note, beyond question or cavil. If it is largely a minor note of sadness—that detracts nothing from its value or its rank, for it is the privilege of the poet to

be sad—in fact, it is almost his duty ... You know
my heart is always with you, and that I have a very
deep and very vital and very reverent affection for
you. Which all the more exacerbates my vain wish
that I might have had you about 40 years ago to
give you a good shaking and lug you to Acoma and
to Zuñi and a few hundred other places that God
Made on Purpose, and among a people who are still
unspoiled as He made 'em![25]

Poet Eufina C. Tompkins also rebuked Ina for her depressed attitude. "One who has accomplished what you have in life; who has made for herself so secure a place in the romance history and poetry of the fairest spot on earth, you should sing a song of thanks and joyfulness, not one of lamentation."[26] Tompkins invited Ina to take a different view. "Let us sit up on the front seat of the go-cart and face the wind."

When Ina's brother congratulated her on the Andrews article, she replied:

Mr. Andrews meant well—but God save the mark
... My work, nearly all done in girlhood, I feel a
failure, a pitiful failure and denial; a blasphemy
against the Altar of the God of Mind and Melody.
No one can realize in the least what a shell it is
to me, because I know what it is and should have
been; what a wickedness my whole life has been
forced to be against its truer self.[27]

Ina was not the only female writer of her time to feel disappointed in her work. By age forty-one, Mary Austin believed she had missed the chance of being a great writer. Mina Loy, a Greenwich Village bohemian poet, was in her thirties when she wrote in her journal, "In the end a woman is defeated by life, whether she cares about others' opinions or not."[28] The Mama of New York's Dada, the Baroness Elsa von Freytag-Loringhoven, ended her days in Germany, lost without her art. She wrote poet Djuna Barnes, "I cannot any more conceive of the idea of a decent artist existence for me, and another is not possible ... Forgive me, but I am mourning destruction of high quality, as I know myself to be ... That is the tragedy; I still feel deep in me glittering wealth."[29]

Not all women writers gave in to despair, and at least one female California writer refused to be vanquished by age. At sixty-four, Gertrude Atherton took hormone therapy to stimulate her ovaries into premenopausal function and get her literary juices flowing. On her eighty-fourth birthday in 1941, Atherton said, "I've buried ten generations of critics, have written forty-five or fifty books and still have something to say."[30]

Ina turned eighty-five years old on March 10, 1926. On her previous birthday, Sterling had brought a bouquet of California wildflowers, and aviatrix Lillian Gatlin flew in from the Sierras with a clump of mistletoe still attached to the branch of an oak. Other visitors included David Starr Jordan, Benjamin Ide Wheeler, Luther Burbank, Charmian London, and Kathleen Norris. But those who came to her door on her eighty-fifth birthday were turned away. She was too ill to receive them.

In June, Ina Lillian moved the household to a two-story brown shingle house in Berkeley so Ina Agnes could be near the university. Ina's rheumatism and bad mood flared. "I am to finish the burial in Berkeley because the *kid* wants to live on campus."[31]

23

"Dew before Dawn"

In late September 1926, Joan London stood next to Ina at a party given in Ina's honor. The room was crowded to capacity when London saw Sterling enter with Rose Travis, a close friend who used the pseudonym Lawrence Zenda for the songs she and Sterling wrote. Sterling saw London and held up ten fingers to signify the number of days he had not had a drink. He and Rose made their way through the crowd to where Ina was sitting, and London noticed Ina's face light up when she saw him. Sterling asked Ina how things were going and she gestured for him to lean closer. London was close enough to hear Ina say, "They're so good to me here, George, but it's damned dull."[1]

Sterling was one of Ina's trues, and visited her frequently. She called him her lieutenant. In response to an invitation to join her for lunch, he accepted in shaky handwriting. She replied, "So glad you can come, George dear." On another occasion, Sterling wrote to apologize that a reporter had been referring to him as the laureate. He protested that it was through no fault of his own, and that he had set the writer straight. The crown was his by right, she replied, and would be passed to his brow soon enough. "Forgive your old friend for hanging on like the last leaf, under the impression of not being yet through with it all," she said.[2] On Sterling's last visit with Ina, they had dinner and talked about a new book about Jack London, *The Soul of Jack London*.

Sterling was on the wagon but was stocking up for a bender with journalist H. L. Mencken, who was coming to town. Sterling had collected bottles of whisky in his room at the Bohemian Club, and planned a dinner party for the evening of Mencken's arrival. But Mencken did not arrive on the expected day or the next, and didn't send word to Sterling for several days. Whether Sterling was upset with Mencken or if he just couldn't wait to have a drink isn't clear. Regardless, he sat in his room by himself and drank the bottles of whiskey.

When Mencken finally did arrive, he found Sterling drunk and ill. Sterling stayed home while Mencken and others met for dinner at writer Idwal Jones's house. Another dinner was planned for the following night, and when Mencken knocked on Sterling's door to see if he was attending, there was no answer. The door was locked and Mencken could see through the transom that Sterling's light was out.

All of Sterling's friends, including Mencken, thought it was just a matter of time before Sterling acted on his obsession with suicide. Joan London said, "When I knew George in those last years he was a bitter, cynical, disillusioned man, with his face set toward death."[3]

On November 18 after no one had seen Sterling for at least twenty-four hours, the Bohemian Club manager entered Sterling's room and found him dead. Police determined that he had ingested cyanide the day before. Scattered on the floor among the empty bottles were bits of burned poems and letters, only a few words of which were readable, such as "And conches faintly blown on haunted shores, heard when the fog's white dusk is on the sea."

In a eulogy written for the *San Francisco Examiner*, Idwal Jones said he had been with Sterling earlier that month in a dense fog at midnight. They had walked arm in arm before saying goodnight on a corner. "I hope the best thing anyone will say about me is that 'George was a Roman for friendship,'" said Sterling. Jones watched him disappear into the fog "with his shapeless hat oddly perched on his gray hair." Jones closed his tribute with a stanza from Sterling's poem that celebrated the healing power of fog:

Though the dark be cold and blind
Yet her sea fog's touch is kind,
And her mightier caress
Is joy and pain thereof;
And great is thy tenderness,
O cool, gray city of love![4]

"What dew before the dawn we are!" Ina wrote Bender. "Poor George! Dear George! Glorious George! Beloved George Sterling!"[5] She said Sterling had no right, for his act deprived the world of what he still had to give. Ina considered him to be the greatest living poet, and felt certain that had he known it, he would not have taken his own life. She mourned the fact that he ended his days before God's plan for him was up, and prayed that God could mend "this broken destiny."[6] Bender replied that he, too, was heartbroken. "I have not the usual attitude toward suicide and feel that he solved his problem in his own way for his own good ... but I am sorry for ourselves, for the loss of an incomparable friend."[7] A reporter asked Ina why poets commit suicide. She replied that suicide was a weakness, and poetry was not to blame. Poetry was satisfying to her, she said, but not her own. If she could start all over again and have the time to write she would. "I feel the longing to work desperately!"[8]

Ina turned eighty-six on March 10, 1927. As was usual, her friends and fans came to her house in Berkeley to wish her well. An *Oakland Tribune* reporter asked if she had a birthday greeting for the people of California. Ina reiterated that she believed California would lead the nation in beauty, achievement, and culture. When the reporter wished Ina many more birthdays, she replied, "Please don't ... I want to live only as long as I am of use to the world. When I am no longer of service, I want to die and make place for someone who can serve."[9]

One visitor that day was W. W. Campbell, the president of the University of California, who came with a proclamation from the governor of California that named Ina the state's representative to the Women's World's Fair at Chicago in May. Several days later, writer Charles Phillips, who had taken a job at Notre Dame University, heard the news and urged her to come. "I'll meet you in Chicago and be your beau all the time you're here ... I have some savings, saved for some sort of a treat or holiday. Let it be this, please, my dear. I'll take care of everything the minute you step from the train."[10] Phillips adored Ina. He was fifty years younger than she, yet his letters to here were as intimate as love letters. In one he said, "Oh, how I long to see you—be with you—talk with you ... You have been always a *light* in my life. I live over again those perfect days when I was able to go to you and draw and draw on the fountain of your love ... I do need you so—just to run to you, and laugh a little—and then rest my old head in your lap ... I love you always! You do know it—believe it—don't you?"[11]

Lummis had asked her what she wanted for her eighty-sixth birthday, and she replied,

> I want lots of things. The blasted *dinero* for one,
> and feet that I can use as I once did, and a head
> that has an idea in it at least once a century, and
> my friends here that I love, and to know a few
> things that God, or whatever stands for God, won't
> let me *know*. Will you answer me one of my ques-
> tions? Why am I given to know so much more than
> ever before what there is to do in this life and the
> value of it now that the *power*, physical and mental,
> are no longer mine? *Dear Man Who Has Lived*, tell
> me that![12]

Lummis replied,

> We have come to the mountaintop, and all the
> kingdoms of the earth are spread at our feet. We
> haven't the sinew to run down the peak to the foot
> and remedy this, that, and the other, there, and
> then skip back to the summit to see how much bet-
> ter we have made the world. But we have the power
> to look on the glory and the wonder of all that is,
> with a certain understanding and richness that

the climber never sees ... God bless you dear Ina!
Cheer up![13]

But that was no longer possible, especially after Seyfforth died on September 26, 1927. Coming as it did within a year of Sterling's suicide, her boy's death rendered Ina faithless. She asked poet Eufina C. Tompkins if she could offer the comfort of "unquestioning faith ... [or] any word of certainty."[14] Tompkins said she put her faith in science.

Ina was unable to attend the Women's World's Fair, so Charles Phillips came to her in late December. He helped finalize plans for her last collection, which included her New York work mixed with a few of her classics. They did not finish and Phillips promised to return the following summer. Ina asked Phillips to finish putting the poems in order, write a foreword, and submit *Wings of Sunset* to Houghton Mifflin if she should not last until summer.

Ina lived two months more. She died on leap day, February 29, 1928, ten days before her eighty-seventh birthday. The memorial service was held two days later in St. Mark's Episcopal Church in Berkeley where UC English professor Lionel Stevenson recited Ina's "Beside the Dead." Two hundred mourners listened to the poem that she had written more than fifty years earlier:

> It must be sweet, O thou, my dead, to lie
> With hands that folded are from every task;
> Sealed with the seal of the great mystery,
> The lips that nothing answer, nothing ask.
> The life-long struggle ended; ended quite
> The weariness of patience, and of pain,
> And the eyes closed to open not again
> On desolate dawn or dreariness of night.
> It must be sweet to slumber and forget;
> To have the poor tired heart so still, at last:
> Done with all yearning, done with all regret,
> Doubt, fear, hope, sorrow, all forever past;
> Past all the hours, or slow of wing or fleet—
> It must be sweet, it must be very sweet![15]

At the beautiful Mountain View Cemetery in Oakland, ten pall-bearers carried Ina's coffin to her resting place next to her mother. The coffin was lowered into a grave that would remain unmarked by a headstone for nearly sixty years.

Four days after Ina's funeral, the *New York Sun* revealed her Mormon ancestry for the first time. The news came as a shock to almost all of her fans and friends. Bob Davis, the reporter who broke the story, said only that his anonymous source was "one who was close to Ina Coobrith."[16] It was likely Bio De Casseres.

After Ina left the Church of Jesus Christ of Latter-day Saints, she didn't subscribe to any one particular religion, although she continued to believe in God. After the deaths of Sterling and Seyfforth, her certainly of God eroded, but she never lost faith in poetry. It was her comfort, her religion, and her savior. She believed in the importance of putting pen to paper, and that fervent belief was her gift to the young state of California. She also had an unwavering love for the natural beauty of the state and its ability to inspire. From her hotel room in New York, she wrote about the trees, mountains, and sunsets in the West. She attempted to capture the essence of the fog rolling in at the Gate, the ephemeral nature of a poppy, and the springtime snow of orchards. Charles Keeler summarized Ina's life best when he wrote:

> The amazing thing to me is how a child of the real Wild West, born in Illinois in the stormy opening years of the Mormon Church, in the family of its founders, crossing the plains in a pioneer wagon train, through herds of bison and antelope, with bands of hostile Indians to threaten them, wandering in pioneer days of California to the Mexican pueblo of Los Angeles, and with the schooling afforded there, blossoming into a poet with the artistry of an English Tennyson—how such a thing could be possible! Yet this miracle actually happened.[17]

Ina was critical of her own work. She held it up to the great poets who had come before her and found it wanting. With just two years of a formal high school education, she was always first in line to admit that she had not reached her potential. And yet, she didn't lose faith in the act itself. When once asked which was her favorite poem, she replied, "The poem I haven't written."[18]

Epilogue:
The Ina Coolbrith Circle

What use the questioning? This thing we are:
A breath called life, housed for a little space
In how infinitesimal a star ...

—Ina Coolbrith, "The Unsolvable," 1919–23

When Ina Donna Coolbrith attended the Ina Coolbrith Circle for the last time on December 18, 1927, she asked the group to "keep the history and the literature—the glory of California—alive in the world."[1] The first thing they did shortly after she died was to petition the national and state geographic boards to name a mountain after her. After two years of wrangling they succeeded in changing the name of Summit Peak, an eight-thousand-foot crest at the junction of Plumas, Lassen, and Sierra counties six miles south of Beckwourth Pass, to Mount Ina Coolbrith.

The Ina Coolbrith Circle still meets today, with its monthly programs and annual poetry contests promoting California and its writers. The Circle also works to keep Ina Coolbrith's memory alive. In the 1980s they installed a plaque at the top of Ina Coolbrith Park on San Francisco's Russian Hill and marked her grave with a pink marble headstone. In 1991 they installed a plaque in the Oakland Public Library, and since 2004 they have maintained an Ina Coolbrith Circle Collection at the California State Library, which as of 2014 consisted of nearly three hundred poetry books by Circle members.[2]

Notes

These abbreviations are used in the notes:

Bancroft—The Bancroft Library, University of California, Berkeley.

C-S Huntington—Coolbrith-Stoddard correspondence. These items are reproduced by permission of The Huntington Library, San Marino, California.

Huntington—These items are reproduced by permission of The Huntington Library, San Marino, California.

IDC Bancroft—Ina Donna Coolbrith Collection of Letters and Papers (ca. 1865–1928), The Bancroft Library, University of California, Berkeley.

IDC Huntington—Ina Donna Coolbrith Papers. These items are reproduced by permission of The Huntington Library, San Marino, California.

LDS Library—Church History Library, The Church of Jesus Christ of Latter-day Saints.

Mills College—Special Collections, F. W. Olin Library, Mills College.

Scrapbooks OPL—Ina Coolbrith Scrapbooks, Volumes I & II. Courtesy Oakland Public Library, Oakland History Room.

Prologue
Epigraph: Ina Coolbrith, "Renewal," *Century Magazine*, May 1909.
1. Nancy Barr Mavity, "California poet symbolizes spirit of days of gold," *San Francisco Chronicle*, September 11, 1921.

2. Edward F. O'Day, "The Laureate of California," *The Lantern*, November 1917.

3. Ina Coolbrith to Don Carlos Pickett, June 14, 1926. IDC Huntington.

4. Ulv Youff, *Ulven* (London: Chapman & Dodd, 1923).

5. Coolbrith to Robert Norman, n.d. [ca. 1919], IDC Bancroft.

6. Coolbrith to Ella Sterling Cummins Mighels, May 30, [1917?], Ina Coolbrith Correspondence, California History Room, California State Library, Sacramento, CA.

Part I: Searching for Home
Epigraph: Edward Pollock, "Chandos Picture," *Outcroppings: Being Selections of California Verse* (San Francisco: A. Roman and Company, 1866).

Chapter 1

1. Ina Coolbrith, "Gossip: Personal Reminiscences of Early California Writers" (lecture, Pacific Coast Women's Press Association, San Francisco, CA, April 10, 1911), IDC Bancroft.

2. Ibid.

3. Ina Coolbrith to Joseph F. Smith, March 19, 1857, LDS Library.

4. Edward F. O'Day, "The Laureate of California," *The Lantern*, November 1917.

5. Ella Sterling Cummins, *The Story of the Files: A Review of Californian Writers and Literature* (San Francisco: World's Fair Commission of California, Columbian Exposition, 1893).

6. Jeanne E. Francoeur, "Ina Coolbrith, Our Poet—In the Past and Present," *The Woman Citizen*, October 1913.

7. Gertrude Atherton, "The Pearls of Loreto," *The Splendid Idle Forties* (Kentfield, CA: Allen Press, 1960).

8. Coolbrith, "Gossip," IDC Bancroft.

9. Ibid.

10. Edward Pollock, "Evening," *Poems of Places, An Anthology in 31 Volumes*, Henry Wadsworth Longfellow, ed. (Boston: James R. Osgood & Co., 1876–79).

11. Coolbrith, "Gossip," IDC Bancroft.

12. Ibid.

13. Pollock, "Chandos Picture," *Outcroppings*.

14. Coolbrith, "My Childhood's Home," *Los Angeles Star*, August 30, 1856.

15. Joseph Smith III called Ina "Cousin Inez" in his memoirs (Mary Audentia Smith Anderson, ed.), *Joseph Smith III and the Restoration* (Independence, MO: Herald Publishing House, 1952). There is some debate whether her first name is pronounced EE-na or Eye-na. See: Aleta George, "The 'Eye' in Ina Coolbrith," *San Francisco Chronicle*, March 28, 2014.

16. Coolbrith, "My Ideal Home," *Los Angeles Star*, August 22, 1857.

17. Coolbrith, "Gossip," IDC Bancroft.

18. John Rollin Ridge, *Marysville Express* (found in Scrapbooks, n.d., Oakland Public Library).

19. Ina Coolbrith, "One," *Wings of Sunset* (Boston: Houghton Mifflin, 1929), first written as an inscription to Charles Fletcher Lummis.

20. George Wharton James, "Ina Donna Coolbrith: An Historical Sketch and Appreciation," *National Magazine*, June 1907.

21. Kenneth N. Owens, *Gold Rush Saints: California Mormons and the Great Rush for Riches* (Norman: University of Oklahoma Press, 2004).

22. Edward Leo Lyman, Susan Ward Payne, and S. George Ellsworth, eds., *No Place to Call Home: The 1807–1857 Life Writings of Caroline Barnes Crosby, Chronicler of Outlying Mormon Communities* (Logan, UT: Utah State University Press, 2005).

23. Joseph F. Smith to Ina Coolbrith, April 20, 1918, JFS-LDS Library.

24. Ibid.

Chapter 2

1. Coolbrith, "Lines on the Recent Massacre," *Los Angeles Star*, January 26, 1857.

2. Jon Krakauer, *Under the Banner of Heaven: A Story of Violent Faith* (New York: Random House, 2003).

3. *San Francisco Daily Alta California*, April 5, 1854.

4. Crosby, *No Place to Call Home*.

5. Coolbrith to Joseph F. Smith, July 22, 1857, LDS Library.
6. Ibid.
7. Ibid.
8. Ibid.
9. Joseph F. Smith to Coolbrith, September 1, 1857, LDS Library.
10. Coolbrith to Joseph F. Smith, July 22, 1857, LDS Library.
11. Ibid.
12. Ibid.
13. Ibid.
14. Joseph F. Smith to Coolbrith, September 1, 1857, LDS Library.
15. Coolbrith to Joseph F. Smith, July 22, 1857, LDS Library.
16. Joseph F. Smith to Coolbrith, September 1, 1857, LDS Library.
17. Coolbrith to Joseph F. Smith, March 19, 1857, LDS Library.
18. Joseph F. Smith to Coolbrith, September 1, 1857, LDS Library.
19. Todd Compton, *In Sacred Loneliness: The Plural Wives of Joseph Smith* (Salt Lake City: Signature Books, 1997).
20. Agnes Smith to George A. Smith, June 3, 1846, George A. Smith papers, LDS Library.
21. Jane Rae Fuller Topham, *In Search of Living Water: Biography of Susanna Mehetable Rogers Sangiovanni Pickett Keate*, unpublished.
22. Ibid.
23. Compton, *In Sacred Loneliness*.
24. Topham, *In Search of Living Water*.
25. Joseph F. Smith to Coolbrith, April 20, 1918, LDS Library.
26. Thomas P. Brown, *Western Pacific News Service*, February 15, 1932.
27. Hampton Sides, *Blood and Thunder: The Epic Story of Kit Carson and the Conquest of the American West* (New York: Anchor Books, 2006).
28. Coolbrith to John Smith, July 30, 1908, LDS Library.

Chapter 3

1. Coolbrith, "Fragment from an Unfinished Poem," in May Wentworth, ed., *Poetry of the Pacific: Selections and Original Poems from the Poets of the Pacific States* (San Francisco: Pacific Publishing Company, 1867).
2. Coolbrith, "Cupid Kissed Me," *Californian*, August 13, 1864.
3. Ina Coolbrith, "Spiders," unpublished, Scrapbooks OPL.
4. Robert Carsley to Abel Stearns, May 27, 1859, Huntington.
5. Ina Cook, "Memories of Ina Coolbrith" (lecture, place unknown, date unknown, note cards for lecture found in Oakland Public Library).
6. Jesse Winter Smith, interview by Norma Ricketts, June 24, 1965, shared with author.
7. Coolbrith, "Rebuke," *Overland Monthly*, February 1869.
8. Coolbrith, "A Mother's Grief," *Californian*, 25 March 1865.
9. Coolbrith, "In the Night, to my Mother," *California Home Journal*, July 1861.
10. Ibid.
11. The details of Agnes's river crossing come from Lucy Mack Smith, *Joseph Smith's History by His Mother*, and H. S. Salisbury, "Josephine Donna Smith—Ina Coolbrith," *The Improvement Era*, 1950.
12. Fawn M. Brodie, *No Man Knows My History: The Life of Joseph Smith* (New York: Alfred A. Knopf, 1945, renewed 1973).
13. Compton, *In Sacred Loneliness*.
14. Ibid.
15. Krakauer, *Under the Banner of Heaven*.
16. Coolbrith, "In the Night, to my Mother," *California Home Journal*, July 1861.
17. Los Angeles County, District Court, Case #853, December 26, 1861, Huntington. (All the quotes during this scene are taken from the divorce trial.)
18. Ibid.
19. Ibid.
20. Coolbrith, "In the Pouts," *Californian*, February 11, 1865.
21. Coolbrith, "Pancho," *Wings of Sunset* (New York: Houghton Mifflin Company, 1929).

22. Coolbrith, "San Francisco: April 18, 1906," *Wings of Sunset.*

Part II: San Francisco
Epigraph: Benjamin De Casseres, "Ina Coolbrith of California's 'Overland Trinity'," *The Sun*, December 7, 1919.

Chapter 4
1. James M. Parker, *San Francisco Directory of 1852–53* (San Francisco: James M. Parker, 1852).
2. Louis Laurent Simonin, "California Women," *More San Francisco Memoirs, 1852–1899: The Ripening Years*, Malcolm E. Barker, ed., (San Francisco: Londonborn Publications, 1996).
3. Josephine Clifford McCrackin, "Reminiscences of Bret Harte and Pioneer Days in the West," *Overland Monthly*, November 1915.
4. Marian Taylor, "Ina Coolbrith, California Poet," *Overland Monthly*, October 1914.
5. Ibid.
6. Coolbrith, "Unrest," *Los Angeles Star*, November 22, 1862.
7. Ina Lillian Cook, "Ina Coolbrith: Some Impressions and Recollections," *The Wasp-News Letter*, December 22–29, 1928.
8. Starr King School for the Ministry, http://www.sksm.edu/.
9. Ibid.
10. Oscar P. Fitzgerald, excerpt from *California Sketches New and Old* (1894); reprinted in *More San Francisco Memoirs (1852–1899): The Ripening Years*, Malcolm E. Barker, compiler and editor (San Francisco: Londonborn Publications, 1996).
11. William Day Simonds, *Starr King in California* (San Francisco: Paul Elder & Company, 1917).
12. Charles Webb, *The Golden Era*, Sunday, March 6, 1864.
13. Thomas Starr King to James T. Fields, January 31, 1862, Huntington Library.
14. Franklin Walker, *San Francisco's Literary Frontier* (New York: Alfred A. Knopf, 1939).
15. Coolbrith, JGW [John Greenleaf Whittier], December 13, 1909, Oakland Public Library.

16. Coolbrith, "Christmas Eve: 1863," *Golden Era*, December 27, 1863.
17. Ibid.
18. Charles Henry Webb, *The Golden Era*, Sunday, March 6, 1864.

Chapter 5
1. Coolbrith to Bio DeCasseras, n.d. [post-1924], LDS Library.
2. Coolbrith, "Gossip," IDC Bancroft.
3. Ibid.
4. Ibid.
5. Ibid. In her speech, Ina said this incident took place just before Webb left for New York, but she also said it happened after he sold the magazine. It makes more sense that it occurred before he went on vacation in Tahoe because Ina already knew Harte before Webb left for New York one year later.
6. Walker, *San Francisco's Literary Frontier*, p. 179.
7. Coolbrith, "Meg Merriliana," *Californian*, February 4, 1865.
8. Ibid.
9. Harte to Coolbrith, June 3, 1865, IDC Bancroft.
10. Walker, *San Francisco's Literary Frontier*.
11. Ibid.
12. *The Nation*, n.d., Scrapbooks OPL.
13. "Longfellow Praises Pomes of Noted California Poetess," *Sacramento, Cal Union*, March 31, 1920.
14. Coolbrith, "Gossip," IDC Bancroft.
15. Ibid.
16. Ibid.
17. Lucy Mack Smith. *Joseph Smith's History by His Mother* (Utah Lighthouse Ministry, 1853).
18. Coolbrith, "Gossip," IDC Bancroft.
19. *Golden Era*, "Three Poets at a Poet's Grave," nd. Scrapbooks OPL.
20. Ina Coolbrith, "A Poet's Grave at Lone Mountain," *Californian*, March 10, 1866.
21. John Rollin Ridge, "October Hills," *Poems* (San Francisco: Henry Payot & Co. Publishers, 1868).

Chapter 6

1. Charles Warren Stoddard, *In the Footprints of the Padres* (San Francisco: A. M. Robertson, 1901).
2. Francis Bret Harte, "Etc." *Overland Monthly*, December 1868.
3. Adeline Knapp, "The Blessed Hills of San Francisco," *San Francisco Call*, February 19, 1896.
4. Coolbrith, "Longing," *Overland Monthly*, July 1868.
5. Coolbrith, introduction to a special printing of Bret Harte, "Plain Language from Truthful James (The Heathen Chinee)" (San Francisco: John Henry Nash, 1924).
6. Ina Lillian Cook, "Ina Coolbrith: Some Impressions and Recollections," *The Wasp-News Letter*, December 22–29, 1928.
7. Coolbrith, notes on a speech about Charles Warren Stoddard, given to Oakland's Ebell Club on November 1, 1923, IDC Bancroft.
8. Stoddard, *In the Footprints of the Padres*.
9. Charles Warren Stoddard, "Ina D. Coolbrith," *The Magazine of Poetry*, 1 (1889).
10. Ibid.
11. Cook, "Ina Coolbrith: Some Impressions and Recollections."
12. Coolbrith to Stoddard, March 11, 1868, C-S Huntington.
13. Ibid.
14. Coolbrith to Stoddard, March 20, 1868, C-S Huntington.
15. Coolbrith, Ebell Club speech, IDC Bancroft.
16. Ibid.
17. Roger Austen, *Genteel Pagan: The Double Life of Charles Warren Stoddard* (Amherst: University of Massachusetts Press, 1991, p. 29).
18. Ibid.
19. *San Francisco Call*, "A Holiday on Olympus," July 28, 1895.
20. Nigey Lennon, *The Sagebrush Bohemian: Mark Twain in California* (New York: Paragon House, 1990).
21. Raine Bennett, "Sappho of the Western Sea," *Touring Topics*, November 1933.
22. Coolbrith, introduction to Harte, "Plain Language from Truthful James (The Heathen Chinee)."
23. In an undated statement from an unidentified source in the

Bancroft Library is an account of Stoddard's performance as Twain's secretary. "It was not required of Mr. Stoddard that he furnish any conversation—it was simply his duty to seem amused at the conversation of Mr. Clemens and Mr. Dolby [his agent]. This duty however he did not adequately perform. Instead of laughing boisterously at the conversation, he merely chuckled now and then, and in no wise earned his salary in this respect. It was expected of him that he should at least keep awake and listen. Again he failed. He did not listen and he did not keep awake. He went to sleep and interrupted the conversation with a species of snore, which he had acquired in some foreign part. Aside from these trifling defects, Mr. Clemens found him a most delightful companion and comrade." IDC Bancroft.

24. Coolbrith to Stoddard, August 27, 1873, C-S Huntington.
25. Lennon, *The Sagebrush Bohemian.*
26. Benjamin De Casseres, "Ina Coolbrith of California's 'Overland Monthly,'" *The Sun*, December 7, 1919.
27. Coolbrith, "Longing," *Overland Monthly*, July 1868.
28. Ambrose Bierce, n.d., *San Francisco News Letter*, Scrapbooks OPL.
29. Coolbrith, "Longing," *Overland Monthly*, July 1868.
30. Harte to Coolbrith (Ina wrote on the back of this letter), July 16, 1868, IDC Bancroft.
31. Harte to Coolbrith, July 22, 1868, IDC Bancroft.
32. Coolbrith, "Gossip," IDC Bancroft.
33. Coolbrith, introduction to Harte, "Plain Language from Truthful James (The Heathen Chinee)."
34. Ina Coolbrith, "In Blossom Time," *Overland Monthly*, August 1868.
35. Coolbrith, A Recollection of Francis Bret Harte and Charles Warren Stoddard, IDC Huntington.
36. Ibid.
37. Coolbrith, "Gossip," IDC Bancroft.
38. Coolbrith, Recollection, IDC Huntington.
39. Josephine Clifford McCracken, "Reminiscences of Bret Harte," *Overland Monthly*, September 1902.
40. Coolbrith, "Gossip," IDC Bancroft.

41. Coolbrith, Recollection, IDC Huntington.
42. "Court of Last Appeal," *Dramatic Chronicle*, Scrapbooks OPL.
43. Coolbrith, "Gossip," IDC Bancroft.
44. Noah Brooks, "Bret Harte: A Biographical and Critical Sketch," *Overland Monthly*, September 1902.
45. Coolbrith to Laurie Haynes Martin, February 9, 1912, IDC Huntington.
46. Ina Coolbrith, "When the Grass Shall Cover Me," *Overland Monthly*, November 1868.
47. Coolbrith to Stoddard, January 9, 1869, C-S Huntington.
48. Roger Austen, *Genteel Pagan* (Citation: Horace Traubel, *With Walt Whitman in Camden*, vol. 4, Philadelphia: University of Pennsylvania Press, 1953, pp. 267–69).
49. Austen, *Genteel Pagan*.
50. Coolbrith to Stoddard, January 9, 1869, IDC Huntington.

Chapter 7
1. Evelyn Wells, "Ina Coolbrith Spurns Another Birthday," *San Francisco Call*, March 8, 1924.
2. Charles Warren Stoddard, "The Magazine of Poetry: A Quarterly Review, Volume 1," January-October 1889.
3. Catharine E. Beecher, *Miss Beecher's Housekeeper and Health-keeper*, (New York: Harper & Bros., 1874).
4. Henry George, "What the Railroad will Bring Us," *Overland Monthly*, October 1868.
5. Bret Harte, "What the Engines Said: Opening of the Pacific Railroad," *Yale Book of American Verse*, Thomas R. Lounsbury, ed. (New Haven: Yale University Press, 1912).
6. Coolbrith, "Gossip," IDC Bancroft.
7. Brett Page, "So This Is San Francisco," 1925 (clipping found in Scrapbooks, OPL, with no publication given).
8. Charles Warren Stoddard, "A South-sea Idyl," *Overland Monthly*, September 1869.
9. Ibid.
10. Austen, *Genteel Pagan*.
11. Franklin Walker, *San Francisco's Literary Frontier* (New York: Alfred A. Knopf, 1939).

12. Coolbrith, "The Coming," *Overland Monthly*, August 1869.
13. Coolbrith, "The Road to School," *Overland Monthly*, February 1872.
14. Coolbrith, "If Only," *Overland Monthly*, July 1870.
15. Coolbrith, "Just for a Day," *Overland Monthly*, January 1871.
16. Horace Traubel, *With Walt Whitman in Camden*, vol. 3 (Philadelphia: University of Pennsylvania Press, 1961).
17. Edwin Haviland Miller, Editor, *Walt Whitman; The Correspondence*, (New York: New York University Press, 1961-69).
18. Coolbrith, lecture, Tribute to Joaquin Miller, IDC Bancroft.
19. Walker, *San Francisco's Literary Frontier*.
20. Charles Warren Stoddard, *Exits and Entrances: A Book of Essays and Sketches* (Boston: Lothrop Publishing Company, 1903).
21. Ibid.
22. Coolbrith, lecture, Tribute to Joaquin Miller, IDC Bancroft.
23. Stoddard, *Exits and Entrances*.
24. Bret Harte, *Overland Monthly*, April 1870.
25. Letter addressed to "My Dear Friend" [Unknown], February 8, 1927, Oakland Public Library.
26. Coolbrith, "With a Wreath of Laurel," *Overland Monthly*, September 1870.
27. Harte to Coolbrith, January 28, 1869, IDC Bancroft.
28. Harte to Coolbrith, May 31, no year, IDC Bancroft.
29. Ibid.
30. Coolbrith, introduction to Harte, "Plain Language from Truthful James (The Heathen Chinee)."
31. Coolbrith, "Gossip," IDC Bancroft.
32. Ibid.
33. Coolbrith, introduction to Harte, "Plain Language from Truthful James (The Heathen Chinee)."
34. Letter from Coolbrith to Laurie Haynes Martin, Feb. 9, 1912, IDC Huntington.
35. Coolbrith, "An Emblem," *Overland Monthly*, February 1871.
36. Coolbrith, "Oblivion," *Overland Monthly*, May 1871.

Chapter 8

1. *San Francisco Call*, July 20, 1871.
2. Coolbrith, "California," July 19, 1871. Not published until included in *Songs from the Golden Gate*.
3. Introduction written by Coolbrith for a special printing of "California" by John Henry Nash and the California Book Club, 1918.
4. Coolbrith, "California."
5. Davidson, Marie Hicks, "Intimate Studies: Ina Coolbrith," *California Writers*, April 22, 1917.
6. Coolbrith, "California."
7. *San Francisco Newsletter*, July 22, 1871.
8. Coolbrith to Stoddard, January 26, 1871, C-S Huntington.
9. Coolbrith, "At the Hill's Base," *Overland Monthly*, January 1872.
10. "An Ending," *Overland Monthly*, May 1872.
11. Stoddard, *Exits and Entrances*.
12. Joaquin Miller, *Life Amongst the Modocs: Unwritten History* (Berkeley: Heyday Books, 1996). Originally published in 1873.
13. Coolbrith to Stoddard, May 4, 1872, C-S Huntington.
14. Miller, *Life Amongst the Modocs*.
15. Ibid.
16. Coolbrith to Stoddard, May 4, 1872, C-S Huntington.
17. Coolbrith to Stoddard, Thursday, January 26 (no year given, but I believe it is 1871), C-S Huntington.
18. Coolbrith to Stoddard, March 12, 1873, C-S Huntington.
19. Coolbrith, "Marah," *Overland Monthly*, June 1873.
20. Coolbrith to John Smith, July 30, 1908, LDS Library.
21. Coolbrith, "Beside the Dead," *Overland Monthly*, May 1875.
22. Coolbrith to Stoddard, August 27, 1873, C-S Huntington.
23. Coolbrith to Stoddard, May 25, 1874, C-S Huntington.
24. Coolbrith to Stoddard, October 1, 1874, C-S Huntington.
25. Coolbrith to Stoddard, Nov. 9, 1874, C-S Huntington.
26. Coolbrith, "A Prayer for Strength," *Overland Monthly*, August 1874.
27. Ibid.

28. Samuel Dickson, "Isadora Duncan," *Virtual Museum of the City of San Francisco*, http://www.sfmuseum.org/bio/isadora.html.
29. Coolbrith, "Freedom," *Songs from the Golden Gate* (New York: Houghton Mifflin Company, 1895).

Part III: Oakland
Epigraph: Coolbrith, "A Night of Storm," *Californian*, 1881.

Chapter 9
1. Coolbrith to Stoddard, May 9, 1875, C-S Huntington.
2. Ibid.
3. Ibid.
4. Ibid.
5. Coolbrith to Stoddard, May 15 [1875] (Ina did not include a year on this letter. The Huntington Library suggests it was written in 1872, but there are clues in the letter that date it at 1875), C-S Huntington.
6. Coolbrith to Stoddard, May 9, 1875, C-S Huntington.
7. Ibid.
8. Coolbrith to Stoddard, May 25, 1874, C-S Huntington
9. Josephine DeWitt Rhodehamel and Raymund Francis Wood, *Ina Coolbrith: Librarian and Laureate of California* (Provo, UT: Brigham Young University Press, 1973).
10. Coolbrith, Scrapbooks OPL.
11. John Muir to Jeanne Carr, May 4, 1875, John Muir Papers, Holt-Atherton Special Collections, University of the Pacific Library. © 1984 Muir-Hanna Trust.
12. Coolbrith to Stoddard, February 16, 1876, C-S Huntington.
13. Coolbrith to Grace Porter Hopkins, 1913, IDC Bancroft.
14. John Muir, "May–July 1877, Travels in Utah," John Muir Papers, Holt-Atherton Special Collections, University of the Pacific Library. © 1984 Muir-Hanna Trust.
15. Letter from Ina Coolbrith to John Muir and Louisa Muir, [1880], John Muir Papers, Holt-Atherton Special Collections, University of the Pacific Library. © 1984 Muir-Hanna Trust.
16. Coolbrith to Jeanne Carr, October 31, 1876, IDC Huntington.

17. Ibid.
18. Clipping (date and source unknown), Scrapbooks, OPL.
19. Coolbrith to Jeanne Carr, October 31, 1876, IDC Huntington.

Chapter 10

1. Coolbrith to Stoddard, no date, C-S Huntington.
2. Coolbrith to Judge Boalt, September 18, 1886, IDC Bancroft.
3. Minutes of the Oakland Library, April 2, 1880, OPL.
4. Minutes of the Oakland Library, August 3, 1880, OPL.
5. Austen, *Genteel Pagan*.
6. Bret Harte to J. H. Carmany, December 10, 1878, OPL.
7. Laura B. Everett to Coolbrith, May 2 [1925?], IDC Huntington.
8. Coolbrith to Stoddard, February 7, 1881, C-S Huntington.
9. Stoddard to Coolbrith, May 6, 1881, IDC Bancroft.
10. Edward Rowland Sill to Coolbrith, July 31, 1881, Scrapbooks, OPL.
11. John Greenleaf Whittier, undated, Scrapbook I, OPL.
12. Ambrose Bierce, *Wasp* (February 1883), Scrapbooks, OPL.
13. *San Francisco Chronicle*, no date, Scrapbooks, OPL.
14. *Oakland Tribune*, no date, Scrapbooks, OPL.
15. *Boston Courier*, June 19, 1881.
16. *Boston Saturday Gazette*, June 25, 1881.
17. *Vanity Fair*, August 13, 1881.
18. *Century Magazine*, December 1881, Scrapbooks, OPL.
19. Coolbrith to Stoddard, August 31, 1881, C-S Huntington.
20. Coolbrith to Stoddard, February 7, 1881, C-S Huntington.
21. Bierce, *Wasp*, February 1883.
22. Coolbrith to Jeanne Carr, October 31, 1876, IDC Huntington.

Chapter 11

1. Minutes of the Oakland Library, June 5, 1883, OPL.
2. Coolbrith to Stoddard, July 17, 1883, C-S Huntington.
3. Coolbrith to Stoddard, September 18, 1883, C-S Huntington.
4. Minutes of the Oakland Library, October 7, 1884, OPL.

5.   Minutes of the Oakland Library, December 4, 1883, OPL.
6.   Coolbrith to Donald McIntyre Graham, August 22, 1881, Margaret Collier Collection, Huntington.
7.   Coolbrith to Stoddard, September 18, 1883, C-S Huntington.
8.   Minutes of the Oakland Library, April 1, 1883, OPL.
9.   Ina Coolbrith to Henry Peterson, September 28, 1884, IDC Bancroft.
10. Coolbrith, JGW [John Greenleaf Whittier], December 13, 1909, Oakland Public Library.
11. Ibid.
12. Ibid.
13. Ibid.
14. Ibid.
15. Ibid.

Chapter 12

1.   Coolbrith to Stoddard, May 12, 1885, C-S Huntington.
2.   Ibid.
3.   Coolbrith to Stoddard, February 16, 1876, C-S Huntington.
4.   Calla Shasta Miller to George Melvin Miller, June 30, 1879. Joaquin Miller Collection, Honnold/Mudd Library, Claremont College.
5.   Calla Shasta Miller to George Miller, August 30, 1879, Claremont.
6.   Calla Shasta Miller to George Miller, November 3, 1879, Claremont.
7.   Ibid.
8.   Coolbrith to Stoddard, February 7, 1881, C-S Huntington.
9.   Calla Shasta Miller to George Miller, November 3, 1879, Claremont.
10. Rhodehamel and Wood, *Ina Coolbrith: Librarian and Laureate of California*.
11. Coolbrith to Stoddard, July 17, 1883, C-S Huntington.
12. Ben Sweeney, "Jack London's Noble Lady," *Pacific Historian*, Fall 1973.
13. Ibid.
14. Coolbrith, "Gossip," IDC Bancroft.

15. Isadora Duncan. *My Life* (New York: Liveright, 1927).
16. Peter Kurth, *Isadora: A Sensational Life* (Boston: Little, Brown and Company, 2001).
17. Duncan, *My Life*.
18. Kurth, *Isadora: A Sensational Life*.
19. Duncan, *My Life*.
20. Coolbrith, "When Love is Dead," *Current Literature: A Magazine of Record and Review*, April–June 1900.
21. Mary Austin, *Earth Horizon: Autobiography* (Albuquerque: University of New Mexico Press, 1932).
22. Ibid.

Chapter 13

1. Women in the Utah Territory had been voting since 1870, but in 1887 the federal government stripped them of the right. Utah returned suffrage to women in 1895.
2. Coolbrith, "The Mariposa Lily," originally published in "A Christmas Greeting," San Francisco, 1886.
3. Coolbrith, "California Rain," *Oakland Tribune*, January 1888, Scrapbooks OPL.
4. Coolbrith to Stoddard, September 18, 1883, C-S Huntington.
5. Ibid.
6. Coolbrith to Stoddard, March 14, 1889, C-S Huntington.
7. Wilder, E. M., August 14, 1853, Oakland Public Library.
8. Smith, Mary Audentia Smith Anderson, ed., *Joseph Smith III and the Restoration*.
9. Coolbrith to Jeanne Carr, October 31, 1876, IDC Huntington.
10. Coolbrith to John Vance Cheney, [May?], 1890, IDC Huntington.
11. Coolbrith to John Vance Cheney, May 2, 1890, IDC Huntington.
12. Coolbrith to John Vance Cheney, July 8, 1890, IDC Huntington.
13. Coobrith to Ina Peterson, February 25, 1890.
14. Coolbrith to Stoddard, August 15, 1892, C-S Huntington.
15. Ibid.

16. Judith A. Allen, *The Feminism of Charlotte Perkins Gilman: Sexualities, Histories, Progressivism* (Chicago: University of Chicago Press, 2009).
17. Charlotte Perkins Gilman, "The Living of Charlotte Perkins Gilman (University of Wisconsin Press, 1935).
18. Ina Lillian Cook to Carey McWilliams, April 4, 1929, OPL.
19. Coolbrith to Stoddard, October 15, 1892, C-S Huntington.
20. Charles Wells Moulton, ed., "The Magazine of Poetry: A Quarterly Review," V1, Buffalo, NY, 1889.
21. "Oakland Free Library: Interview with Miss Ina D. Coolbrith, Librarian," *Oakland Times*, September 4 1892, Scrapbooks OPL.
22. Rhodehamel and Wood, *Ina Coolbrith: Librarian and Laureate of California.*
23. *Oakland Enquirer*, September 29, 1892, Scrapbooks OPL
24. "Ina D. Coolbrith: No Longer the Public Librarian," *Oakland Enquirer*, 29 September 1892.
25. "Sudden: Ina D. Coolbrith Discharged: Only Three Day's Grace Given Her: No Direct Charges Made by the Trustees: History of the Disagreeable Outburst at the Library," *Oakland Daily Evening Tribune*, September 28, 1892. Scrapbooks OPL.
26. Minutes of the Oakland Library, October 4, 1892.
27. "She Resigns. Ina D. Coolbrith Writes to the Library Trustees," *Oakland Tribune*, October 5, 1892.
28. "Oakland News: Miss Ina Coolbrith Tenders Her Resignation," *San Francisco Chronicle*, October 5, 1892.
29. "The Coolbrith Episode," *Blue Lake Advocate*, October 15, 1892.
30. "The Free Library: Miss Ina Coolbrith to go Out as Librarian January 1st," *Oakland Times*, September 30, 1892, Scrapbooks OPL.
31. "The Quaker Poet," *Oakland Enquirer*, October 10, 1892, Scrapbooks OPL
32. Ambrose Bierce, "Prattle," *San Francisco Examiner*, October 16, 1892, Scrapbooks OPL.
33. Coolbrith to Stoddard, October 15, 1892, C-S Huntington.
34. Ibid.

35. Coolbrith, "Millennium," *San Francisco Examiner*, December 25, 1892.

36. Coolbrith to Stoddard, October 15, 1892, C-S Huntington.

Part IV: San Francisco Redux
Epigraph: Ina Coolbrith, "The Flight of Song," *Century Magazine*, October 1894.

Chapter 14

1. "An Eminent California Poet and Her Work," *Chicago Inter-Ocean*, November 11, 1893, and, "She is a True Poet," *Chicago Evening Post*, July 14, 1894.

2. Charles S. Scofield, "The Poet of the Sierras: His Mountain Home on the Heights Above Oakland," *Stockton Evening Mail*, April 29, 1893.

3. Adeline Knapp, "Neighboring with a Poet," *San Francisco Call* (Scrapbooks OPL, no date, but likely c. 1894).

4. George Wharton James, *San Francisco Call*, no date, Scrapbooks OPL.

5. Scofield, "The Poet of the Sierras."

6. Lawrence Ferlinghetti and Nancy J. Peters, *Literary San Francisco: A Pictorial History from Its Beginnings to the Present Day* (San Francisco: City Lights Books and Harper & Row, 1980).

7. Ina Coolbrith, "Some Wildflowers of California," no date, no publication, Scrapbooks OPL.

8. Ina Coolbrith, "La Copa de Oro (California Poppy)," *San Francisco Bulletin*, May 24, 1893.

9. Information about the Queen Isabella statue is from *Literary and other exercises in California state building* (Chicago: Rand, McNally & Company, 1893); Mae Silver, "1894 Midwinter Fair: Women Artists," foundsf.org.

10. *Chicago Evening Post*, no date, Scrapbooks OPL.

11. Jeanne E. Francoeur, "Ina Coolbrith, Our Poet—In the Past and Present," *Woman Citizen*, October 1913.

12. Coolbrith, "Concha," *Wings of Sunset* (Boston: Houghton Mifflin Company, 1929).

13. Coolbrith, "The Captive of the White City," *Songs from the Golden Gate* (Boston: Houghton Mifflin, 1895).
14. "Authors' Club to the Ladies," *New York Times,* January 18, 1894.
15. "Authors' Club of New York: Its Annual Reception for Literary Women," *Boston Herald,* January 20, 1894.
16. Coolbrith, Lecture, "Tribute to Joaquin Miller," IDC Bancroft.
17. Letter from Aurora Esmeralda (Ella Sterling Cummins Mighels) to Childe Carlton, March 12, 1928, Ella Sterling Mighels Papers, 1870–1934 (MS 1470, Box 3, Folder 11). Courtesy California Historical Society.

Chapter 15

1. Ella Sterling Cummins, *The Story of the Files: A review of* Californian Writers and Literature (World's Fair Commission of California, Columbian Exposition, 1893).
2. J. Golden Taylor, Thomas J. Lyon, George F. Day, Gerald W. Haslam, James H. Maguire, and William T. Pilkington, eds., *A Literary History of the American West* (Fort Worth: Texas Christian University Press, 1987).
3. "Books and Bookmakers," *San Francisco Call,* April 7, 1895.
4. Coolbrith to Charles Augustus Keeler, April 29, 1895, Charles Augustus Keeler Papers, The Huntington Library, San Marino, California.
5. Ambrose Bierce, "Idle Chatter," n.d., Scrapbooks OPL.
6. Evelyn Wells, "Ina Coolbrith Spurns Birthday," *San Francisco Call,* March 8, 1924.
7. Coolbrith, "A Paper for the Convention: or The Attitude of the Muse Toward Poems of Occasion," *Oakland Examiner,* September 8, 1896.
8. Ibid.
9. Ibid.
10. Charles Augustus Keeler, "Friends Bearing Torches," unpublished manuscript, Guide to the Charles Augustus Keeler Papers, 1858–1949, Bancroft.
11. Coolbrith to Edwin Bliss Hill, Edwin Bliss Hill Papers, Huntington.
12. Coolbrith to Hill, Huntington.

13. *San Francisco Call*, "A Holiday on Olympus," July 28, 1895.

14. *Oakland Times*, November 9, 1895, Scrapbooks OPL.

15. *San Francisco Chronicle*, October 27, 1895, Scrapbooks OPL.

16. *Portland Maine Transcript*, (no date), Scrapbooks OPL.

17. *Los Angeles Herald*, November 24, 1895, Scrapbooks OPL.

18. *New York Times*, November 1895, Scrapbooks OPL.

19. Virginia Woolf, "A Room of One's Own," October 24, 1929, Hogarth Press, England.

20. Coolbrith to Charles Keeler, 26 December 26, 1897, Charles Augustus Keeler Papers, Huntington.

21. In 1906, the Mercantile Library Association merged with the Mechanics' Institute Library, founded in 1854. Today, the Mechanics' Institute Library and Chess Room serves as a cultural event center, library, and chess club. It's located on Post Street in San Francisco.

22. *San Francisco Chronicle*, January 17, 1898, Scrapbooks OPL

23. *San Francisco Examiner*, January 17, 1898.

24. Coolbrith to Stoddard, 15 February 1898, C-S Huntington.

25. Coolbrith to T. R. Bannerman, c. 1898, IDC Bancroft.

26. Albert Kinross, "Views and Reviews: Ina Coolbrith," *London Outlook*, August 20, 1898.

27. Gertrude Atherton, letter to the editor, *London Outlook*, August 27, 1898.

28. Coolbrith to Charles Keeler, October 1, 1998, Charles Augustus Keeler Papers, Huntington.

29. W. [H.?] Smith, Jr. to Charles Keeler, April 18, 1907, Charles Augustus Keeler Papers, Huntington.

30. Charles Fletcher Lummis Manuscript, 1899–1904, Braun Research Library Collection, Autry National Center, Los Angeles, MS.1.1.891A, Letter, Coolbrith to Lummis, December 13, 1899.

31. Charles Fletcher Lummis Manuscript, 1899–1904, Braun Research Library Collection, Autry National Center, Los Angeles, MS.1.1.891A, Letter, Coolbrith to Lummis, September 24, 1899.

Chapter 16

1. James Marie Hopper, "Our San Francisco," *Everybody's Magazine*, June 1906, found in Malcolm E. Barker, *Three Fearful Days: San Francisco Memoirs of the 1906 Earthquake & Fire* (San Francisco: Londonborn Publications, 1998).

2. Edmund Clarence Stedman to Coolbirth, November 17, 1903, IDC Bancroft.

3. J. Winter Smith, interview by Norma Ricketts, June 24, 1965, notes from interview shared with the author.

4. Hopper, "Our San Francisco," June 1906.

5. Emily Wortis Leider, *California's Daughter: Gertrude Atherton and Her Times* (Stanford, CA: Stanford University Press: 1991).

6. Ibid.

7. Jack London, "The Story of an Eyewitness," *Collier's Weekly*, May 5, 1906, reprinted in "Jack London and the Great Earthquake and Fire," The Virtual Museum of the City of San Francisco, www.sfmuseum.net.

8. Henry Anderson Lafler, "Poets of the Far West," *New York Evening Post*, n.d., Scrapbooks OPL.

9. *Los Angeles Herald*, April 16, 1906, Scrapbooks OPL.

10. Mary Austin to Coolbrith, May 29, 1906, IDC Bancroft.

11. Otis Notman, "Visits to Californian Authors," *New York Times*, October 18, 1907.

12. Ibid.

13. Coolbrith, "Carmel-by-the-Sea," *Oakland Tribune*, August 22, 1909.

14. Gertrude Atherton, "San Francisco's Tragic Dawn," *Harper's Weekly*, May 12, 1906.

15. Coolbrith to Keeler, June 4, 1906, IDC Huntington.

16. Coolbrith to Keeler, June 5, 1906, IDC Huntington.

17. Coolbrith, "San Francisco, April 18, 1906." *Putnam's Magazine*, October 1906.

18. Coolbrith to Eleanor Davenport, n.d. [ca. 1907], IDC Bancroft.

19. Coolbrith to Grenville S. Pettis, June 14, 1906, IDC Huntington.

20. *Oakland Enquirer*, October 30, 1906, Scrapbooks OPL.

21. Coolbrith to George Sterling, February 18, 1907, George Sterling Papers, Huntington.

22. George Sterling to Coolbrith, March 16, 1907, IDC Bancroft.
23. George Wharton James, "Mark Twain—An Appreciation of His Pioneer Writings on Fasting and Health (Part I), *Physical Culture*, May 1919, reprinted in "The Story Behind the A. F. Bradley Photos," www.twainquotes.com.
24. Ibid.
25. Stoddard to Coolbrith, February 16, 1907, C-S Bancroft.
26. This event was recreated using three sources: "Authors' reading proves great success," *Evening Bulletin*, November 28, 1907; "A Notable Gathering of Western Writers," *Sunset*, January 1908; Leider, *California's Daughter*.
27. Coolbrith, lecture, Gertrude Franklin Atherton [given to the Pacific Coast Women's Press Association in September 1911], Gertrude Franklin Horn Atherton Papers, Bancroft.

Chapter 17

1. Sterling to Coolbrith, October 11, 1910, IDC Bancroft.
2. Josephine Rhodehamel, lecture, Ina Coolbrith Circle, September 28, 1947, Oakland Public Library.
3. Marian Taylor, "Ina Coolbrith, California Poet," *Overland Monthly*, October 1914.
4. Unidentified, undated newspaper clipping, Scrapbooks OPL.
5. "Ina Coolbrith—A Biography," *Notre Dame Quarterly*, 1912.
6. Coolbrith to Keeler, April 16, 1907, IDC Huntington.
7. Ina Coolbrith, "Charles Warren Stoddard" (lecture, Ebell Society, Oakland, CA, November 1, 1923).
8. M. E. Grenander, "Ambrose Bierce and Charles Warren Stoddard: Some Unpublished Correspondence," *Huntington Library Quarterly*, May 23, 1960.
9. William Keith to Coolbrith, n. d., IDC Bancroft.
10. Brother Cornelius, *Keith: Old Master of California* (New York: G. P. Putnam's Sons, 1942).
11. Coolbrith to Herbert Bashford, February 25, 1913, IDC Bancroft.
12. Coolbrith to John Muir, November 19, 1894, John Muir Papers, Holt-Atherton Special Collections, University of the Pacific Library. © 1984 Muir-Hanna Trust.
13. Coolbrith to Sterling, February 21, 1909, IDC Huntington.

14. Mark Thompson, *American Character: The Curious Life of Charles Fletcher Lummis and the Rediscovery of the Southwest* (Arcade Publishing: New York, 2001).

15. Charles Fletcher Lummis to Coolbrith, November 18, 1912, Huntington.

16. Ina Coolbrith, President's Report, Year Book of the Pacific Coast Women's Press Association, 1916–17, Oakland Public Library.

17. Charles John Hyne to Coolbrith, May 28, 1915, IDC Bancroft.

18. Gertrude M. Reynolds to Coolbrith, June 7, 1915, IDC Bancroft.

19. Enrique Loynaz del Castillo, December 10, 1915, IDC Bancroft.

20. George Wharton James, "Ina Donna Coolbrith: An Historical Sketch and Appreciation," *National Magazine*, June 1907.

21. Coolbrith to George Wharton James, February 9, 1912, IDC Huntington.

22. Kate Kennedy, "Ina Coobrith—Poet, Friend. An Appreciation," *Pacific Short Story Club Magazine*, January 1912.

23. Marian Taylor, "Ina Coolbrith, California Poet," *Overland Monthly*, October 1914.

24. Coolbrith to Ella Sterling Mighels, January 31, 1915, California Historical Society.

25. Coolbrith to Lorenzo Sosso, March 2, 1915, Society of California Pioneers.

26. Marian Taylor, "Congress of Authors and Journalists," *Overland Monthly*.

27. *Los Angeles Graphic*, July 31, 1915, Scrapbooks OPL.

28. Marian Taylor, "Congress of Authors and Journalists," *Overland Monthly*.

29. *New York Times Book Review*, July 18 1915.

30. Taylor, "Congress of Authors and Journalists."

31. Charles Phillips, "Books and Writers. The Laurel Wreath," *The Monitor*, July 10, 1915.

32. Ibid.

33. *New York Times Book Review*, July 18, 1915.

34. Charles Fletcher Lummis Manuscript, 1905–16, Braun Research Library Collection, Autry National Center, Los Angeles, MS.1.1.891B, Letter, Coolbrith to Lummis, November 2, 1915.

35. Coolbrith to Mrs. Alexander T. Leonard, August 27, 1915, IDC Bancroft.

36. Coolbrith to Keeler, February 11, 1914, IDC Huntington.

Chapter 18

1. Ina Coolbrith, "From Russian Hill," *Sunset Magazine*, August 1915.

2. Lummis to Coolbrith, November 10, 1917, Braun Research Library.

3. Coolbrith to Charles Keeler, January 7, 1910, IDC Huntington.

4. Charles Keeler, "Friends Bearing Torches," (unpublished manuscript), Bancroft.

5. Charles Fletcher Lummis Manuscript, 1899–1904, Braun Research Library Collection, Autry National Center, Los Angeles, MS.1.1.891A, Letter, Ina Coolbrith to Lummis, September 24, 1899.

6. Josephine Clifford McCracken to Coolbrith, November 21, 1909, IDC Huntington.

7. Joan [London] Miller, (lecture, Ina Coolbrith Circle, March 1968 and September 1969).

8. George Sterling to Coolbrith, September 15, 1923, IDC Bancroft.

9. *Elsie Whitaker Martinez: San Francisco Bay Area Writers and Artists*, An Interview Conducted by Franklin D. Walker and Willa Klug Baum, The Bancroft Library, UC Berkeley.

10. Ulv Youff, *Ulven: Written During Retirement in Switzerland* (London: Chapman & Dodd, LTD., 1923).

11. Ibid.

12. Ibid.

13. Gertrude Atherton to Coolbrith, October 12, 1918, IDC Bancroft.

14. Atherton to Coolbrith, December 5, 1898, IDC Bancroft.

15. Youff, *Ulven*.

16. Coolbrith to Bender, n.d., Special Collections, F. W. Olin Library, Mills College.

17. Youff, *Ulven*.

18. Lummis to Coolbrith, September 29, 1919, IDC Huntington.
19. Coolbrith to Joseph F. Smith, January 13, 1916, LDS Library.
20. Coolbrith to Joseph F. Smith, April 28, 1914, LDS Library.
21. Coolbrith to Joseph F. Smith, May 22, 1916, LDS Library.
22. Coolbrith to Bio (Adele Terrill Jones) DeCasseras, Adele T. De Casseres correspondence, LDS Library.
23. Coolbrith to Joseph F. Smith, January 9, 1917, LDS Library.
24. Coolbrith to Joseph F. Smith, February 18, 1917, LDS Library. (Ina does not cite the article in her letter, and I was unable to find the article she is referring to.)
25. Coolbrith to Joseph F. Smith, July 31, 1914, LDS Library.
26. There is a dating problem with the letters. His letter, written April 20, 1918, says, "Your letter of May 3rd, reached me on the 6th inst."
27. Joseph F. Smith to Ina Coolbrith, April 20, 1918. LDS Library.
28. Compton, *In Sacred Loneliness*.
29. Joseph F. Smith to Coolbrith, April 20, 1918. LDS Library.
30. Coolbrith to Joseph F. Smith, February 18, 1917, LDS Library.
31. Coolbrith to Mighels, n.d., Ina Coolbrith Letters, California State Library.
32. Coolbrith to Bender, October 26, 1919, Mills College.
33. Coolbrith to Grenville Pettis, February 5, 1920, IDC Huntington.
34. Ibid.
35. Coolbrith to Bio De Casseres, n.d. (c. 1923–27), LDS Library.
36. Coolbrith to Grenville Pettis, February 5, 1920, IDC Huntington.
37. *Sacramento Bee*, May 5, 1919.

Part V: New York

Epigraph: Coolbrith to Bender, November 30, 1925, Special Collections, F. W. Olin Library, Mills College.

Chapter 19

1. Coolbrith to Bender, December 19, 1919, Mills College.
2. Charles Beebe Turrill to Coolbrith, November 15, 1919, Society of California Pioneers.

3. Edwin Markham to Coolbrith, November 22, 1919, IDC Huntington.

4. Benjamin De Casseres, "Ina Coolbrith of California's 'Overland Trinity,'" *The Sun*, December 7, 1919.

5. De Casseres, *The Sun*, December 1919.

6. Robert S. Norman to Coolbrith, December 29, 1919, IDC Bancroft.

7. Booth & Lincoln's hand story: Sharpe, Roy, "Ina Coolbrith will prepare her memoirs," *Oakland Tribune*, 1921.

8. Coolbrith to Joseph F. Smith, January 20, 1916, LDS Library.

9. Edna St. Vincent Millay, "Figs from Thistles," *Poetry: A Magazine of Verse*, June 1918.

10. "Ina Coolbrith in New York: Honored by the Literary Critics and by the Poetry Society of America," *San Francisco Bulletin*, January 6, 1920.

11. Nathan Newmark, *San Francisco Star*, March 25, 1916, Scrapbooks OPL.

12. Coolbrith, "Gossip," IDC Bancroft.

13. Coolbrith, lecture, Tribute to Joaquin Miller, IDC Bancroft.

14. "Ina Coolbrith in New York," *San Francisco Bulletin*, January 6, 1920.

15. Coolbrith to Bender, February 20, 1920, Mills College.

16. Ibid.

17. Charles Phillips (Joseph MacConaghy) to Coolbrith, January 28, 1920, IDC Bancroft.

18. Phillips to Coolbrith, January 28, 1920, IDC Bancroft.

19. Coolbrith to Charles Beebe Turrill, April 8, 1920, Society of California Pioneers.

20. Coolbrith, *Wings of Sunset* (New York: Houghton Mifflin Company, 1929).

21. Coolbrith to Bender, November 16, 1920, Mills College.

22. Coolbrith, "Love's Age," *Wings of Sunset*.

23. Coolbrith to Charles Beebe Turrill, April 8, 1920, Society of California Pioneers.

24. Turrill to Coolbrith, March 28, 1920, Society of California Pioneers.

25. Coolbrith to Ella Sterling Cummins Mighels, August 28, 1916, California State Library.
26. Ella Sterling Mighels (note on back of letter), Coolbrith to Mighels, August 28, 1916, California State Library.
27. Coolbrith to Mighels, August 28, 1916, California State Library.
28. Ella Sterling Mighels (note on back of letter), Coolbrith to Mighels, November 30, 1917, California State Library.
29. Coolbrith to Turrill, June 17, 1919, Society of California Pioneers.
30. The Mighels-Coolbrith spat and the resulting formation of the Ina Coolbrith Circle was pieced together from letters found at Bancroft Library, Coolbrith Correspondence and Papers Additions; Ella Sterling Mighels Collection, California Historical Society, Manuscript Collection; and the California State Library.
31. Coolbrith to Ina Coolbrith Circle, March 12, 1920, Society of California Pioneers.
32. Coolbrith to Turrill, April 8, 1920, Society of California Pioneers.
33. Lummis to Coolbrith, September 29, 1919, IDC Huntington.
34. Charles Fletcher Lummis Housebook, 1899–1928, Braun Research Library Collection, Autry National Center, Los Angeles, MS.1.10.1, Page 382, June 12, 1920.

Chapter 20

1. Coolbrith to Bender, October 30, 1920, Mills College.
2. Henry Staats Moore to Coolbrith, March 28 (no year), IDC Bancroft.
3. Ina Lillian Cook to Coolbrith, November 28, 1921, Coolbrith Correspondence and Papers Additions, The Bancroft Library, University of California, Berkeley.
4. Coolbrith to Turrill, November 6, 1920, Society of CA Pioneers.
5. Ibid.
6. Maynard Dixon to Coolbrith, August 26, 1920, IDC Bancroft.
7. Coolbrith to Bender, March 14, 1921, Mills College.
8. "Modernistic Free Verse 'Idiotic,' says Cal. Poet," n.d., Scrapbooks OPL.

9. Nancy Barr Mavity, "California Poet Symbolizes Spirit of Days of Gold," *San Francisco Chronicle*, September 11, 1921.

10. Charles Keeler, "Friends Bearing Torches," unpublished ms., Bancroft.

11. Charles Fletcher Lummis Manuscript, 1916–20, Braun Research Library Collection, Autry National Center, Los Angeles, MS.1.1.891C, Letter, Lummis to Coolbrith, November 9, 1920.

12. Charles Fletcher Lummis Manuscript, 1921–27, Braun Research Library Collection, Autry National Center, Los Angeles, MS.1.1.891D, Letter, Lummis to Coolbrith, January 6, 1921.

13. Edward Francis O'Day to Coolbrith, December 20, 1920.

14. *Bookman*, December 1920, Scrapbooks OPL.

15. Coolbrith to Turrill, February 11, 1921, Society of California Pioneers.

16. Program, Poetry Society of America 11th Annual Dinner, January 27, 1921, IDC Bancroft.

17. Coolbrith to Turrill, February 11, 1921, Society of California Pioneers.

18. Josephine Clifford McCracken to Coolbrith, August 11, 1917, IDC Huntington.

19. Coolbrith, "Alien," *Overland Monthly*, March 1921.

20. Coolbrith to Bender, April 13, 1921, Mills College.

21. Youff, *Ulven*.

22. Charles Fletcher Lummis Manuscript, 1921–27, Braun Research Library Collection, Autry National Center, Los Angeles, MS.1.1.891D, Letter, Lummis to Coolbrith, July 29, 1921.

23. Coolbrith to Dr. Alex and Mrs. Leonard, August 23, 1921, Alexander Thomas Leonard, Collection of letters and clippings relating to California authors, circa 1909–42, Bancroft.

24. Coolbrith to Mildred Leo Clemens, October 15, 1921, IDC Bancroft.

25. Ibid.

26. Coolbrith to Sterling, November 8, 1921, IDC Huntington.

27. Sterling to Coolbrith, November 14, 1921, IDC Bancroft.

28. Sterling to Coolbrith, March 5, 1922, IDC Bancroft.

29. Coolbrith to Mildred Leo Clemens, December 1921, IDC Bancroft.

30. Turrill to Coolbrith, December 27, 1921, Society of CA Pioneers.
31. Ibid.
32. Coolbrith to Turrill, October 19, 1921, Society of CA Pioneers.
33. Coolbrith to Bender, January 4, 1922, Mills College.
34. Ina Agnes (Cook) to Coolbrith, February 8, 1922, IDC Bancroft.
35. Coolbrith to Bender, May 2, 1922, Mills College.

Chapter 21

1. Ulv Youff, *Ulven*.
2. Coolbrith to Bender, September 28, 1922, Mills College.
3. Coolbrith to Mrs. Leonard, October 17, 1922, IDC Bancroft.
4. Coolbrith, "My Kindred" and "Songs of Content," *Wings of Sunset*.
5. Coolbrith, "Honey Throats," *Wings of Sunset*.
6. Coolbrith, "Haunted," *Wings of Sunset*.
7. Coolbrith, "If I Have Never Loved Before," *Wings of Sunset*.
8. Coolbrith, "Atom," *Wings of Sunset*.
9. Coolbrith, "With the Caravan," *Wings of Sunset*.
10. Coolbrith, "Sahara," *Wings of Sunset*.
11. Coolbrith, "Concha," *Wings of Sunset*.
12. Ibid.
13. Coolbrith to Lummis, January 12, 1923, Braun Library.
14. *The Bookman*, November 23, 1922.
15. Coolbrith to Sterling, January 3, 1923, IDC Huntington.
16. Sterling to Coolbrith, January 11, 1923, IDC Bancroft.
17. Coolbrith to Bender, December 16, 1922, Mills College.
18. H. O. Houghton and Company (signature illegible), Dec. 20, 1922, IDC Bancroft.
19. Coolbrith to Bender, March 26, 1923, Mills College.
20. Coolbrith to Sterling, January 3, 1923, IDC Huntington.
21. Coolbrith to Grenville Pettis, February 16, 1923, IDC Huntington.
22. Ina's address book, Oakland Public Library.
23. Coolbrith to Clemens, April 20, 1923, IDC Bancroft.
24. Youff, *Ulven*.
25. Ibid.
26. Ibid.

27. Thompson, *American Character*.

28. Nancy Barr Mavity, "California Poet Symbolizes Spirit of Days of Gold," *San Francisco Chronicle*, September 11, 1921.

29. Program for "The Covered Wagon" at the Criterion, OPL.

30. Bio De Casseras, "Pioneer Relives Girlhood Scenes at 'Covered Wagon,'" *New York Times*, 1923, Scrapbooks OPL.

31. Coolbrith to Turrill, October 9, 1921, Society of California Pioneers.

32. Coolbrith, "Unheeded," *Wings of Sunset*.

Part VI: Poetry as Home

Epigraph: Evelyn Wells, "Ina Coolbrith Spurns Birthday," *San Francisco Call*, March 8, 1924.

Chapter 22

1. Wells, "Ina Coolbrith Spurns Birthday," *San Francisco Call*, March 8, 1924.

2. Ina Cook Graham to Bud Heide, July 21, 1968, Oakland Public Library.

3. Evelyn Wells, "Ina Coolbrith Spurns Birthday," *San Francisco Call*.

4. Coolbrith to Mrs. Leonard, February 8, 1924, Alexander Thomas Leonard, "Collection of letters and clippings relating to California authors, circa 1909-1942, The Bancroft Library, University of California, Berkeley.

5. Coolbrith to Sterling, May 20, 1924, IDC Huntington.

6. Coolbrith to Turrill, Sunday, no date, Society of California Pioneers.

7. Coolbrith to Mrs. Drum, July 17, 1923, Oakland Public Library.

8. Bio (Terrill) De Casseres to Ina Cook Graham, May 20, 1928, IDC Huntington.

9. Coolbrith to Bio (Terrill) De Casseres, n.d. [c. 1924–27], LDS Library.

10. *San Francisco Chronicle*, October 6, 1923.

11. Coolbrith to Bender, November 22, 1923, and Coolbrith to Bender, n.d., Mills College.

12. Coolbrith to Sterling, October 14, 1924, IDC Huntington.
13. Clark Ashton Smith to Coolbrith, March 12, 1925, IDC Bancroft.
14. Coolbrith, introduction to Harte, "Plain Language from Truthful James (The Heathen Chinee)."
15. Ibid.
16. Coolbrith to Bender, December 27, 1924, Mills College.
17. Coolbrith to Bender, November 30, 1925, Mills College.
18. Carlton Waldo Kendall, "California's Pioneer Poetess," *Overland Monthly*, August 1929.
19. Charles Fletcher Lummis Manuscript, 1921–27, Braun Research Library Collection, Autry National Center, Los Angeles, MS.1.1.891D, Letter, Lummis to Coolbrith, June 9, 1926.
20. J. Torrey Connor to Coolbrith, December 22, 1925, IDC Bancroft.
21. Charles Fletcher Lummis Manuscript, 1921–27, Braun Research Library Collection, Autry National Center, Los Angeles, MS.1.1.891D, Postcard, Lummis to Coolbrith, 1926.
22. Coolbrith to Phelan, December 25, 1925, IDC Huntington.
23. James Alexander Miller to Coolbrith, March 9, 1926, IDC Bancroft.
24. Maurice Andrews to Coolbrith, January 29, 1926, IDC Bancroft.
25. Charles Fletcher Lummis Manuscript, 1921–27, Braun Research Library Collection, Autry National Center, Los Angeles, MS.1.1.891D, Letter, Lummis to Coolbrith, June 9, 1926.
26. Eufina Tompkins, February 28, 1927, IDC Bancroft.
27. Coolbrith to Don Carlos Pickett, June 14, 1926, IDC Huntington.
28. Andrea Barnet, *All Night Party: The Women of Bohemian Greenwich Village and Harlem, 1913–1930* (Chapel Hill, NC: Algonquin Books of Chapel Hill, 2004).
29. Ibid.
30. *New York Post*, October 30, 1941.
31. Coolbrith to Don Carlos Pickett, June 14, 1926, IDC Huntington.

Chapter 23

1. Joan [London] Miller to Dalton Gross, October 12, 1965, IDC Huntington.
2. Coolbrith to Sterling, May 1, 1925, IDC Huntington.
3. Joan [London] Miller to Dalton Gross, October 12, 1965, IDC Huntington.
4. George Sterling, "Cool, Gray City of Love," *San Francisco Bulletin*, December 11, 1920.
5. Coolbrith to Bender, November 20, 1926, Mills College.
6. Ibid.
7. Bender to Coolbrith, November (no date), and November 29, 1926, Mills College.
8. Evelyn Wells, "Poet Suicides Victims of Lost Hope," *San Francisco Call*, November 28, 1927.
9. *Oakland Tribune*, March 10, 1927.
10. Phillips to Coolbrith, March 20, 1927, IDC Bancroft.
11. Phillips to Coolbrith, November 25, 1926, IDC Bancroft.
12. Charles Fletcher Lummis Manuscript, 1921–27, Braun Research Library Collection, Autry National Center, Los Angeles, MS.1.1.891D, Letter, Coolbrith to Lummis, March 23, 1927.
13. Charles Fletcher Lummis Manuscript, 1921-1927, Braun Research Library Collection, Autry National Center, Los Angeles, MS.1.1.891D, Letter, Lummis to Coolbrith, March 25, 1927.
14. Eufina Tompkins to Coolbrith, February 28, 1927, IDC Bancroft.
15. Coolbrith, "Beside the Dead," *Overland Monthly*, May 1875.
16. Bob Davis, "Bob Davis Recalls: Origin of Ina Coolbrith, California's Poet Laureate," *The New York Sun*, Tuesday, March 6, 1928.
17. Charles Keeler, "Friends Bearing Torches," Unpublished, IDC Bancroft.
18. Edward F. O'Day, "The Laureate of California," *The Lantern*, November 1917.

Epilogue

Epigraph: Coolbrith, "The Unsolvable," *Wings of Sunset*.

1. Ina Lillian Cook, "Ina Coolbrith: Some Impressions and Recollections," *The Wasp-News Letter*, December 22–29, 1928.

2. Learn more about the Ina Coolbrith Circle at www.coolpoetry.org.

Selected Bibliography
and Further Reading

This list contains the nonfiction books I read or consulted for the book, with a few related fiction books (*) included. Letters, lectures, poems, and articles from magazines or newspapers are in the notes.

Austen, Roger. *Genteel Pagan: The Double Life of Charles Warren Stoddard*. Crowley, John W., ed. Amherst, MA: University of Massachusetts Press, 1991.

Austin, Mary. *Earth Horizon: Autobiography*. Albuquerque, NM: University of New Mexico Press, 1932.

Bagwell, Beth. *Oakland: The Story of a City*. Novato, CA: Presidio Press, 1982.

Barker, Malcolm E., ed. *More San Francisco Memoirs 1852–1899*. San Francisco: Londonborn Publications, 1996.

Barnet, Andrea. *All Night Party: The Women of Bohemian Greenwich Village & Harlem, 1913–1930*. Chapel Hill, NC: Algonquin Books of Chapel Hill, 2004.

Beckwourth, James P. *The Life and Adventures of James P. Beckwourth, as told to Thomas D. Bonner*. Lincoln, NE: University of Nebraska Press, 1972.

Beebe, Lucius. *The Overland Limited*. Berkeley, CA: Howell North Books, 1963.

Beecher, Catharine Esther. *Miss Beecher's Housekeeper and Healthkeeper*. New York: Harper & Bros., 1874.

Bibliography

Benfey, Christopher. *A Summer of Hummingbirds: Love, Art, and Scandal in the Intersecting Worlds of Emily Dickinson, Mark Twain, Harriet Beecher Stowe, & Martin Johnson Heade*. New York: Penguin, 2008.

* Boyle, T. C. *The Women*. New York: Penguin, 2009.

Brechin, Gray. *Imperial San Francisco: Urban Power, Earthly Ruin*. Berkeley, CA: University of California Press, 1999.

Brodie, Fawn M. *No Man Knows My History: The Life of Joseph Smith*. New York: Alfred A. Knopf, 1945.

Chase, Marilyn. *The Barbary Plague: The Black Death in Victorian San Francisco*. New York: Random House, 2003.

Cleland, Robert Glass. *El Molino Viejo*, 2nd ed. Los Angeles: Ward Ritchie Press, 1951.

Cohen, Rachel. *A Chance Meeting: Intertwined Lives of American Writers and Artists, 1854–1967*. New York: Random House, 2004.

Compton, Todd. *In Sacred Loneliness: The Plural Wives of Joseph Smith*. Salt Lake City, UT: Signature Books, 1997

Coolbrith, Ina. *A Perfect Day and Other Poems*. San Francisco: Carmany and Co., 1881.

———. *Songs from the Golden Gate*. Boston: Houghton Mifflin, 1895.

———. *Wings of Sunset*. Boston: Houghton Mifflin, 1929.

———. *At the Heart of the Circle: The Life and Selected Poetry of Ina Coolbrith*. Alpaugh, David, and Clifford Wolfe, eds. Richmond Heights, CA: The Ina Coolbrith Circle, 2002.

Crosby, Caroline Barnes. *No Place to Call Home: The 1807–1857 Life Writings of Caroline Barnes Crosby*. Lyman, Edward Leo, Susan Ward Payne, and S. George Ellsworth, eds. Logan, UT: Utah State University Press, 2005.

Cummins, Ella Sterling. *The Story of the Files: A Review of California Writers and Literature*. World's Fair Commission of California, Columbian Exposition, 1893.

Dickson, Samuel. *Tales of San Francisco*. Stanford, CA: Stanford University Press, 1947.

Dinkelspiel, Frances. *Towers of Gold: How One Jewish Immigrant Named Isaias Hellman Created California*. New York: St. Martin's Press, 2008.

Duckett, Margaret. *Mark Twain and Bret Harte*. Norman, OK: University of Oklahoma Press, 1964.

Estrada, William David. *The Los Angeles Plaza: Sacred and Contested Space*. Austin, TX: University of Texas Press, 2008.

Farquhar, Francis P., ed. *Up and Down California in 1860–1864: The Journal of William H. Brewer*. Berkeley, CA: University of California Press, 1966.

Ferrier, William Warren. *Berkeley, California: The Story of the Evolution of a Hamlet into a City of Culture and Commerce*. Berkeley, CA: William Warren Ferrier, 1933.

* Finney, Jack. *Time and Again*. New York: Simon & Schuster, 1970.

Fitzpatrick, Kevin C. *A Journey into Dorothy Parker's New York*. Berkeley, CA: Roaring Forties Press, 2005.

Goodman, Matthew. *Eighty Days: Nellie Bly and Elizabeth Bisland's History-Making Race Around the World*. New York: Ballantine, 2013.

* Gold, Glen David, *Carter Beats the Devil*. New York: Hyperion, 2001.

Goodman, Susan, and Carl Dawson. *Mary Austin and the American West*. Berkeley, CA: University of California Press, 2008.

Gordon, Mary McDougall, ed. *Overland to California with the Pioneer Trail: The Gold Rush Diary of Bernard J. Reid*. Champaign, IL: University of Illinois Press, 1987.

Gordon, Charlotte. *Mistress Bradstreet: The Untold Life of America's First Poet*. New York: Little, Brown, 2005.

Hahn, Emily. *Romantic Rebels*. Boston: Houghton Mifflin, 1967.

* Hall, Oakley. *Separations*. Reno, NV: University of Nevada Press, 1997.

Harlan, George. *San Francisco Bay Ferryboats*. Berkeley, CA: Howell-North Books, 1967.

Heilbrun, Carolyn G. *Writing a Woman's Life*. New York: Ballantine, 1988.

Bibliography

* Horan, Nancy. *Loving Frank*. New York: Ballantine, 2007.

* Houston, James D. *Snow Mountain Passage: A Novel of the Donner Party*. New York: Alfred A. Knopf, 2001.

Hunt, Linda Lawrence. *Bold Spirit: Helga Estby's Forgotten Walk across Victorian America*, New York: Anchor, 2005.

Kershaw, Alex. *Jack London: A Life*. New York: St. Martin's, 1997.

Krakauer, Jon. *Under the Banner of Heaven: A Story of Violent Faith*. New York: Random House, 2003.

Larson, Erik. *The Devil in the White City*. New York: Crown, 2003.

Leider, Emily Wortis. *California's Daughter: Gertrude Atherton and Her Times*. Stanford, CA: Stanford University Press, 1991.

Lennon, Nigey. *The Sagebrush Bohemian: Mark Twain in California*. New York: Paragon House, 1990.

Lewis, Oscar, ed. *This Was San Francisco*. New York: David McKay Co., 1962.

Lyman, Edward Leo. *The Rise and Fall of a California Community*. Salt Lake City, UT: Signature Books, 1996.

Malcolm, Janet. *The Silent Woman: Sylvia Plath and Ted Hughes*. New York: Vintage, 1993.

* Markovits, Benjamin. *A Quiet Adjustment*. New York: W. W. Norton, 2008.

Mead, Marion. *Bobbed Hair and Bathtub Gin: Writers Running Wild in the Twenties*. New York: Harcourt, 2004.

Miller, Joaquin. *Life Amongst the Modocs: Unwritten History*. Berkeley, CA: Heyday, 1996. (Originally published by Richard Bentley and Son, London, 1873.)

Miller, Jon, ed. *San Francisco Stories*. San Francisco: Chronicle Books, 1990.

* Moses, Kate. *Wintering: A Novel of Sylvia Plath*. New York: Anchor, 2003.

Muir, John. *My First Summer in the Sierra*. Boston: Houghton Mifflin, 1911.

Neville, Amelia Ransome. *The Fantastic City: Memoirs of the Social and Romantic Life of Old San Francisco*. Boston: Houghton Mifflin, 1932.

* Newman, Janis Cooke. *Mary*. San Francisco: Macadam/Cage, 2006.

Bibliography

Newmark, Harris. *Sixty Years in Southern California, 1853–1913*. New York: Knickerbocker Press, 1916.

* Norris, Frank. *McTeague*. New York: Doubleday & McClure, 1899.

———. *The Octopus: A Story of California*. New York: Doubleday, Page and Co., 1901.

O'Brien, Edna. *Byron in Love*. New York: W. W. Norton, 2010.

Owens, Kenneth N. *Gold Rush Saints*. Norman, OK: University of Oklahoma Press, 2004.

Parins, James W. *John Rollin Ridge: His Life and Works*. Lincoln, NE: University of Nebraska Press, 1991.

* Pearl, Matthew. *The Dante Club*. New York: Random House, 2004.

Phillips, Kate. *Helen Hunt Jackson: A Literary Life*. Berkeley, CA: University of California Press, 2003.

Poole, Jean Bruce. *El Pueblo: The Historic Heart of Los Angeles*. Ball, Tevvy, ed. Los Angeles: Getty Conservation Institute, 2002.

Rathmell, George. *Realms of Gold: The Colorful Writers of San Francisco, 1850–1950*. Berkeley, CA: Creative Arts, 1998.

Rhodehamel, Josephine DeWitt and Raymund Francis Wood. *Ina Coolbrith: Librarian and Laureate of California*. Provo, UT: Brigham Young University Press, 1973.

Rich, Adrienne. *On Lies, Secrets and Silence: Selected Prose 1966–1978*. New York: W. W. Norton, 1979.

Robinson, John W. *Los Angeles in Civil War Days, 1860–1865*. Los Angeles: Dawson's Book Shop, 1977.

Sides, Hampton. *Blood and Thunder: The Epic Story of Kit Carson and the Conquest of the American West*. New York: Anchor, 2006.

Smith, Lucy Mack. *Joseph Smith's History by His Mother*. Photo reprint of 1853 original. Salt Lake City, UT: Utah Lighthouse Ministry.

Smith, Joseph Smith III. *Joseph III and the Restoration*. Independence, MO: Herald House, 1952.

Soulé, Frank, John H. Gihon, and James Nisbet, eds. *The Annals of San Francisco*. Berkeley, CA: Berkeley Hills Books, 1999.

Spalding, William A. *History and Reminiscences, Los Angeles City and County, California*, Vol. I. Los Angeles: J. R. Finnell and Sons, 1931.

Stewart, George R., Jr. *Bret Harte: Argonaut and Exile*. Boston: Houghton Mifflin, 1931.

Stoddard, Charles Warren. *In the Footprints of the Padres*. San Francisco: A. M. Robertson, 1901.

* Stone, Irving. *Jack London: Sailor on Horseback*. New York: Doubleday, 1938.

Tarnoff, Ben. *The Bohemians: Mark Twain and the San Francisco Writers Who Reinvented American Literature*. New York: Penguin, 2014.

Taylor, J. Golden, *A Literary History of the American West*. Lyon, Thomas J., ed. Fort Worth, TX: Texas Christian University Press, 1987.

Thompson, Mark. *American Character: The Curious Life of Charles Fletcher Lummis and the Rediscovery of the Southwest*. New York: Arcade Publishing, 2001.

Twain, Mark. *The Autobiography of Mark Twain: Including Chapters Now Published for the First Time*. New York: Harper Perennial, 1917. (Neider, Charles, ed., 1959.)

———. *Roughing It*. Hartford, CT: American Publishing Company, 1872.

Walker, Franklin. *San Francisco's Literary Frontier*. New York: Alfred A. Knopf, 1939.

———. *A Literary History of Southern California*. Berkeley, CA: University of California Press, 1950.

Walker, Cheryl. *The Nightingale's Burden: Women Poets and American Culture before 1900*. Bloomington, IN: Indiana University Press, 1983.

Worster, Donald. *A Passion for Nature: The Life of John Muir*. New York: Oxford University Press, 2008.

* Yellowbird (Ridge), John Rollin. *The Life and Adventures of Joaquin Murieta, the Celebrated California Bandit*. San Francisco: W. R. Cooke and Company, 1854.

Youff, Ulv. *Ulven*. London: Chapman & Dodd, Ltd, 1923.

Illustration Credits

p. 111   William Keith, painter. Photograph by Thomas Houseworth & Co.: por. 9. California Faces: Selections from The Bancroft Library Portrait Collection, The Bancroft Library, University of California, Berkeley.

p. 116   The Oakland Public Library. Courtesy Oakland Public Library, Oakland History Room.

p. 132   Calla Shasta Miller, 1879. Joaquin Miller Collection. Special Collections, Honnold/Mudd Library, Claremont University Consortium.

p. 136   Jack London portrait with dog, age 9. Courtesy Oakland Public Library, Oakland History Room.

p. 142   Ina Coolbrith portrait, age 50, c. 1885. Courtesy Oakland Public Library, Oakland History Room.

p. 147   Ambrose Bierce [inscribed to Ina Lillian Peterson, Oct. 7, 1892]: por. 2. California Faces: Selections from The Bancroft Library Portrait Collection, The Bancroft Library, University of California, Berkeley.

p. 158   Joaquin Miller. Photograph by Herman Ulutoken [?]: por. 56. California Faces: Selections from The Bancroft Library Portrait Collection, The Bancroft Library, University of California, Berkeley.

p. 194   Joaquin Miller, George Sterling, and Charles Warren Stoddard: por. 34. California Faces: Selections from The Bancroft Library Portrait Collection, The Bancroft Library, University of California, Berkeley.

p. 207   Carl Seyfforth. Courtesy Oakland Public Library, Oakland History Room.

p. 252   Portrait of Ina Coolbrith with cat, no date. Photographer: Ansel Adams. Gelatin silver copyprint. Photograph by Ansel Adams. Courtesy, California Historical Society, CHS2014.1753. © 2015 The Ansel Adams Publishing Rights Trust.

Author photo by David George.

Index

About the Author

Aleta George writes about nature and culture in California. Her work has appeared in *Smithsonian.com*, the *Los Angeles Times*, *High Country News*, the *San Francisco Chronicle*, and *Bay Nature*. George graduated with honors from San Francisco State University and lives at the northeastern edge of the San Francisco Bay where land meets water and city meets farm. This is her first book.